Alexander Dyce, William Gifford, John Ford

Works

Vol. II

Alexander Dyce, William Gifford, John Ford

Works
Vol. II

ISBN/EAN: 9783744710633

Printed in Europe, USA, Canada, Australia, Japan

Cover: Foto ©Thomas Meinert / pixelio.de

More available books at **www.hansebooks.com**

CONTENTS OF VOL. II.

LOVE'S SACRIFICE.

I cannot ascertain when this tragedy was first given to the stage; but it was printed in the same year as *The Broken Heart*. The old title is "Loues Sacrifice. A tragedie Receiued generally well. Acted by the Queenes Majesties Seruants at the Phœnix in Drury-lane. London: Printed by I. B. for Hvgh Beeston, dwelling next the Castle in Cornhill. 1633." 4to. It has neither prologue nor epilogue.

TO

MY TRUEST FRIEND, MY WORTHIEST KINSMAN,

JOHN FORD, OF GRAY'S INN, ESQ.

THE title of this little work, my good cousin, is in sense but the argument of a dedication;[1] which being in most writers a custom, in many a compliment, I question not but your clear knowledge of my intents will, in me, read as the earnest of affection. My ambition herein aims at a fair flight, borne up on the double wings of gratitude for a received, and acknowledgment for a continued love. It is not so frequent to number many kinsmen, and amongst them some friends, as to presume on some friends, and amongst them little friendship. But in every fulness of these particulars I do not more partake through you, my cousin, the delight than enjoy the benefit of them. This inscription to your name is only a faithful deliverance to memory of the truth of my respects to

[1] *The* title *of this little work, my good cousin, is in sense but the argument of a dedication;*] i.e. LOVE'S SACRIFICE. The affection between the cousins appears to be mutual; for, on the appearance of *Perkin Warbeck*, this gentleman returned the compliment with an introductory copy of verses, which are neither the best nor the worst called forth by that drama.

virtue, and to the equal in honour with virtue, desert. The contempt thrown on studies of this kind by such as dote on their own singularity[2] hath almost so out-faced invention and proscribed[3] judgment, that it is more safe, more wise, to be suspectedly silent than modestly confident of opinion herein. Let me be bold to tell the severity of censurers how willingly I neglect their practice, so long as I digress from no becoming thankfulness. Accept, then, my cousin, this witness to posterity of my constancy to your merits; for no ties of blood, no engagements of friendship, shall more justly live a precedent than the sincerity of both in the heart of

JOHN FORD.

[2] Here is an allusion to Prynne, who is also noticed by Shirley in the complimentary verses prefixed to this play. That restless "paper worm," as Needham calls him, had the year before produced his *Histriomastix, or Actor's Tragedy*, to the sore annoyance of the stage; and was at this time before the Star-Chamber for the scurrilous and libellous language in that "voluminous" farrago of puritanic rancour.—There is a quaintness in the style of this little piece; but the frank and grateful tone of affection which it displays is truly pleasing. It is not his dramatic powers that Ford is solicitous to assert; but his respect to virtue and desert, and his boldness to avow and praise them in a dear relation.

[3] *proscribed*] The 4to has "prescrib'd." D.

DRAMATIS PERSONÆ.

PHILIPPO CARAFFA, duke of Pavy.
PAULO BAGLIONE, uncle to the duchess.
FERNANDO, favourite to the duke.
FERENTES, a wanton courtier.
ROSEILLI, a young nobleman.
PETRUCHIO, } two counsellors of state.
NIBRASSA, }
RODERICO D'AVOLOS, secretary to the duke.
MAURUCCIO, an old antic.
GIACOPO, servant to Mauruccio.

BIANCA, the duchess.
FIORMONDA, the duke's sister.
COLONA, daughter to Petruchio.
JULIA, daughter to Nibrassa.
MORONA, an old lady.

Attendants, Courtiers, Officers, &c.

SCENE—*Pavy* (Pavia).

LOVE'S SACRIFICE.

ACT I.

SCENE I. *A room in the palace.*

Enter ROSEILLI *and* RODERICO D'AVOLOS.

Ros. Depart the court?
D'Av. Such was the duke's command.
Ros. You're secretary to the state and him,
Great in his counsels, wise, and, I think, honest:
Have you, in turning over old recórds,
Read but one name descended of the house
Of Lesui[1] in his loyalty remiss?
D'Av. Never, my lord.
Ros. Why, then, should I now, now when glorious peace
Triumphs in change of pleasures, be wip'd off,
Like to a useless moth, from courtly ease?—
And whither must I go?
D'Av. You have the open world before you.
Ros. Why, then 'tis like I'm banish'd?
D'Av. Not so: my warrant is only to command

[1] *Of Lesui*] *Lesus*, or *Lelus*, would be just as near to the traces of the original. As the "records" of this illustrious house have never fallen in my way, I cannot pretend to say which is the genuine word. The text is evidently a misprint.

you from the court; within five hours to depart after notice taken, and not to live within thirty miles of it, until it be thought meet by his excellence to call you back. Now I have warned you, my lord, at your peril be it, if you disobey. I shall inform the duke of your discontent. [*Exit.*

Ross. Do, politician, do! I scent the plot
Of this disgrace; 'tis Fiormonda, she,[2]
That glorious widow, whose commanding check
Ruins my love:[3] like foolish beasts, thus they
Find danger that prey too near the lions' den.

Enter FERNANDO *and* PETRUCHIO.

Fern. My noble lord, Roseilli!
Ros. Sir, the joy
I should have welcom'd you with is wrapt up
In clouds of my disgrace; yet, honour'd sir,
Howsoe'er frowns of great ones cast me down,
My service shall pay tribute in my lowness
To your uprising virtues.
Fern. Sir, I know
You are so well acquainted with your own,
You need not flatter mine: trust me, my lord,
I'll be a suitor for you.
Pet. And I'll second
My nephew's suit with importunity.
Ros. You are, my Lord Fernando, late return'd
From travels; pray instruct me:—since the voice
Of most supreme authority commands

[2] *'tis Fiormonda, she,*] Ford, as has been already observed, escapes no better than his contemporaries from Italian names. "*Fiormonda*" is here a quadrisyllable.

[3] *Ruins my love,* &c.] There is corruption here: a couplet would seem to have been intended by the author. Qy.

"*Ruins my love: like foolish beasts, thus they*
Find danger that too near the lions prey"? D.

My absence, I determine to bestow
Some time in learning languages abroad;
Perhaps the change of air may change in me
Remembrance of my wrongs at home: good sir,
Inform me; say I meant to live in Spain,
What benefit of knowledge might I treasure?

Fern. Troth, sir, I'll freely speak as I have found.
In Spain you lose experience; 'tis a climate
Too hot to nourish arts;[4] the nation proud,
And in their pride unsociable; the court
More pliable to glorify itself
Than do a stranger grace: if you intend
To traffic like a merchant, 'twere a place
Might better much your trade; but as for me,
I soon took surfeit on it.

Ros. What for France?

Fern. France I more praise and love.[5] You are, my lord,

[4] Fernando's character of the Spanish nation is somewhat tinctured with severity; yet not unjust in the main. James had, with much political foresight and some success, strove to cultivate the friendship of Spain; but the culpable capriciousness of Charles, aggravated by the ruffian insolence of Buckingham, abruptly checked his endeavours, and by rendering the Spanish party unpopular, as well as unfashionable at court, occasioned a fatal reaction in politics, which in no long process of time threw that country and its resources into the arms of France, to be constantly directed against us. Ford seems to be indebted to Howell for a part of his description.

[5] *France I more praise and love*, &c.] Here again we have the prevailing language of the day; though it must be admitted that Ford (with some assistance from Massinger) has selected his traits of character with impartiality and judgment. The excellence of the French in horsemanship is noticed by most of our old writers. Thus, the King in *Hamlet*;

"I have seen myself and serv'd against the French,
And they can well on horseback; but this gallant
Had witchcraft in't, he grew unto his seat," &c.

And in *The White Devil* [by Webster];

"Hee told mee of a *restie* Barbarie horse
Which he would faine haue brought to the carreere,
The sault, and the ring-galliard: now, my lord,
I haue a *rare French rider*."

There is more of this in the same play; but enough on so trite a

Yourself for horsemanship much fam'd ; and there
You shall have many proofs to show your skill.
The French are passing courtly, ripe of wit,
Kind, but extreme dissemblers ; you shall have
A Frenchman ducking lower than your knee,
At th' instant mocking even your very shoe-ties.
To give the country due, it is on earth
A paradise ; and if you can neglect
Your own appropriaments, but praising that
In others wherein you excel yourself,
You shall be much belov'd there.

Ros. Yet methought
I heard you and the duchess, two nights since,
Discoursing of an island thereabouts,
Call'd—let me think—'twas—

Fern. England ?

Ros. That : pray, sir—
You have been there, methought I heard you praise it.

Fern. I'll tell you what I found there ; men as neat,
As courtly as the French, but in condition
Quite opposite.[6] Put case that you, my lord,
Could be more rare on horseback than you are,
If there—as there are many—one excell'd
You in your art as much as you do others,
Yet will the English think their own is nothing

---

subject. It seems, indeed, that about this period the English were surpassed by most nations in this noble art ; nor was it till James I. wisely encouraged horse-races, that we thought of improving the old heavy, short-winded breed of horses, by the introduction of Barbary and other stallions, and that the consequent improvement in managing them took place, which long since rendered us the most skilful and daring riders of Europe.

[6] *but in* condition
Quite opposite, &c.] i.e. in *disposition*. We have the word in the same sense in page 13, where Petruchio says of the Duchess that she is

"right noble
In her *condition*" [*conditions*. D.].

Compar'd with you, a stranger; in their habits
They are not more fantastic [t]han uncertain;
In short, their fair abundance, manhood, beauty,[7]
No nation can disparage but itself.

Ros. My lord, you have much eas'd me; I resolve.

Fern. And whither are you bent?

Ros. My lord, for travel;
To speed for England.

Fern. No, my lord, you must not:
I have[8] yet some private conference
T' impart unto you for your good; at night
I'll meet you at my Lord Petruchio's house:
Till then be secret.

Ros. Dares my cousin trust me?[9]

Pet. Dare I, my lord! yes, 'less your fact were greater
Than a bold woman's spleen.

Ros. The duke's at hand,
And I must hence: my service to your lordships.
[*Exit.*

Pet. Now, nephew, as I told you, since the duke
Hath held the reins of state in his own hand,
Much alter'd from the man he was before,—

* * * * * * * *

As if he were transformèd in his mind,[10]—

[7] *In short, their* fair *abundance, manhood, beauty.*] The old copy reads "their *fare* abundance:" a slighter change would be to place a comma after "*fare;*" but the text as it now stands seems to me more in the author's manner.

[8] *I have*] Qy. "For *I have*"? D.

[9] *Dares my cousin trust me?*] It does not appear what plan Fernando had formed to serve Roseilli, who, like his friend, seems already to have forgotten that he was ordered to leave the court that morning.

[10] Here, or rather, perhaps, after the preceding verse, a line or more has dropt out at the press. The purport of the lost passage is easily collected from the context. The duke, since his accession, has drawn round him a set of profligate parasites, who, &c. It is scarcely necessary to observe that no part of the duke's conduct jus-

To soothe him in his pleasures, amongst whom
Is fond Ferentes; one whose pride takes pride
In nothing more than to delight his lust;
And he—with grief I speak it—hath, I fear,
Too much besotted my unhappy daughter,
My poor Colona; whom, for kindred's sake,
As you are noble, as you honour virtue,
Persuade to love herself: a word from you
May win her more than my entreats[11] or frowns.

Fern. Uncle, I'll do my best: meantime, pray tell me,
Whose mediation wrought the marriage
Betwixt the duke and duchess,—who was agent.

Pet. His roving eye and her enchanting face,
The only dower nature had ordain'd
T' advance her to her bride-bed. She was daughter
Unto a gentleman of Milán—no better—
Preferr'd to serve i' th' Duke of Milan's court;
Where for her beauty she was greatly fam'd:
And passing late from thence to Monaco,
To visit there her uncle, Paul Baglione
The abbot, Fortune—queen to such blind matches—
Presents her to the duke's eye, on the way,
As he pursues the deer: in short, my lord,
He saw her, lov'd her, woo'd her, won her, match'd her;[12]
No counsel could divert him.

Fern. She is fair.

---

tifies the reproach here laid upon him; he is rather a well-meaning dotard, a better Bassanes, than a follower of debauched society: but Ford seems to have lost his way through a great part of this drama.

11 *entreats*] The 4to has "entreaties." D.

12 *in short, my lord,*
He saw her, lov'd her, &c.] The duke is "a thriving wooer." In this rapid abstract of his success the poet seems to have had another bold and fortunate adventurer in view;

"Mars videt hanc, visamque cupit, potiturque cupita."

Pet. She is; and, to speak truth, I think right noble
In her conditions.[13]

Fern. If, when I should choose,
Beauty and virtue were the fee propos'd,
I should not pass[14] for parentage.

Pet. The duke
Doth come.

Fern. Let's break-off talk.—[*Aside*] If ever, now,
Good angel of my soul, protect my truth!

Enter the Duke, BIANCA, FIORMONDA, NIBRASSA, FERENTES, JULIA, *and* D'AVOLOS.

Duke. Come, my Bianca, revel in mine arms;
Whiles I, wrapt in my admiration, view
Lilies and roses growing in thy cheeks.—
Fernando! O, thou half myself! no joy
Could make my pleasures full without thy presence:
I am a monarch of felicity,
Proud in a pair of jewels, rich and beautiful,—
A perfect friend, a wife above compare.

Fern. Sir, if a man so low in rank may hope,
By loyal duty and devoted zeal,
To hold a correspondency[15] in friendship
With one so mighty as the Duke of Pavy,
My uttermost ambition is to climb
To those deserts may give the style of servant.

Duke. Of partner in my dukedom, in my heart,
As freely as the privilege of blood
Hath made them mine; Philippo and Fernando
Shall be without distinction.—Look, Bianca,
On this good man; in all respects to him
Be as to me: only the name of husband,

[13] *conditions.*] See note, p. 10. D.
[14] *pass*] i.e. care. D.
[15] *correspondency*] The 4to has "Correspondence." D.

And reverent observance of our bed,
Shall differ us in persons, else in soul
We are all one.

Bian. I shall, in best of love,
Regard the bosom-partner of my lord.

Fior. [*aside to Fer.*] Ferentes,—

Fer. [*aside to Fior.*] Madam?

Fior. [*aside to Fer.*] You are one loves courtship:
He hath[16] some change of words,[17] 'twere no lost labour
To stuff your table-books;[18] the man speaks wisely!

Fer. [*aside to Fior.*] I'm glad your highness is so pleasant.

Duke. Sister,—

Fior. My lord and brother?

Duke. You are too silent,
Quicken your sad remembrance:[19] though the loss
Of your dead husband be of more account
Than slight neglect, yet 'tis a sin against
The state of princes to exceed a mean
In mourning for the dead.

Fior. Should form, my lord,
Prevail above affection? no, it cannot.
You have yourself here a right noble duchess,
Virtuous at least; and should your grace now pay—
Which heaven forbid!—the debt you owe to nature,
I dare presume she'd not so soon forget
A prince that thus advanc'd her.—Madam, could you?

D'Av. [*aside*] Bitter and shrewd.

[16] *hath*] The 4to has "had." D.

[17] *change of words,*] Is plenty of words, fluency of language.

[18] *To stuff your table-books;*] i.e. to set down in your memorandum or pocket-book. She speaks ironically, and affects to characterise Fernando as a ready talker, a mere man of words. It is in this sense that Ferentes understands her.

[19] Quicken *your sad remembrance:*] i.e. *Enliven* your melancholy recollections by the admission of pleasanter thoughts.

Bian. Sister, I should too much bewray my weakness,
To give a resolution on a passion
I never felt nor fear'd.[20]
Nib. A modest answer.
Fern. If credit may be given to a face,
My lord, I'll undertake on her behalf;
Her words are trusty heralds to her mind.
Fior. [*aside to D'Av.*] Exceeding good; the man will "undertake"!
Observe it, D'Avolos.
D'Av. [*aside to Fior.*] Lady, I do;[21]
'Tis a smooth praise.
Duke. Friend, in thy judgment I approve thy love,
And love thee better for thy judging mine.
Though my gray-headed senate in the laws
Of strict opinion and severe dispute
Would tie the limits of our free affects,[22]—
Like superstitious Jews,—to match with none
But in a tribe of princes like ourselves,
Gross-nurtur'd slaves, who force their wretched souls
To crouch to profit; nay, for trash and wealth
Dote on some crookèd or misshapen form;
Hugging wise nature's lame deformity,
Begetting creatures ugly as themselves:—
But why should princes do so, that command
The storehouse of the earth's hid minerals?—

[20] *I should too much bewray my weakness*
To give a resolution (to speak *decisively*) *on a* passion
I never felt nor fear'd.] i.e. ingratitude. It is well answered; "but she'll keep her word!"

[21] *Lady, I do;*] The 4to has "I doe, Lady." D.

[22] *Would tie the limits of our free* affects,] i.e. affections. So in *The Case is Alter'd* [Jonson's *Works*, vol. vi. p. 345]:

"Rachel, I hope I shall not need to urge
The sacred purity of our *affects*."

And see *Jonson*, vol. ii. p. 281. [Here the 4to has "effects." D.]

No, my Bianca, thou'rt to me as dear
As if thy portion had been Europe's riches;
Since in thine eyes lies more than these are worth.
Set on; they shall be strangers to my heart
That envy thee thy fortunes.—Come, Fernando,
My but divided self; what we have done
We are only deb[i]tor to heaven for.—On!

Fior. [*aside to D'Av.*] Now take thy time, or never, D'Avolos;
Prevail, and I will raise thee high in grace.

D'Av. [*aside to Fior.*] Madam, I will omit no art.

[*Exeunt all but D'Av., who recals Fern.*

My honour'd Lord Fernando!

Fern. To me, sir?

D'Av. Let me beseech your lordship to excuse me, in the nobleness of your wisdom, if I exceed good manners: I am one, my lord, who in the admiration of your perfect virtues do so truly honour and reverence your deserts, that there is not a creature bears life shall more faithfully study to do you service in all offices of duty and vows of due respect.

Fern. Good sir, you bind me to you: is this all?

D'Av. I beseech your ear a little; good my lord, what I have to speak concerns your reputation and best fortune.

Fern. How's that! my reputation? lay aside
Superfluous ceremony; speak; what is't?

D'Av. I do repute myself the blessedest man alive, that I shall be the first gives your lordship news of your perpetual comfort.

Fern. As how?

D'Av. If singular beauty, unimitable virtues, honour, youth, and absolute goodness be a fortune, all those are at once offered to your particular choice.

Fern. Without delays, which way?

D'Av. The great and gracious Lady Fiormonda love[s] you, infinitely loves you.—But, my lord, as ever you tendered a servant to your pleasures, let me not be revealed that I gave you notice on't.

Fern. Sure, you are strangely out of tune, sir.

D'Av. Please but to speak to her; be but courtly-ceremonious with her, use once but the language of affection, if I misreport aught besides my knowledge, let me never have place in your good opinion. O, these women, my lord, are as brittle metal as your glasses, as smooth, as slippery,—their very first substance was quicksands:[23] let 'em look never so demurely, one fillip chokes them. My lord, she loves you; I know it.—But I beseech your lordship not to discover me; I would not for the world she should know that you know it by me.

Fern. I understand you, and to thank your care
Will study to requite it; and I vow
She never shall have notice of your news
By me or by my means. And, worthy sir,
Let me alike enjoin you not to speak
A word of that I understand her love;
And as for me, my word shall be your surety
I'll not as much as give her cause to think
I ever heard it.

D'Av. Nay, my lord, whatsoever I infer, you may break with her in it, if you please; for, rather than silence should hinder you one step to such a fortune, I will expose myself to any rebuke for your sake, my good lord.

Fern. You shall not indeed, sir; I am still your friend, and will prove so. For the present I am forced

[23] *their very* first *substance was* quicksands:] This is said in allusion to the traditionary stories of the first discovery of glass by the Phœnician mariners in consequence of their lighting a fire on the sand.

to attend the duke: good hours befall ye! I must leave you. [*Exit.*

D'Av. Gone already? 'sfoot, I ha' marred all! this is worse and worse; he's as cold as hemlock. If her highness knows how I have gone to work, she'll thank me scurvily: a pox of all dull brains! I took the clean contrary course. There is a mystery in this slight carelessness of his; I must sift it, and I will find it. Ud's me, fool myself out of my wit! well, I'll choose some fitter opportunity to inveigle him, and till then smooth her up that he is a man overjoyed with the report. [*Exit.*

SCENE II. *Another room in the same.*

Enter FERENTES *and* COLONA.

Fer. Madam, by this light I vow myself your servant; only yours, inespecially yours. Time, like a turncoat, may order and disorder the outward fashions of our bodies, but shall never enforce a change on the constancy of my mind. Sweet Colona, fair Colona, young and sprightful lady, do not let me in the best of my youth languish in my earnest affections.

Col. Why should you seek, my lord, to purchase glory
By the disgrace[s] of a silly maid?

Fer. That I confess too. I am every way so unworthy of the first-fruits of thy embraces, so far beneath the riches of thy merit, that it can be no honour to thy fame to rank me in the number of thy servants; yet prove me how true, how firm I will stand to thy pleasures, to thy command; and, as time shall serve, be ever thine. Now, prithee, dear Colona,—

Col. Well, well, my lord, I have no heart of flint;

Or if I had, you know by cunning words
How to outwear it :—but—

Fer. But what? do not pity thy own gentleness, lovely Colona. Shall I? Speak, shall I?—say but ay, and our wishes are made up.

Col. How shall I say ay, when my fears say no?

Fer. You will not fail to meet [me] two hours hence, sweet?

Col. No;
Yes, yes, I would have said: how my tongue trips!

Fer. I take that promise and that double *yes* as an assurance of thy faith. In the grove; good sweet, remember; in any case alone,—d'ye mark, love?—not as much as your duchess' little dog;—you'll not forget?—two hours hence—think on't, and miss not: till then—

Col. O, if you should prove false, and love another!

Fer. Defy me, then! I'll be all thine, and a servant only to thee, only to thee. [*Exit Col.*]—Very passing good! three honest women in our courts here of Italy are enough to discredit a whole nation of that sex. He that is not a cuckold or a bastard is a strangely happy man; for a chaste wife, or a mother that never stept awry, are wonders, wonders in Italy. 'Slife! I have got the feat on't, and am every day more active in my trade: 'tis a sweet sin, this slip of mortality, and I have tasted enough for one passion of my senses.—Here comes more work for me.

Enter JULIA.

And how does my[24] own Julia? Mew upon this sadness! what's the matter you are melancholy?—Whither away, wench?

[24] *my*] Gifford printed "mine." D.

Jul. 'Tis well; the time has been when your smooth tongue
Would not have mock'd my griefs; and had I been
More chary of mine honour,[25] you had still
Been lowly as you were.

Fer. Lowly! why, I am sure I cannot be much more lowly than I am to thee; thou bringest me on my bare knees, wench, twice in every four-and-twenty hours, besides half-turns instead of bevers.[26] What must we next do, sweetheart?

Jul. Break vows on your side; I expect no other,
But every day look when some newer choice
May violate your honour and my trust.

Fer. Indeed, forsooth! how say ye by that, la?[27] I hope I neglect no opportunity to your *nunquam satis*, to be called in question for. Go, thou art as fretting as an old grogram:[28] by this hand, I love thee[29] for't; it becomes thee so prettily to be angry. Well, if thou shouldst die, farewell all love with me for ever! go; I'll meet thee soon in thy lady's back-lobby, I will, wench; look for me.

Jul. But shall I be resolv'd you will be mine?

Fer. All thine; I will reserve my best ability, my heart, my honour only to thee, only to thee. Pity of my blood, away! I hear company coming on: remember, soon I am all thine, I will live perpetually only to thee: away! [*Exit Jul.*] 'Sfoot! I wonder about

25 *mine honour,*] Gifford printed "*mine* own *honour.*" D.

26 *bevers.*] A slight intermediate repast between breakfast and dinner, or sometimes between dinner and the *undermele.*

27 *how say ye by that, la?*] A colloquial expression, common in our old dramatists, for "what do you mean by that?" There is a slight error in the old copy, which for "*say ye*" reads "*shey.*"

28 *thou art as fretting as an old grogram:*] A coarse kind of silk taffety, usually stiffened with gum, and peculiarly liable, after some wearing, to fret and lose its gloss. It is often alluded to by our old writers.

29 *thee*] Gifford printed "you." D.

what time of the year I was begot; sure, it was when the moon was in conjunction, and all the other planets drunk at a morris-dance: I am haunted above patience; my mind is not as infinite to do as my occasions are proffered of doing. Chastity! I am an eunuch if I think there be any such thing; or if there be, 'tis amongst us men, for I never found it in a woman throughly tempted yet. I have a shrewd hard task coming on; but let it pass.—Who comes now? My lord, the duke's friend! I will strive to be inward with him.

Enter FERNANDO.

My noble[30] Lord Fernando!—

Fern. My Lord Ferentes, I should change some words
Of consequence with you; but since I am,
For this time, busied in more serious thoughts,
I'll pick some fitter opportunity.

Fer. I will wait your pleasure, my lord. Good-day to your lordship. [*Exit.*

Fern. Traitor to friendship, whither shall I run,
That, lost to reason, cannot sway the float
Of the unruly faction in my blood?
The duchess, O, the duchess! in her smiles
Are all my joys abstracted.—Death to my thoughts!
My other plague comes to me.

Enter FIORMONDA *and* JULIA.

Fior. My Lord Fernando, what, so hard at study!
You are a kind companion to yourself,
That love to be alone so.

Fern. Madam, no;
I rather chose this leisure to admire
The glories of this little world, the court,

[30] *noble*] Omitted by Gifford. D.

Where, like so many stars, on several thrones
Beauty and greatness shine in proper orbs;
Sweet matter for my meditation.

Fior. So, so, sir!—Leave us, Julia [*Exit Jul.*]—
your own proof,
By travel and prompt observation,
Instruct[s] you how to place the use of speech.—
But since you are at leisure, pray let's sit:
We'll pass the time a little in discourse.
What have you seen abroad?

Fern. No wonders, lady,
Like these I see at home.

Fior. At home! as how?

Fern. Your pardon, if my tongue, the voice of truth,
Report but what is warranted by sight.

Fior. What sight?

Fern. Look in your glass, and you shall see
A miracle.

Fior. What miracle?

Fern. Your beauty,
So far above all beauties else abroad
As you are in your own superlative.

Fior. Fie, fie! your wit hath too much edge.

Fern. Would that,
Or any thing that I could challenge mine,
Were but of value to express how much
I serve in love the sister of my prince!

Fior. 'Tis for your prince's sake, then, not for mine?

Fern. For you in him, and much for him in you.
I must acknowledge, madam, I observe
In your affects[31] a thing to me most strange,
Which makes me so much honour you the more.

Fior. Pray, tell it.

Fern. Gladly, lady:

[31] *In your* affects] See [note], p. 15.

I see how opposite to youth and custom
You set before you, in the[32] tablature
Of your remembrance, the becoming griefs
Of a most loyal lady for the loss
Of so renown'd a prince as was your lord.

Fior. Now, good my lord, no more of him.

Fern. Of him!
I know it is a needless task in me
To set him forth in his deservèd praise;
You better can record it; for you find
How much more he exceeded other men
In most heroic virtues of account,
So much more was your loss in losing him.
Of him! his praise should be a field too large,
Too spacious, for so mean an orator
As I to range in.

Fior. Sir, enough: 'tis true
He well deserv'd your labour. On his deathbed
This ring he gave me, bade me never part
With this but to the man I lov'd as dearly
As I lov'd him: yet since you know which way
To blaze his worth so rightly, in return
To your deserts wear this for him and me.

[*Offers him the ring.*

Fern. Madam!

Fior. 'Tis yours.

Fern. Methought you said he charg'd you
Not to impart it but to him you lov'd
As dearly as you lov'd him.

Fior. True, I said so.

Fern. O, then, far be it my unhallow'd hand
With any rude intrusion should annul[33]
A testament enacted by the dead!

[32] *the*] The 4to has "your." D.
[33] *annul*] The 4to has "vnuaile;" and Gifford printed "unveil." D.

Fior. Why, man, that testament is disannull'd
And cancell'd quite by us that live. Look here,
My blood is not yet freez'd; for better instance,
Be judge yourself; experience is no danger—
Cold are my sighs; but, feel, my lips are warm.
[*Kisses him.*

Fern. What means the virtuous marquess?

Fior. To new-kiss
The oath to thee, which whiles he liv'd was his:
Hast thou yet power to love?

Fern. To love!

Fior. To meet
Sweetness of language in discourse as sweet?

Fern. Madam, 'twere dulness past the ignorance
Of common blockheads not to understand
Whereto this favour tends; and 'tis a fortune
So much above my fate, that I could wish
No greater happiness on earth: but know
Long since I vow'd to live a single life.

Fior. What was 't you said?

Fern. I said I made a vow—

Enter BIANCA, PETRUCHIO, COLONA, *and* D'AVOLOS.

[*Aside*] Blessèd deliverance!

Fior. [*aside*] Prevented? mischief on this interruption!

Bian. My Lord Fernando, you encounter fitly;
I have a suit t'ye.

Fern. 'Tis my duty, madam,
To be commanded.

Bian. Since my lord the duke
Is now dispos'd to mirth, the time serves well
For mediation, that he would be pleas'd
To take the Lord Roseilli to his grace.
He is a noble gentleman; I dare

Engage my credit, loyal to the state;—
And, sister, one that ever strove, methought,
By special service and obsequious care,
To win respect from you: it were a part
Of gracious favour, if you pleas'd to join
With us in being suitors to the duke
For his return to court.

Fior. To court! indeed,
You have some cause to speak; he undertook,
Most champion-like, to win the prize at tilt,
In honour of your picture; marry, did he.
There's not a groom o' th' querry could have match'd
The jolly riding-man: pray, get him back;
I do not need his service, madam, I.

Bian. Not need it, sister! why, I hope you think
'Tis no necessity in me to move it,
More than respect of honour.

Fior. Honour! puh!
Honour is talk'd of more than known by some.

Bian. Sister, these words I understand not.

Fern. [*aside*] Swell not, unruly thoughts!—
Madam, the motion you propose proceeds
From the true touch of goodness; 'tis a plea
Wherein my tongue and knee shall jointly strive
To beg his highness for Roseilli's cause.
Your judgment rightly speaks him; there is not
In any court of Christendom a man
For quality or trust more absolute.

Fior. [*aside*] How! is't even so?

Pet. I shall for ever bless
Your highness for your gracious kind esteem
Of my dishearten'd kinsman; and to add
Encouragement to what you undertake,
I dare affirm 'tis no important fault
Hath caus'd the duke's distaste.

Bian. I hope so too.

D'Av. Let your highness, and you all, my lords, take advice how you motion his excellency on Roseilli's behalf; there is more danger in that man than is fit to be publicly reported. I could wish things were otherwise for his own sake; but I'll assure ye, you will exceedingly alter his excellency's disposition he now is in, if you but mention the name of Roseilli to his ear; I am so much acquainted in the process of his actions.

Bian. If it be so, I am the sorrier, sir:
I'm loth to move my lord unto offence;
Yet I'll adventure chiding.

Fern. [*aside*] O, had I India's gold, I'd give it all
T' exchange one private word, one minute's breath,
With this heart-wounding beauty!

Enter the Duke, FERENTES, *and* NIBRASSA.

Duke. Prithee, no more, Ferentes; by the faith
I owe to honour, thou hast made me laugh
Beside my spleen.[34]—Fernando, hadst thou heard
The pleasant humour of Mauruccio's dotage
Discours'd, how in the winter of his age
He is become a lover, thou wouldst swear
A morris-dance were but a tragedy
Compar'd to that: well, we will see the youth.—
What council hold you now, sirs?

Bian. We, my lord,
Were talking of the horsemanship in France,[35]

[34] *thou hast made me laugh*
Beside my spleen.] i.e. "beyond my usual custom of laughter." The spleen seems to have been considered as the source of any sudden and violent ebullition, whether of mirth or anger.

[35] *We, my lord,*
Were talking of the horsemanship in France, &c.] See p. 9. This topic is skilfully introduced by the duchess, as it leads directly to the mention of Roseilli's excellence in the art. It does not appear how the duke reckoned time, but he evidently supposes some days to have passed since the opening of the play, though we are but in

Which, as your friend reports, he thinks exceeds
All other nations.

Duke. How! why, have not we
As gallant riders here?

Fern. None that I know.

Duke. Pish, your affection leads you; I dare wage
A thousand ducats, not a man in France
Outrides Roseilli.

Fior. [*aside*] I shall quit this wrong.

Bian. I said as much, my lord.

Fern. I have not seen
His practice since my coming back.

Duke. Where is he?
How is't we see him not?

Pet. [*aside*] What's this? what's this?

Fern. I hear he was commanded from the court.

D'Av. [*aside*] O, confusion on this villanous occasion!

Duke. True; but we meant a day or two at most
Should be his furthest term. Not yet return'd?
Where's D'Avolos?

D'Av. My lord?

Duke. You know our mind:
How comes it thus to pass we miss Roseilli?

D'Av. My lord, in a sudden discontent I hear he departed towards Benevento, determining, as I am given to understand, to pass to Seville, minding to visit his cousin, Don Pedro de Toledo, in the Spanish court.

Duke. The Spanish court! now, by the blessèd bones
Of good Saint Francis, let there posts be sent

---

the second scene, and, as appears from Petruchio's speech in the next page, not yet arrived at the close of the first day!

30 *mind*] The 4to has "minds." D.

To call him back, or I will post thy head
Beneath my foot: ha, you! you know my mind;
Look that you get him back: the Spanish court!
And without our commission!—[37]

Pet. [*aside*] Here's fine juggling!

Bian. Good sir, be not so mov'd.

Duke. Fie, fie, Bianca,
'Tis such a gross indignity; I'd rather
Have lost seven years' revenue:—the Spanish court!—
How now, what ails our sister?

Fior. On the sudden
I fall a-bleeding; 'tis an ominous sign,
Pray heaven it turn to good!—Your highness' leave.
[*Exit.*

Duke. Look to her.—Come, Fernando,—come, Bianca,—
Let's strive to overpass this choleric heat.—
Sirrah, see that you trifle not. [*To D'Av.*]—How we
Who sway the manage of authority
May be abus'd by smooth officious agents!—
But look well to our sister.
[*Exeunt all but Pet. and Fern.*

Pet. Nephew, please you
To see your friend to-night?

Fern. Yes, uncle, yes. [*Exit Pet.*
Thus bodies walk unsoul'd![38] mine eyes but follow
My heart entomb'd in yonder goodly shrine:
Life without her is but death's subtle snares,
And I am but a coffin to my cares. [*Exit.*

[37] *And without our commission!—*] The 4to has "*And without our Commission,*— say!" D.

[38] *unsoul'd*] Spenser has this word in *The Faery Queene;*

"Ne ought to see, but like a shade to weene,
Unbodied, *unsoul'd*, unheard, unseene."

[B. vii. C. vii. 46.—Gifford quoted Spenser here because Weber had said that "*unsoul'd*" was "a very quaint word, coined by Ford." D.]

ACT II.

SCENE I. *A room in* MAURUCCIO'S *house.*

MAURUCCIO *looking in a glass, trimming his beard;* GIACOPO *brushing him.*

Maur. Beard, be confin'd to neatness, that no hair
May stover up[1] to prick my mistress' lip,
More rude than bristles of a porcupine.—
Giacopo!

Gia. My lord?

Maur. Am I all sweet behind?

Gia. I have no poulterer's nose; but your apparel sits about you most debonairly.

Maur. But, Giacopo, with what grace do my words proceed out of my mouth? Have I a moving countenance? is there harmony in my voice? canst thou perceive, as it were, a handsomeness of shape in my very breath, as it is formed into syllable[s], Giacopo?

Enter above[2] Duke, BIANCA, FIORMONDA, FERNANDO, Courtiers, *and* Attendants.

Gia. Yes, indeed, sir, I do feel a savour as pleasant as—a glister-pipe [*aside*]—calamus, or civet.

Duke. Observe him, and be silent.

Maur. Hold thou the glass, Giacopo, and mark me with what exceeding comeliness I could court the lady marquess, if it come to the push.

[1] *May* stover *up*] i.e. *bristle* up, *stiffen*, &c.; in which sense the word is still familiarly used in the western counties.

[2] *Enter above*, &c.] i.e. as has been already observed, on the raised platform of the old stage, which served as a gallery to a room, or a balcony to a street.

Duke. Sister, you are his aim.

Fior. A subject fit
To be the stale of laughter!

Bian. That's your music.[3]

Maur. Thus I reverse my pace, and thus stalking in courtly gait, I advance one, two, and three.—Good! I kiss my hand, make my congee, settle my countenance, and thus begin.—Hold up the glass higher, Giacopo.

Gia. Thus high, sir?

Maur. 'Tis well; now mark me.

"Most excellent marquéss, most fair la-dy,
Let not old age or hairs that are sil-vér
Disparage my desire; for it may be
I am than other green youth nimblé-er.[4]
Since I am your gra-cé's servánt so true,
Great lady, then, love me for my vir-tue."

O, Giacopo, Petrarch was a dunce, Dante a jig-maker, Sanazzar a goose, and Ariosto a puck-fist,[5] to me! I tell thee, Giacopo, I am rapt with fury; and have been for these six nights together drunk with the pure liquor of Helicon.

Gia. I think no less, sir; for you look as wild, and talk as idly, as if you had not slept these nine years.

Duke. What think you of this language, sister?

Fior. Sir,
I think in princes' courts no age nor greatness

[3] *That's your music.*] This appears to be an incidental observation on the perpetual tone of wrangling sustained by this captious, jealous, malevolent woman, who turns everything to poison.

[4] *nimblé-er:*] Rather, "nimbeler."—The 4to has "nimb-ler." D.

[5] *Ariosto a* puck-fist,] i. e. an *empty* boaster. The word is common in our old writers for anything vile or worthless. The fungus so called is better known to our villagers by the name of *puff-ball.*

But must admit the fool; in me 'twere folly
To scorn what greater states[6] than I have been.

Bian. O, but you are too general—

Fior. A fool!
I thank your highness: many a woman's wit
Have thought themselves much better was much worse.

Bian. You still mistake me.

Duke. Silence! note the rest.

Maur. God-a'-mercy, brains! Giacopo, I have it.

Gia. What, my lord?

Maur. A conceit, Giacopo, and a fine one—down on thy knees, Giacopo, and worship my wit. Give me both thy ears. Thus it is; I will have my picture drawn most compositiously, in a square table[7] of some two foot long, from the crown of the head to the waist downward, no further.

Gia. Then you'll look like a dwarf, sir, being cut off by the middle.

Maur. Speak not thou, but wonder at the conceit that follows. In my bosom, on my left side, I will have a leaf of blood-red crimson velvet—as it were part of my doublet—open; which being opened, Giacopo,—now mark!—I will have a clear and most transparent crystal in the form of a heart.—Singular-admirable!—When I have framed this, I will, as some rare outlandish piece of workmanship, bestow it on the most fair and illustrious Lady[8] Fiormonda.

Gia. But now, sir, for the conceit.

Maur. Simplicity and ignorance, prate no more!

[6] *states*] See note, vol. i. p. 191. D.

[7] *table*] The board, or strained canvas, on which the picture was to be painted.

[8] *Lady*] Omitted by Gifford. D.

blockhead, dost not understand yet? Why, this being to her instead of a looking-glass, she shall no oftener powder her hair, surfel her cheeks,[9] cleanse her teeth, or conform the hairs of her eyebrows, but having occasion to use this glass—which for the rareness and richness of it she will hourly do—but she shall as often gaze on my picture, remember me, and behold the excellence of her excellency's beauty in the prospective and mirror, as it were, in my heart.

Gia. Ay, marry, sir, this is something.

All above except Fior. Ha, ha, ha! [*Exit Fior.*

Bian. My sister's gone in anger.

Maur. Who's that laughs? search with thine eyes, Giacopo.

Gia. O, my lord, my lord, you have gotten an everlasting fame! the duke's grace, and the duchess' grace, and my Lord Fernando's grace, with all the rabble of courtiers, have heard every word; look where they stand! Now you shall be made a count for your wit, and I lord for my counsel.

Duke. Beshrew the chance! we are discover'd.

Maur. Pity—O, my wisdom! I must speak to them.—
O, duke most great, and most renownèd duchess!
Excuse my apprehension, which not much is;
'Tis love, my lord, that's all the hurt you see;

[9] surfel *her cheeks,*] Thus Broome; "Her eye artificially spirited, her cheek *surfelled*, her teeth blanched, her lips painted," &c. *City Wit.* To *surphule* or *surfel* the cheeks is to wash them with mercurial or sulphur water, as it was called, one of those pernicious compounds which, under the name of cosmetics, found their way to the ladies' toilets. They were generally applied, that is, rubbed in, with Spanish wool or a piece of scarlet cloth. The word itself is very common, as indeed was the practice in Ford's time, which in the variety of those deleterious washes yields in nothing to ours. In that interminable old drama, *The Spanish Bawd,* there are more lotions and cosmetics enumerated than our modern Gowlands perhaps ever dreamed of.

Angelica herself [doth] plead for me.

Duke. We pardon you, most wise and learnèd lord;
And, that we may all glorify your wit,
Entreat your wisdom's company to-day
To grace our table with your grave discourse :[10]
What says your mighty eloquence?

Maur. Giacopo, help me; his grace has put me out [of] my own bias, and I know not what to answer in form.

Gia. Ud's me, tell him you'll come.

Maur. Yes, I will come, my lord the duke, I will.

Duke. We take your word, and wish your honour health.—
Away, then! come, Bianca, we have found
A salve for melancholy,—mirth and ease.

[*Exit the Duke, followed by all but Bian. and Fern.*

Bian. I'll see the jolly lover and his glass
Take leave of one another.

Maur. Are they gone?

Gia. O, my lord, I do now smell news.

Maur. What news, Giacopo?

Gia. The duke has a smackering towards you, and you shall clap-up with his sister the widow suddenly.

Maur. She is mine, Giacopo, she is mine! Advance the glass, Giacopo, that I may practise, as I pass, to walk a portly grace like a marquis, to which degree I am now a-climbing.

[10] *Entreat your wisdom's company to-day
To grace our* table *with your grave discourse* :] The old copy reads "To grace our *talk*," which renders the metre as imperfect as the sense. I flatter myself that the text is restored to its genuine state.

Thus do we march to honour's haven of bliss,
To ride in triumph through Persepolis.[11]
[*Exit Gia., going backward with the glass, followed by Maur. complimenting.*[12]

Bian. Now, as I live, here's laughter
Worthy our presence! I'll not lose him so. [*Going.*

Fern. Madam,—

Bian. To me, my lord?

Fern. Please but to hear
The story of a castaway in love;
And, O, let not the passage of a jest
Make slight a sadder subject, who hath plac'd
All happiness in your diviner eyes!

Bian. My lord, the time—

Fern. The time! yet hear me speak,
For I must speak or burst: I have a soul
So anchor'd down with cares in seas of woe,
That passion and the vows I owe to you
Have chang'd me to a lean anatomy:[13]
Sweet princess of my life,—

Bian. Forbear, or I shall—

Fern. Yet, as you honour virtue, do not freeze
My hopes to more discomfort than as yet
My fears suggest; no beauty so adorns

[11] *To ride in triumph through Persepolis.*] To my surprise, it has escaped Gifford that here Mauruccio is quoting Marlowe's *Tamburlaine;*

"*Mean.* Your majesty shall shortly have your wish,
And *ride in triumph through Persepolis.*
[*Exeunt all except Tamb. Ther. Tech. and Usum.*
Tamb. And *ride in triumph through Persepolis!*—
Is it not brave to be a king, Techelles?—
Usumcasane and Theridamas,
Is it not passing brave to be a king,
And *ride in triumph through Persepolis?*"
First Part of Tamburlaine, act ii. sc. 5,—*Works*, p. 17, ed. Dyce, 1858. D.

[12] *Mauruccio* complimenting.] i.e. practising the airs of a courtier.

[13] *anatomy:*] i.e. skeleton. D.

The composition of a well-built mind
As pity: hear me out.
Bian. No more! I spare
To tell you what you are, and must confess
Do almost hate my judgment, that it once
Thought goodness dwelt in you. Remember now,
It is the third time since your treacherous tongue
Hath pleaded treason to my ear and fame;
Yet, for the friendship 'twixt my lord and you,
I have not voic'd your follies: if you dare
To speak a fourth time, you shall rue your lust;
'Tis all no better:—learn and love yourself. [*Exit.*
Fern. Gone! O, my sorrows! how am I undone!
Not speak again? no, no, in her chaste breast
Virtue and resolution have discharg'd
All female weakness: I have su'd and su'd,
Knelt, wept, and begg'd; but tears and vows and words
Move her no more than summer-winds a rock.
I must resolve to check this rage of blood,
And will: she is all icy to my fires,
Yet even that ice inflames in me desires. [*Exit.*

SCENE II. *A room in* PETRUCHIO'S *house.*

Enter PETRUCHIO *and* ROSEILLI.

Rose. Is't possible the duke should be so mov'd?
Pet. 'Tis true; you have no enemy at court
But her for whom you pine so much in love;
Then master your affections: I am sorry
You hug your ruin so.—
What say you to the project I propos'd?
Rose. I entertain it with a greater joy
Than shame can check.

Enter FERNANDO.

Pet. You're come as I could wish;
My cousin is resolv'd.
Fern. Without delay
Prepare yourself, and meet at court anon,
Some half-hour hence; and Cupid bless your joy!
Rose. If ever man was bounden to a friend,—
Fern. No more; away! [*Exeunt Pet. and Rose.*
Love's rage is yet unknown;
In his—ay me![13]—too well I feel my own!—
So, now I am alone; now let me think.
She is the duchess; say she be; a creature
Sew'd-up in painted[14] cloth might so be styl'd;
That's but a name: she's married too; she is,
And therefore better might distinguish love:
She's young and fair; why, madam, that's the bait
Invites me more to hope: she's the duke's wife;
Who knows not this?—she's bosom'd to my friend;
There, there, I am quite lost: will not be won;
Still worse and worse: abhors to hear me speak;
Eternal mischief! I must urge no more;
For, were I not be-leper'd in my soul,
Here were enough to quench the flames of hell.
What then? pish! [if] I must not speak, I'll write.
Come, then, sad secretary to my plaints,
Plead thou my faith, for words are turn'd to sighs.
What says this paper? [*Takes out a letter, and reads.*

Enter D'AVOLOS *behind with two pictures.*

D'Av. [*aside*] Now is the time. Alone? reading a letter? good; how now! striking his breast! what, in the name of policy, should this mean? tearing his

[13] *ay me!*] See note, vol. i. p. 165. D.
[14] *in painted*] Gifford printed "*in a painted.*" D.

hair! passion; by all the hopes of my life, plain passion! now I perceive it. If this be not a fit of some violent affection, I am an ass in understanding; why, 'tis plain,—plainer and plainer; love in the extremest. O, for the party who, now! The greatness of his spirits is too high cherished to be caught with some ordinary stuff, and if it be my Lady Fiormonda, I am strangely mistook. Well, that I have fit occasion soon to understand. I have here two pictures newly drawn, to be sent for a present to the Abbot of Monaco, the duchess' uncle, her own and my lady's: I'll observe which of these may, perhaps, bewray him—he turns about.—My noble lord!—

Fern. You're welcome, sir; I thank you.

D'Av. Me, my lord! for what, my lord?

Fern. Who's there? I cry you mercy, D'Avolos,
I took you for another; pray, excuse me.
What is't you bear there?

D'Av. No secret, my lord, but may be imparted to you: a couple of pictures, my good lord,—please you see them?

Fern. I care not much for pictures; but whose are they?

D'Av. Th' one is for my lord's sister, the other is the duchess.

Fern. Ha, D'Avolos! the duchess's?

D'Av. Yes, my lord.—[*Aside*] Sure, the word startled him: observe that.

Fern. You told me, Master Secretary, once,
You ow'd me love.

D'Av. Service, my honoured lord; howsoever you please to term it.

Fern. 'Twere rudeness to be suitor for a sight;
Yet trust me, sir, I'll be all secret.

D'Av. I beseech your lordship;—they are, as I

am, constant to your pleasure. [*Shows Fiormonda's picture.*] This, my lord, is the widow marquess's, as it now newly came from the picture-drawer's, the oil yet green: a sweet picture; and, in my judgment, art hath not been a niggard in striving to equal the life. Michael Angelo himself needed not blush to own the workmanship.

Fern. A very pretty picture; but, kind signior,
To whose use is it?

D'Av. For the duke's, my lord, who determines to send it with all speed as a present to Paul[15] Baglione, uncle to the duchess, that he may see the riches of two such lustres as shine in the court of Pavy.

Fern. Pray, sir, the other?

D'Av. [*shows the picture of the Duchess*] This, my lord, is for the Duchess Bianca: a wondrous sweet picture, if you well observe with what singularity the artsman hath strove to set forth each limb in exquisitest proportion, not missing a hair.

Fern. A hair!

D'Av. She cannot more formally, or—if it may be lawful to use the word—more really, behold her own symmetry in her glass than in taking a sensible view of this counterfeit. When I first saw it, I verily almost was of a mind that this was her very lip.

Fern. Lip!

D'Av. [*aside*] How constantly he dwells upon this portraiture!—Nay, I'll assure your lordship there is no defect of cunning.—[*Aside*] His eye is fixed as if it were incorporated there.—Were not the party herself alive to witness that there is a creature composed of flesh and blood as naturally enriched with such harmony of admirable beauty as is here artificially counterfeited, a very curious eye might repute

[15] *Paul*] Gifford printed "Paulo:" but see p. 12. D.

it as an imaginary rapture of some transported conceit, to aim at an impossibility; whose very first gaze is of force almost to persuade a substantial love in a settled heart.

Fern. Love! heart!

D'Av. My honoured lord,—

Fern. O heavens!

D'Av. [*aside*] I am confirmed.—What ails your lordship?

Fern. You need not praise it, sir; itself is praise.—
[*Aside*] How near had I forgot myself!—I thank you.
'Tis such a picture as might well become
The shrine of some fam'd[16] Venus; I am dazzled
With looking on't:—pray, sir, convey it hence.

D'Av. I am all your servant.—[*Aside*] Blessed, blessed discovery!—Please you to command me?

Fern. No, gentle sir.—[*Aside*] I'm lost beyond my senses.—
D'ye hear, sir? good, where dwells the picture-maker?

D'Av. By the castle's farther drawbridge, near Galiazzo's statue; his name is Alphonso Trinultio.—[*Aside*] Happy above all fate!

Fern. You say enough; my thanks t'ye! [*Exit D'Av.*]—Were that picture
But rated at my lordship, 'twere too cheap.
I fear I spoke or did I know not what;
All sense of providence was in mine eye.

Enter FERENTES, MAURUCCIO, *and* GIACOPO.

Fer. [*aside*] Youth in threescore years and ten!—Trust me, my Lord Mauruccio, you are now younger in the judgment of those that compare your former age with your latter by seven-and-twenty years than

[16] *fam'd*] The 4to has "fain'd." D.

you were three years ago: by all my fidelity, 'tis a miracle! the ladies wonder at you.

Maur. Let them wonder; I am wise as I am courtly.

Gia. The ladies, my lord, call him the Green Broom of the court,—he sweeps all before him,—and swear he has a stabbing wit: it is a very glister to laughter.

Maur. Nay, I know I can tickle 'em at my pleasure; I am stiff and strong, Ferentes.

Gia. [*aside*] A radish-root is a spear of steel in comparison of I know what.

Fer. The marquess doth love you.

Maur. She doth love me.

Fer. And begins to do you infinite grace, Mauruccio, infinite grace.

Fern. I'll take this time.—[*Comes forward*] Good hour, my lords, to both!

Maur. Right princely Fernando, the best of the Fernandos; by the pith of generation, the man I look for. His highness hath sent to find you out: he is determined to weather his own proper individual person for two days' space in my Lord Nibrassa's forest, to hunt the deer, the buck, the roe, and eke the barren doe.

Fern. Is his highness preparing to hunt?

Maur.[17] Yes, my lord, and resolved to lie forth for the breviating the prolixity of some superfluous transmigration of the sun's double cadence to the western horizon, my most perspicuous good lord.

Fern. O, sir, let me beseech you to speak in your own mother tongue.—[*Aside*] Two days' absence, well. —My Lord Mauruccio, I have a suit t'ye,—

Maur. My Lord Fernando, I have a suit to you.

[17] *Maur.*] The 4to has "Feren." D.

Fern. That you will accept from me a very choice token of my love: will you grant it?

Maur. Will you grant mine?

Fern. What is't?

Maur. Only to know what the suit is you please to prefer to me.

Fern. Why, 'tis, my lord, a fool.

Maur. A fool!

Fern. As very a fool as your lordship is—hopeful to see in any time of your life.

Gia. Now, good my lord, part not with the fool on any terms.

Maur. I beseech you, my lord, has the fool qualities?

Fern. Very rare ones: you shall not hear him speak one wise word in a month's converse; passing temperate of diet, for, keep him from meat four-and-twenty hours, and he will fast a whole day and a night together; unless you urge him to swear, there seldom comes an oath from his mouth; and of a fool, my lord, to tell ye the plain truth, had he but half as much wit as you, my lord, he would be in short time three quarters as arrant wise as your lordship.

Maur. Giacopo, these are very rare elements in a creature of little understanding. O, that I long to see him!

Fern. A very harmless idiot;—and, as you could wish, look where he comes.

Enter PETRUCHIO, *and* ROSEILLI *dressed like a fool.*[18]

Pet. Nephew, here is the thing you sent for.—Come hither, fool; come, 'tis a good fool.

[18] *dressed like a* fool.] i.e. in the long petticoats with which innocents, or natural fools, were furnished for the sake of decency. The passion of our ancestors for retaining these mortifying and disgusting spectacles about them can only be accounted for from the

Fern. Here, my lord, I freely give you the fool; pray use him well for my sake.

Maur. I take the fool most thankfully at your hands, my lord.—Hast any qualities, my pretty fool? wilt dwell with me?

Ros. A, a, a, a, ay.

Pet. I never beheld a more natural creature in my life.

Fern. Uncle, the duke, I hear, prepares to hunt;
Let's in and wait.—Farewell, Mauruccio.

[*Exeunt Fern. and Pet.*

Maur. Beast that I am, not to ask the fool's name! 'tis no matter; fool is a sufficient title to call the greatest lord in the court by, if he be no wiser than he.

Gia. O, my lord, what an arrant excellent pretty creature 'tis!—Come, honey, honey, honey, come!

Fer. You are beholding to my Lord Fernando for this gift.

Maur. True. O, that he could but speak methodically!—Canst speak, fool?

Ros. Can speak; de e e e e—

Fer. 'Tis a present for an emperor. What an excellent instrument were this to purchase a suit or a monopoly from the duke's ear!

Maur. I have it, I am wise and fortunate.—Giacopo, I will leave all conceits, and instead of my picture, offer the lady marquess this mortal man of weak brain.

---

superstitious belief, then widely spread, that they brought a blessing to the house that cherished them. It is not easy to surmise why Roseilli took upon himself this repulsive character. He could scarcely expect to win his mistress by inarticulate drivelling; yet he assigns no other motive for his gratuitous degradation: at all events, he contributes nothing to the perfection of the story, nor do his discoveries in his disguise advance or retard the fortunes of his friend, or facilitate the progress of the action in a single instance.

Gia. My lord, you have most rarely bethought you; for so shall she no oftener see the fool but she shall remember you better than by a thousand looking-glasses.

Fer. She will most graciously entertain it.

Maur. I may tell you, Ferentes, there's not a great woman amongst forty but knows how to make sport with a fool.—Dost know how old thou art, sirrah?

Ros. Dud—a clap cheek for nown sake, gaffer; hee e e e e.

Fer. Alas, you must ask him no questions, but clap him on the cheek; I understand his language: your fool is the tender-heartedest creature that is.

Enter FIORMONDA *and* D'AVOLOS *in close conversation.*

Fior. No more; thou hast in this discovery
Exceeded all my favours, D'Avolos.
Is't Mistress Madam Duchess? brave revenge!

D'Av. But had your grace seen the infinite appetite of lust in the piercing adultery of his eye, you would—

Fior. Or change him, or confound him: prompt dissembler!
Is here the bond of his religious vow?
And that, "now when the duke is rid abroad,
My gentleman will stay behind, is sick—or so"?

D'Av. "Not altogether in health;"—it was the excuse he made.

Maur. [*seeing them*] Most fit opportunity! her grace comes just i' th' nick; let me study.

Fer. Lose no time, my lord.

Gia. To her, sir.

Maur. Vouchsafe to stay thy foot, most Cynthian hue,

And from a creature ever vow'd thy servant
Accept this gift, most rare, most fine, most new;
The earnest-penny of a love so fervent.

Fior. What means the jolly youth?

Maur. Nothing, sweet princess, but only to present your grace with this sweet-faced fool; please you to accept him to make you merry: I'll assure your grace he is a very wholesome fool.

Fior. A fool! you might as well ha' given yourself. Whence is he?

Maur. Now, just very now, given me out of special favour by the Lord Fernando, madam.

Fior. By him? well, I accept him; thank you for't:
And, in requital, take that toothpicker;
'Tis yours.

Maur. A toothpicker! I kiss your bounty: no quibble now?—And, madam,
If I grow sick, to make my spirits quicker,
I will revive them with this sweet toothpicker.

Fior. Make use on't as you list.—Here, D'Avolos,
Take in the fool.

D'Av. Come, sweetheart, wilt along with me?

Ros. U u umh,—u u umh,—wonnot, wonnot—u u umh.

Fior. Wilt go with me, chick?

Ros. Will go, te e e—go will go—

Fior. Come, D'Avolos, observe to-night; 'tis late:
Or I will win my choice, or curse my fate.

[*Exeunt Fior. Ros. and D'Av.*

Fer. This was wisely done, now. 'Sfoot, you purchase a favour from a creature, my lord, the greatest king of the earth would be proud of.

Maur. Giacopo!—

Gia. My lord?

Maur. Come behind me, Giacopo; I am big with

conceit, and must be delivered of poetry in the eternal commendation of this gracious toothpicker: —but, first, I hold it a most healthy policy to make a slight supper—

For meat's the food that must preserve our lives,
And now's the time when mortals whet their knives—

on thresholds, shoe-soles, cart-wheels, &c.—Away, Giacopo! [*Exeunt.*

SCENE III. *The palace. The Duchess's apartment.*

Enter COLONA *with lights,* BIANCA, FIORMONDA, JULIA, FERNANDO, *and* D'AVOLOS; COLONA *places the lights on a table, and sets down a chess-board.*

Bian. 'Tis yet but early night, too soon to sleep:
Sister, shall's have a mate at chess?

Fior. A mate!
No, madam, you are grown too hard for me;
My Lord Fernando is a fitter match.

Bian. He's a well-practis'd gamester: well, I care not
How cunning soe'er he be.—To pass an hour
I'll try your skill, my lord: reach here the chess-board.

D'Av. [*aside*] Are you so apt to try his skill, Madam Duchess? Very good!

Fern. I shall bewray too much my ignorance
In striving with your highness; 'tis a game
I lose at still by oversight.

Bian. Well, well,
I fear you not; let's to't.

Fior. You need not, madam.

D'Av. [*aside to Fior.*] Marry, needs she not; how gladly will she to't! 'tis a rook to a queen she heaves a pawn to a knight's place; by'r lady, if all be truly noted, to a duke's place; and that's beside the play,[19] I can tell ye.

[*Fern. and the Duchess play.*

Fior. Madam, I must entreat excuse; I feel
The temper of my body not in case
To judge the strife.

Bian. Lights for our sister, sirs!—
Good rest t'ye; I'll but end my game, and follow.

Fior. [*aside to D'Av.*] Let 'em have time enough; and, as thou canst,
Be near to hear their courtship, D'Avolos.

D'Av. [*aside to Fior.*] Madam, I shall observe 'em with all cunning secrecy.

Bian. Colona, attend our sister to her chamber.

Col. I shall, madam.

[*Exit Fior., followed by Col. Jul. and D'Av.*

Bian. Play.

Fern. I must not lose th' advantage of the game:
Madam, your queen is lost.

Bian. My clergy help me![20]
My queen! and nothing for it but a pawn?
Why, then, the game's lost too: but play.

Fern. What, madam?

[*Fern. often looks about.*

Bian. You must needs play well, you are so studious.—
Fie upon't! you study past patience:—
What do you dream on? here is demurring
Would weary out a statue!—Good, now, play.

Fern. Forgive me; let my knees for ever stick

[*Kneels.*

[19] *to a duke's* place; and that's beside the play, &c.] i.e. that's no part of the game; in other words, there is no piece of this name. The allusion is sufficiently clear.

[20] *My clergy help me!*] i.e. my bishops: but those who understand the game do not need these modicums of information, and upon all others they are thrown away.

Nail'd to the ground, as earthy as my fears,
Ere I arise, to part away so curs'd
In my unbounded anguish as the rage
Of flames beyond all utterance of words
Devour me, lighten'd by your sacred eyes.

Bian. What means the man?

Fern. To lay before your feet
In lowest vassalage the bleeding heart
That sighs the tender of a suit disdain'd.
Great lady, pity me, my youth, my wounds;
And do not think that I have cull'd this time
From motion's swiftest measure to unclasp
The book of lust: if purity of love
Have residence in virtue's breast,[21] lo here,
Bent lower in my heart than on my knee,
I beg compassion to a love as chaste
As softness of desire can intimate.

Re-enter D'AVOLOS *behind.*

D'Av. [*aside*] At it already! admirable haste!

Bian. Am I again betray'd? bad man!—

Fern. Keep in,
Bright angel, that severer breath, to cool
That heat of cruelty which sways the temple
Of your too stony breast: you cannot urge
One reason to rebuke my trembling plea,
Which I have not with many nights' expense
Examin'd; but, O, madam, still I find
No physic strong to cure a tortur'd mind,
But freedom from the torture it sustains.

D'Av. [*aside*] Not kissing yet? still on your knees? O, for a plump bed and clean sheets, to comfort the

[21] in virtue's *breast*,] The 4to reads "in virtue's *quest*:" of which I can make nothing.

aching of his shins! We shall have 'em clip[22] anon and lisp kisses; here's ceremony with a vengeance!

Bian. Rise up; we charge you, rise! [*He rises.*
Look on our face:
What see you there that may persuade a hope
Of lawless love? Know, most unworthy man,
So much we hate the baseness of thy lust,
As, were none living of thy sex but thee,
We had much rather prostitute our blood
To some envenom'd serpent than admit
Thy bestial dalliance. Couldst thou dare to speak
Again, when we forbade? no, wretched thing,
Take this for answer: if thou henceforth ope
Thy leprous mouth to tempt our ear again,
We shall not only certify our lord
Of thy disease in friendship, but revenge
Thy boldness with the forfeit of thy life.
Think on't.

D'Av. [*aside*] Now, now, now the game is a-foot! your gray jennet with the white face is curried, forsooth;—please your lordship leap up into the saddle, forsooth.—Poor duke, how does[23] thy head ache now!

Fern. Stay; go not hence in choler, blessèd woman!
You've school'd me; lend me hearing: though the float
Of infinite desires swell to a tide
Too high so soon to ebb, yet, by this hand,
[*Kisses her hand.*
This glorious, gracious hand of yours,—

D'Av. [*aside*] Ay, marry, the match is made; clap hands and to't, ho!

Fern. I swear,

[22] *clip*] See note, vol. i. p. 172. D.
[23] *does*] Gifford printed "must." D.

Henceforth I never will as much in word,
In letter, or in syllable, presume
To make a repetition of my griefs.
Good-night t'ye! If, when I am dead, you rip
This coffin of my heart, there shall you read
With constant eyes, what now my tongue defines,
Bianca's name carv'd out in bloody lines.
For ever, lady, now good-night!

Bian. Good-night!
Rest in your goodness.—Lights there!—

Enter Attendants *with lights.*

Sir, good-night!

[*Exeunt sundry ways, with Attendants, Bia. and Fern.*

D'Av. So, via!—To be cuckold—mercy and providence—is as natural to a married man as to eat, sleep, or wear a nightcap. Friends!—I will rather trust mine arm in the throat of a lion, my purse with a courtesan, my neck with the chance on a die, or my religion in a synagogue of Jews, than my wife with a friend. Wherein do princes exceed the poorest peasant that ever was yoked to a sixpenny strumpet but that the horns of the one are mounted some two inches higher by a choppine[24] than the other? O Actæon! the goodliest-headed beast of the forest amongst wild

[24] by a *choppine*] i. e. clogs or pattens, of cork or light framework covered with leather, and worn under the shoe. The practice never prevailed in this country, but seems to have been fashionable at Venice, and places where walking was not required, for which choppines were totally unfit, as no woman could drag them after her; at least, if we may trust Lessels, who says that he has often seen them of "a full half-yard high." Ford's choppines, however, are of a very moderate description, and do not reach the altitude of the high-heeled shoes which were fashionable in this country about half a century ago. They derive their origin, as well as their name, from Spain, the region of cork; but our poets generally draw their examples from Italy. See *Jonson*, vol. ii. p. 258.

cattle is a stag; and the goodliest beast amongst tame fools in a corporation is a cuckold.

Re-enter FIORMONDA.

Fior. Speak, D'Avolos, how thrives intelligence?

D'Av. Above the prevention of fate, madam. I saw him kneel, make pitiful faces, kiss hands and fore-fingers, rise,—and by this time he is up, up, madam. Doubtless the youth aims to be duke, for he is gotten into the duke's seat an hour ago.

Fior. Is't true?

D'Av. Oracle, oracle! Siege was laid, parley admitted, composition offered, and the fort entered; there's no interruption. The duke will be at home to-morrow, gentle animal!—what d'ye resolve?

Fior. To stir-up tragedies as black as brave,
And send[25] the lecher panting to his grave. [*Exeunt.*

SCENE IV. *A bedchamber in the same.*

Enter BIANCA, *her hair loose, in her night-mantle. She draws a curtain, and* FERNANDO *is discovered in bed, sleeping; she sets down the candle, and goes to the bedside.*

Bian. Resolve, and do; 'tis done.—What! are those eyes,
Which lately were so overdrown'd in tears,
So easy to take rest? O happy man!
How sweetly sleep hath seal'd-up sorrows here!
But I will call him.—What, my lord, my lord,
My Lord Fernando!

Fern. Who calls me?

Bian. My lord,
Sleeping or waking?

[25] *send*] The 4to has "sending." D.

Fern. Ha! who is't?
Bian. 'Tis I:
Have you forgot my voice? or is your ear
But useful to your eye?
Fern. Madam, the duchess!
Bian. She, 'tis she; sit up,
Sit up and wonder, whiles my sorrows swell:
The nights are short, and I have much to say.
Fern. Is't possible 'tis you?
Bian. 'Tis possible:
Why do you think I come?
Fern. Why! to crown joys,
And make me master of my best desires.
Bian. 'Tis true, you guess aright; sit up and listen.
With shame and passion now I must confess,
Since first mine eyes beheld you, in my heart
You have been only king; if there can be
A violence in love, then I have felt
That tyranny: be record to my soul
The justice which I for this folly fear!
Fernando, in short words, howe'er my tongue
Did often chide thy love, each word thou spak'st
Was music to my ear; was never poor,
Poor wretched woman liv'd that lov'd like me,
So truly, so unfeignedly.
Fern. O, madam!
Bian. To witness that I speak is truth, look here!
Thus singly I adventure[26] to thy bed,
And do confess my weakness: if thou tempt'st
My bosom to thy pleasures, I will yield.
Fern. Perpetual happiness!

[26] *Thus* singly *I adventure*, &c.] By *singly* this paragon of modesty does not, I believe, mean *alone*, without *attendants*, but thus lightly clad, or rather thus undressed: she had, in short, but one garment, "a robe of shame," as she calls it, of which she bids him take note—"look here!" &c.

Bian. Now hear me out.
When first Caraffa, Pavy's duke, my lord,
Saw me, he lov'd me ; and without respect
Of dower took me to his bed and bosom ;
Advanc'd me to the titles I possess,
Not mov'd by counsel or remov'd by greatness ;
Which to requite, betwixt my soul and heaven
I vow'd a vow to live a constant wife :
I have done so ; nor was there in the world
A man created could have broke that truth
For all the glories of the earth but thou,
But thou, Fernando ! Do I love thee now?
Fern. Beyond imagination.
Bian. True, I do,
Beyond imagination : if no pledge
Of love can instance what I speak is true
But loss of my best joys, here, here, Fernando,
Be satisfied, and ruin me.
Fern. What d'ye mean ?
Bian. To give my body up to thy embraces,
A pleasure that I never wish'd to thrive in
Before this fatal minute. Mark me now ;
If thou dost spoil me of this robe of shame,
By my best comforts, here I vow again,
To thee, to heaven, to the world, to time,
Ere yet the morning shall new-christen day,
I'll kill myself!
Fern. How, madam, how !
Bian. I will :
Do what thou wilt, 'tis in thy choice : what say ye?
Fern. Pish! do you come to try me? tell me, first,
Will you but grant a kiss?
Bian. Yes, take it ; that,
Or what thy heart can wish : I am all thine.
[*Fern. kisses her.*

Fern. O, me!—Come, come; how many women, pray,
Were ever heard or read of, granted love,
And did as you protest you will?
Bian. Fernando,
Jest not at my calamity. I kneel: [*Kneels.*
By these dishevell'd hairs, these wretched tears,
By all that's good, if what I speak my heart
Vows not eternally, then think, my lord,
Was never man su'd to me I denied,—
Think me a common and most cunning whore;
And let my sins be written on my grave,
My name rest in reproof! [*Rises.*]—Do as you list.
Fern. I must believe ye,—yet I hope anon,[27]
When you are parted from me, you will say
I was a good, cold, easy-spirited man,
Nay, laugh at my simplicity: say, will ye?
Bian. No, by the faith I owe my bridal vows!
But ever hold thee much, much dearer far
Than all my joys on earth, by this chaste kiss.
[*Kisses him.*
Fern. You have prevail'd; and Heaven forbid that I
Should by a wanton appetite profane
This sacred temple! 'tis enough for me
You'll please to call me servant.
Bian. Nay, be thine:
Command my power, my bosom; and I'll write
This love within the tables of my heart.
Fern. Enough: I'll master passion, and triúmph

[27] *yet I* hope anon, &c.] *Hope* is apparently used here for *expect*, in which sense it [the substantive, at least] also occurs in *Henry IV.* where the Prince says;

"By how much better than my word I am,
By so much shall I falsify men's *hopes*."

In being conquer'd; adding to it this,
In you my love as it begun shall end.
Bian. The latter I new-vow. But day comes on;
What now we leave unfinish'd of content,
Each hour shall perfect up: sweet, let us part.
Fern. This kiss,—best life, good rest! [*Kisses her.*
Bian. All mine to thee!
Remember this, and think I speak thy words;
"When I am dead, rip up my heart, and read
With constant eyes, what now my tongue defines,
Fernando's name carv'd out in bloody lines."
Once more, good rest, sweet!
Fern. Your most faithful servant!
[*Exit Bia.—Scene closes.*

ACT III.

SCENE I. *An apartment in the palace.*

Enter NIBRASSA *chafing, followed by* JULIA *weeping.*

Nib. Get from me, strumpet, infamous whore, leprosy of my blood! make thy moan to ballad-singers and rhymers; they'll jig-out thy wretchedness and abominations to new tunes: as for me, I renounce thee; thou'rt no daughter of mine; I disclaim the legitimation of thy birth, and curse the hour of thy nativity.

Jul. Pray, sir, vouchsafe me hearing.

Nib. With child! shame to my grave! O, whore, wretched beyond utterance or reformation, what wouldst say?

Jul. Sir, by the honour of my mother's hearse,
He has protested marriage, pledg'd his faith;
If vows have any force, I am his wife.

Nib. His faith! Why, thou fool, thou wickedly-credulous fool, canst thou imagine luxury is observant of religion?[1] no, no; it is with a frequent lecher as usual to forswear as to swear; their piety is in making idolatry a worship; their hearts and their tongues are as different as thou, thou whore! and a virgin.

Jul. You are too violent; his truth will prove
His constancy, and so excuse my fault.

Nib. Shameless woman! this belief will damn thee. How will thy Lady Marquess justly reprove me for preferring to her service a monster of so lewd and impudent a life! Look to't; if thy smooth devil leave thee to thy[2] infamy, I will never pity thy mortal pangs, never lodge thee under my roof, never own thee for my child; mercy be my witness!

Enter PETRUCHIO, *leading* COLONA.

Pet. Hide not thy folly by unwise excuse,
Thou art undone, Colona; no entreaties,
No warning, no persuasion, could put off
The habit of thy dotage on that man
Of much deceit, Ferentes. Would thine eyes
Had seen me in my grave, ere I had known
The stain of this thine honour!

Col. Good my lord,
Reclaim your incredulity: my fault
Proceeds from lawful composition
Of wedlock; he hath seal'd his oath to mine
To be my husband.

Nib. Husband! hey-day! is't even so? nay, then, we have partners in affliction: if my jolly gallant's long

[1] *canst thou imagine* luxury *is observant of religion?*] i. e. *lust*. One example for all; "To my journey's end I hasten, and descend to the second continent of Delicacy, which is *Lust* or *Luxury*." [Nash's] *Christ's Tears over Jerusalem*, p. 157.

[2] *thy*] Gifford printed "thine." D.

clapper have struck on both sides, all is well.—Petruchio, thou art not wise enough to be a paritor:[2] come hither, man, come hither; speak softly; is thy daughter with child?

Pet. With child, Nibrassa!

Nib. Foh! do not trick me off; I overheard your gabbling. Hark in thine ear, so is mine too.

Pet. Alas, my lord, by whom?

Nib. Innocent! by whom? what an idle question is that! One cock hath trod both our hens: Ferentes, Ferentes; who else? How dost take it? methinks thou art wondrous patient: why, I am mad, stark mad.

Pet. How like you this, Colona? 'tis too true:
Did not this man protest to be your husband?

Col. Ay me! to me he did.

Nib. What else, what else, Petruchio?—and, madam, my quondam daughter, I hope h'ave[3] passed some huge words of matrimony to you too.

Jul. Alas! to me he did.

Nib. And how many more the great incubus of hell knows best.—Petruchio, give me your hand; mine own daughter in this arm,—and yours, Colona, in this:—there, there, sit ye down together. [*Jul. and Col. sit down.*] Never rise, as you hope to inherit our blessings, till you have plotted some brave revenge; think upon it to purpose, and you shall want no seconds to further it; be secret one to another.—Come, Petruchio, let 'em alone; the wenches will demur on't, and for the process we'll give 'em courage.[4]

[2] *thou art not wise enough to be a* paritor:] An inferior officer, Blount says, that summoned delinquents to a spiritual court. These officers seem, from our dramatic poets, to have been a great terror to the waist-coaters of their days.

[3] *h'ave*] Gifford printed "he has." D.

[4] *and for the process we'll give 'em courage.*] i. e. when the women have agreed on their plan of vengeance, we'll aid them in the performance of it.

Pet. You counsel wisely; I approve your plot.—
Think on your shames, and who it was that wrought 'em.

Nib. Ay, ay, ay, leave them alone.—To work, wenches, to work! [*Exeunt Nib. and Pet.*

Col. We are quite ruin'd.

Jul. True, Colona,
Betray'd to infamy, deceiv'd, and mock'd,
By an unconstant villain: what shall's do?
I am with child.

Col. Heigh-ho! and so am I:
But what shall's do now?

Jul. This: with cunning words
First prove his love; he knows I am with child.

Col. And so he knows I am; I told him on't
Last meeting in the lobby, and, in troth,
The false deceiver laugh'd.

Jul. Now, by the stars,
He did the like to me, and said 'twas well
I was so happily sped.

Col. Those very words
He us'd to me; it fretted me to th' heart:
I'll be reveng'd.

Jul. Peace! here's a noise, methinks.
Let's rise; we'll take a time to talk of this.
[*They rise, and walk aside.*

Enter FERENTES *and* MORONA.

Fer. Will ye hold? death of my delights, have ye lost all sense of shame? You're[5] best roar about the court that I have been your woman's-barber and trimmed ye, kind Morona.

Mor. Defiance to thy kindness! thou'st robbed me of my good name; didst promise to love none but me,

[5] *You're*] Gifford printed "You were" (the 4to has "*y'are*"): but see note, vol. i. p. 131. D.

me, only me; sworest, like an unconscionable villain, to marry me the twelfth day of the month two months since; didst make my bed thine own, mine house thine own, mine all and everything thine own. I will exclaim to the world on thee, and beg justice of the duke himself, villain! I will.

Fer. Yet again? nay, an if you be in that mood, shut up your fore-shop, I'll be your journeyman no longer. Why, wise Madam Dryfist, could your mouldy brain be so addle to imagine I would marry a stale widow at six-and-forty? Marry gip! are there not varieties enough of thirteen? come, stop your clap-dish,[6] or I'll purchase a carting for you. By this light, I have toiled more with this tough carrion hen than with ten quails scarce grown into their first feathers.

Mor. O, treason to all honesty or religion!—Speak, thou perjured, damnable, ungracious defiler of women, who shall father my child which thou hast begotten?

Fer. Why, thee, countrywoman; thou'st a larger purse to pay for the nursing. Nay, if you'll needs have the world know how you, reputed a grave, matron-like, motherly madam, kicked up your heels like a jennet whose mark is new come into her mouth, e'en do, do! the worst can be said of me is, that I was ill advised to dig for gold in a coal-pit. Are you answered?

Mor. Answered!

Jul. Let's fall amongst 'em. [*Comes forward with Col.*]—Love, how is't, chick? ha?

[6] *come, stop your* clap-dish] Thus in [Cooke's] *Greene's Tu Quoque;*

"Widow, hold your *clap-dish*, fasten your tongue
Under your roof, and do not dare to call."

For the word itself, see *Jonson*, vol. i. p. 44. [Where Gifford notices "the custom which prevailed in this country two or three centuries ago, and, not improbably, even so late as Jonson's time, when diseased or infectious wretches wandered up and down with a *clap-dish*, a wooden vessel with a movable cover, to give the charitable warning at once of their necessities and their infectious condition. To this mode of begging our old writers frequently advert," &c. D.]

Col. My dear Ferentes, my betrothèd lord!

Fer. [*aside*] Excellent! O, for three Barbary stone-horses to top three Flanders mares!—Why, how now, wenches! what means this?

Mor. Out upon me! here's more of his trulls.

Jul. Love, you must go with me.

Col. Good love, let's walk.

Fer. [*aside*] I must rid my hands of 'em, or they'll ride on my shoulders.—By your leave, ladies; here's none but is of common counsel one with another; in short, there are three of ye with child, you tell me, by me. All of you I cannot satisfy, nor, indeed, handsomely any of ye. You all hope I should marry you; which, for that it is impossible to be done, I am content to have neither of ye: for your looking big on the matter, keep your own counsels, I'll not bewray ye; but for marriage,—heaven bless ye, and me from ye! This is my resolution.

Col. How, not me!

Jul. Not me!

Mor. Not me!

Fer. Nor you, nor you, nor you: and to give you some satisfaction, I'll yield you reasons.—You, Colona, had a pretty art in your dalliance; but your fault was, you were too suddenly won.—You, Madam Morona, could have pleased well enough some three or four-and-thirty years ago; but you are too old.—You, Julia, were young enough; but your fault is, you have a scurvy face.—Now, everyone knowing her proper defect, thank me that I ever vouchsafed you the honour of my bed once in your lives. If you want clouts, all I'll promise is to rip-up an old shirt or two. So, wishing a speedy deliverance to all your burdens, I commend you to your patience. [*Exit.*

Mor. Excellent!

Jul. Notable!
Col. Unmatchèd villain!
Jul. Madam, though strangers, yet we understand
Your wrongs do equal ours; which to revenge,
Please but to join with us, and we'll redeem
Our loss of honour by a brave exploit.

Mor. I embrace your motion, ladies, with gladness, and will strive by any action to rank with you in any danger.

Col. Come, gentlewomen, let's together, then.—
Thrice-happy maids that never trusted men! [*Exeunt.*

SCENE II. *The state-room in the palace.*

Enter DUKE, BIANCA *supported by* FERNANDO, FIORMONDA, PETRUCHIO, NIBRASSA, FERENTES, *and* D'AVOLOS.

Duke. Roseilli will not come, then! will not? well;
His pride shall ruin him.[7]—Our letters speak
The duchess' uncle will be here to-morrow,—
To-morrow, D'Avolos.

D'Av. To-morrow night, my lord, but not to make more than one day's abode here; for his Holiness has commanded him to be at Rome the tenth of this month, the conclave of cardinals not being resolved to sit till his coming.

Duke. Your uncle, sweetheart, at his next return
Must be saluted cardinal.—Ferentes,
Be it your charge to think on some device

[7] Some months must have elapsed since the Duke sent for Roseilli, whose pretended answer he now learns for the first time. Our author plays as many strange tricks with the unities, as they are called, as any of his contemporaries. In this there may not, perhaps, be much to blame; but Ford's peculiar fault is, that he always appears unconscious, or at least careless, of his want of congruity: the mention of Roseilli here, for instance, is altogether uncalled for, and merely adds one inconsistency more to the fable.

To entertain the present[8] with delight.
Fern. My lord, in honour to the court of Pavy
I'll join with you. Ferentes, not long since
I saw in Brussels, at my being there,
The Duke of Brabant welcome the Archbishop
Of Mentz with rare conceit, even on a sudden,
Perform'd by knights and ladies of his court,
In nature of an antic;[9] which methought—
For that I ne'er before saw women-antics—
Was for the newness strange, and much commended.
Bian. Now, good my Lord Fernando, further this
In any wise; it cannot but content.
Fior. [*aside*] If she entreat, 'tis ten to one the man
Is won beforehand.
Duke. Friend, thou honour'st me:
But can it be so speedily perform'd?
Fern. I'll undertake it, if the ladies please,
To exercise in person only that:
And we must have a fool, or such an one
As can with art well act him.
Fior. I shall fit ye;
I have a natural.
Fern. Best of all, madam:
Then nothing wants.—You must make one, Ferentes.
Fer. With my best service and dexterity,
My lord.
Pet. [*aside to Nib.*] This falls out happily, Nibrassa.

8 *To entertain the present*] i.e. the *present* time. So in *The Tempest*, "If you can . . . . work the peace of the *present*, we will not hand a rope more."

9 *In nature of an* antic;] i.e. of an anti-masque, in which the characters were always grotesque and extravagant. It will appear from the preparatory arrangements of this "antic" (for otherwise it is impossible to account for them), that Fernando had been made acquainted with the disgrace of his cousin Colona, and adopted her plans of revenge. It must be confessed, however, that he has fallen upon a very extraordinary mode of "entertaining the Abbot of Monaco."

Nib. [*aside to Pet.*] We could not wish it better:
Heaven is an unbrib'd justice.

Duke. We'll meet our uncle in a solemn grace
Of zealous presence, as becomes the church:
See all the quire be ready, D'Avolos.

D'Av. I have already made your highness' pleasure known to them.

Bian. Your lip, my lord!

Fern. Madam?

Bian. Perhaps your teeth have bled; wipe't with my handkercher: give me, I'll do't myself.—[*Aside to Fern.*] Speak, shall I steal a kiss? believe me, my lord, I long.

Fern. Not for the world.

Fior. [*aside*] Apparent impudence!

D'Av. Beshrew my heart, but that's not so good.

Duke. Ha, what's that thou mislikest, D'Avolos?

D'Av. Nothing, my lord;—but I was hammering a conceit of mine own, which cannot, I find, in so short a time thrive as a day's practice.

Fior. [*aside*] Well put off, secretary.

Duke. We are too sad; methinks the life of mirth
Should still be fed where we are: where's Mauruccio?

Fer. An't please your highness, he's of late grown so affectionately inward with my Lady Marquess's fool, that I presume he is confident there are few wise men worthy of his society, who are not as innocently harmless as that creature. It is almost impossible to separate them, and 'tis a question which of the two is the wiser man.

Duke. 'Would he were here! I have a kind of dulness
Hangs on me since my hunting, that I feel
As 'twere a disposition to be sick;
My head is ever aching.

D'Av. A shrewd ominous token; I like not that neither.

Duke. Again! what is't you like not?

D'Av. I beseech your highness excuse me; I am so busy with this[10] frivolous project, and can bring it to no shape, that it almost confounds my capacity.

Bian. My lord, you were best to try a set at maw:[11]
I and your friend, to pass away the time,
Will undertake your highness and your sister.

Duke. The game's too tedious.

Fior. 'Tis a peevish play;[12]
Your knave will heave the queen out[12] or your king;
Besides, 'tis all on fortune.

Enter MAURUCCIO *with* ROSEILLI *disguised as before, and* GIACOPO.

Maur. Bless thee, most excellent duke! I here present thee as worthy and learned a gentleman as ever I—and yet I have lived threescore years—conversed with. Take it from me, I have tried him, and [he] is worthy to be privy-counsellor to the greatest

[10] *this*] The 4to has "his." D.

[11] *a set at maw:*] Gifford, by a strange oversight, printed "to *set* a *maw*." D.

[12] '*Tis a peevish play;*
Your knave will *heave* your *queen* out] This game (maw) is treated with equal contempt, and nearly in the same terms, by Sir John Harington;

"Then thirdly follow'd '*heaving* of the maw,'
A game without civility or law;
An odious play, and yet in court oft seen,
A saucy knave to trump both king and queen."

I can give the reader no account of this "*peevish* (pettish) play;" it bears apparently some resemblance to *reversi*, a burlesque of whist, which, though unknown in this country, is a favourite game with the lower orders in France. I have frequently looked on, and seen the players slide the *quinola*, the knave of trumps, under the king or queen (both its inferiors), and *heave* them respectively out of the circle. As the object is to *lose* as many tricks as possible, the game is sufficiently noisy and indecorous for a court. Ford adds, "Besides, 'tis all on fortune." This would apply very well to *reversi*.

Turk in Christendom; of a most apparent and deep understanding, slow of speech, but speaks to the purpose.—Come forward, sir, and appear before his highness in your own proper elements.

Ros. Will—tye—to da new toate sure la now.

Gia. A very senseless gentleman, and, please your highness, one that has a great deal of little wit, as they say.

Maur. O, sir, had you heard him, as I did, deliver whole histories in the Tangay tongue, you would swear there were not such a linguist breathed again; and did I but perfectly understand his language, I would be confident in less than two hours to distinguish the meaning of bird, beast, or fish naturally as I myself speak Italian, my lord. Well, he has rare qualities!

Duke. Now, prithee, question him, Mauruccio.

Maur. I will, my lord.—

Tell me, rare scholar, which, in thy opinion,
Doth cause the strongest breath, garlic or onion.

Gia. Answer him, brother-fool; do, do; speak thy mind, chuck, do.

Ros. Have bid seen all da fine knack, and de, e, naghtye tat-tle of da kna-ve, dad la have so.

Duke. We understand him not.

Maur. Admirable, I protest, duke; mark, O, duke, mark!—What did I ask him, Giacopo?

Gia. What caused the strongest breath, garlic or onions, I take it, sir.

Maur. Right, right, by Helicon! and his answer is, that a knave has a stronger breath than any of 'em: wisdom — or I am an ass — in the highest; a direct figure; put it down, Giacopo.

Duke. How happy is that idiot whose ambition
Is but to eat and sleep, and shun the rod!

Men that have more of wit, and use it ill,
Are fools in proof.

Bian. True, my lord, there's many
Who think themselves most wise that are most fools.

D'Av. Bitter girds,[13] if all were known;—but—

Duke. But what? speak out; plague on your muttering, grumbling!
I hear you, sir; what is't?

D'Av. Nothing, I protest, to your highness pertinent to any moment.

Duke. Well, sir, remember.—Friend, you promis'd study.—
I am not well in temper.—Come, Bianca.—
Attend our friend, Ferentes.

[*Exeunt all but Fern. Ros. Fer. and Maur.*

Fern. Ferentes, take Mauruccio in with you;
He must be one in action.

Fer. Come, my lord,
I shall entreat your help.

Fern. I'll stay the fool,
And follow instantly.

Maur. Yes, pray, my lord.

[*Exeunt Fer. and Maur.*

Fern. How thrive your hopes now, cousin?

Ros. Are we safe?
Then let me cast myself beneath thy foot,
True, virtuous lord. Know, then, sir, her proud heart
Is only fix'd on you, in such extremes
Of violence and passion, that I fear,
Or she'll enjoy you, or she'll ruin you.

[13] *Bitter* girds,] i.e. sarcasms, strokes of satire. Ford has contrived, by several direct quotations from Shakespeare, to put the reader in mind of Iago, to whom, for his misfortune, D'Avolos bears about the same degree of resemblance that the poor Duke does to Othello. D'Avolos, in short, is a mere spy, a pander to the bad passions of others, without one supportable quality to redeem the baseness of his sycophancy, or relieve the dull uniformity of his malice.

Fern. Me, coz? by all the joys I wish to taste,
She is as far beneath my[14] thought as I
In soul above her malice.
Ros. I observ'd
Even now a kind of dangerous pretence[15]
In an unjointed phrase from D'Avolos.
I know not his[16] intent; but this I know,
He has a working brain, is minister
To all my lady's counsels; and, my lord,
Pray heaven there have not anything befall'n
Within the knowledge of his subtle art
To do you mischief!
Fern. Pish! should he or hell
Affront me in the passage of my fate,
I'd crush them into atomies.
Ros. I do admit you could: meantime, my lord,
Be nearest to yourself; what I can learn,
You shall be soon inform'd of: here is all
We fools can catch the wise in,—to unknot,
By privilege of coxcombs,[17] what they plot. [*Exeunt.*

Scene III. *Another room in the same.*

Enter Duke *and* D'Avolos.

Duke. Thou art a traitor: do not think the gloss
Of smooth evasion, by your cunning jests

[14] *my*] The 4to has "thy." D.

[15] *a kind of dangerous* pretence] i. e. intent, design. Thus, in *Macbeth;*

"Against the undivulg'd *pretence* I fight
Of treasonous malice."

Atomies, which occurs in the next speech, is frequently used by our old writers for *atoms*, motes, &c.

[16] *his*] The 4to has "hir." Gifford printed "her." D.

[17] *By privilege of* coxcombs,] i. e. of fool-caps.

And coinage of your politician's brain,
Shall jig me off; I'll know't, I vow I will.
Did not I note your dark abrupted ends
Of words half-spoke? your "wells, if all were known"?
Your short "I like not that"? your girds and "buts"?
Yes, sir, I did; such broken language argues
More matter than your subtlety shall hide:
Tell me, what is't? by honour's self, I'll know.

D'Av. What would you know, my lord? I confess I owe my life and service to you, as to my prince; the one you have, the other you may take from me at your pleasure. Should I devise matter to feed your distrust, or suggest likelihoods without appearance? what would you have me say? I know nothing.

Duke. Thou liest, dissembler! on thy brow I read
Distracted horrors figur'd in thy looks.
On thy allegiance, D'Avolos, as e'er
Thou hop'st to live in grace with us, unfold
What by the[18] parti-halting of thy speech
Thy knowledge can discover. By the faith
We bear to sacred justice, we protest,
Be it or good or evil, thy reward
Shall be our special thanks and love unterm'd:[19]
Speak, on thy duty; we, thy prince, command.

D'Av. O, my disaster! my lord, I am so charmed by those powerful repetitions of love and duty, that I cannot conceal what I know of your dishonour.

Duke. Dishonour! then my soul is cleft with fear;
I half presage my misery: say on,
Speak it at once, for I am great with grief.

D'Av. I trust your highness will pardon me; yet I

[18] *the*] The 4to has "thy." D.

[19] *and love* unterm'd:] i.e. inexpressible, or rather, perhaps, interminable [the latter, surely. D.].

will not deliver a syllable which shall be less innocent than truth itself.

Duke. By all our wish of joys, we pardon thee.

D'Av. Get from me, cowardly servility! my service is noble, and my loyalty an armour of brass: in short, my lord, and plain discovery, you are a cuckold.

Duke. Keep in the word,—a *cuckold!*

D'Av. Fernando is your rival, has stolen your duchess' heart, murdered friendship, horns your head, and laughs at your horns.

Duke. My heart is split!

D'Av. Take courage, be a prince in resolution: I knew it would nettle you in the fire of your composition, and was loth to have given the first report of this more than ridiculous blemish to all patience or moderation: but, O, my lord, what would not a subject do to approve his loyalty to his sovereign? Yet, good sir, take it as quietly as you can: I must needs say 'tis a foul fault; but what man is he under the sun that is free from the career of his destiny? May be she will in time reclaim the errors of her youth; or 'twere a great happiness in you, if you could not believe it; that's the surest way, my lord, in my poor counsel.

Duke. The icy current of my frozen blood
Is kindled up in agonies as hot
As flames of burning sulphur. O, my fate!
A cuckold! had my dukedom's whole inheritance
Been rent, mine honours levell'd in the dust,
So she, that wicked woman, might have slept
Chaste in my bosom, 't had been all a sport.
And he, that villain, viper to my heart,
That he should be the man![20] death above utterance!
Take heed you prove this true.

[20] *That he should be the man!*] This hemistich is repeated in the 4to, apparently by mistake, as it destroys the metre.

D'Av. My lord,—

Duke. If not,
I'll tear thee joint by joint.—Phew! methinks
It should not be:—Bianca! why, I took her
From lower than a bondage:—hell of hells!—
See that you make it good.

D'Av. As for that, 'would it were as good as I would make it! I can, if you will temper your distractions, but bring you where you shall see it; no more.

Duke. See it!

D'Av. Ay, see it, if that be proof sufficient. I, for my part, will slack no service that may testify my simplicity.

Duke. Enough.

Enter FERNANDO.

What news, Fernando?

Fern. Sir, the abbot
Is now upon arrival; all your servants
Attend your presence.

Duke. We will give him welcome
As shall befit our love and his respect.
Come, mine own best Fernando, my dear friend.
[*Exit with Fern.*

D'Av. Excellent! now for a horned moon. [*Music within.*] But I hear the preparation for the entertainment of this great abbot. Let him come and go, that matters nothing to this; whiles he rides abroad in hope to purchase a purple hat, our duke shall as earnestly heat the pericranion[21] of his noddle with a yellow hood at home. I hear 'em coming.

[21] *pericranion*] Gifford printed "pericranium." D.

Loud music. Enter Servants *with torches; then the* Duke, *followed by* FERNANDO, BIANCA, FIORMONDA, PETRUCHIO, *and* NIBRASSA, *at one door; two* Friars, *the* Abbot *and* Attendants, *at the other. The* Duke *and* Abbot *meet and salute;* BIANCA *and the rest salute, and are saluted; they rank themselves, and pass over the stage; the* Quire *singing.*

On to your victuals; some of ye, I know, feed upon wormwood. [*Exit.*

SCENE IV. *Another apartment in the same.*

Enter PETRUCHIO *and* NIBRASSA *with napkins, as from supper.*

Pet. The duke's on rising: are you ready? ho!

[*Within*] All ready.

Nib. Then, Petruchio, arm thyself with courage and resolution; and do not shrink from being stayed on thy own virtue.

Pet. I am resolv'd.—Fresh lights!—I hear 'em coming.

Enter Attendants *with lights, before the* Duke, Abbot, BIANCA, FIORMONDA, FERNANDO, *and* D'AVOLOS.

Duke. Right reverend uncle, though our minds be scanted
In giving welcome as our hearts would wish,
Yet we will strive to show how much we joy
Your presence with a courtly show of mirth.
Please you to sit.

Abbot. Great duke, your worthy honours
To me shall still have place in my best thanks:
Since you in me so much respect the church,
Thus much I'll promise,—at my next return

His Holiness shall grant [you] an indulgence
Both large and general.

Duke. Our humble duty!—
Seat you, my lords.—Now let the masquers enter.

Enter, in an antic fashion, FERENTES, ROSEILLI, *and* MAURUCCIO *at several doors; they dance a short time. Suddenly enter to them* COLONA, JULIA, *and* MORONA *in odd shapes, and dance: the men gaze at them, are at a stand, and are invited by the women to dance. They dance together sundry changes; at last they close* FERENTES *in,*—MAURUCCIO *and* ROSEILLI *being shook off, and standing at several ends of the stage gazing. The women hold hands and dance about* FERENTES *in divers complimental offers of courtship; at length they suddenly fall upon him and stab him; he falls, and they run out at several doors. The music ceases.*

Fer. Uncase me; I am slain in jest. A pox upon your outlandish feminine antics! pull off my visor; I shall bleed to death ere I have time to feel where I am hurt.—Duke, I am slain: off with my visor; for heaven's' sake, off with my visor!

Duke. Slain!—Take his[22] visor off [*They unmask Fer.*]:—we are betray'd:
Seize on them! two are yonder: hold Ferentes:
Follow the rest: apparent treachery!

Abbot. Holy Saint Bennet, what a sight is this!

Re-enter JULIA, COLONA, *and* MORONA *unmasked, each with a child in her arms.*

Jul. Be not amaz'd, great princes, but vouchsafe
Your audience: we are they have done this deed.

[22] *his*] The 4to has "this." D.

Look here, the pledges of this false man's lust,
Betray'd in our simplicities: he swore,
And pawn'd his truth, to marry each of us;
Abus'd us all; unable to revenge
Our public shames but by his public fall,
Which thus we have contriv'd: nor do we blush
To call the glory of this murder ours;
We did it, and we'll justify the deed;
For when in sad complaints we claim'd his vows,
His answer was reproach:—Villain, is't true?

Col. I was *too quickly won*, you slave!

Mor. I was *too old*, you dog!

Jul. I,—and I never shall forget the wrong,—
I was *not fair enough; not fair enough*
For thee, thou monster!—let me cut his gall—
Not fair enough! O, scorn! *not fair enough!*
[*Stabs him.*

Fer. O, O, O!—

Duke. Forbear, you monstrous women! do not add
Murder to lust: your lives shall pay this forfeit.

Fer. Pox upon all cod-piece extravagancy! I am peppered—O, O, O!—Duke, forgive me!—Had I rid any tame beasts but Barbary wild colts, I had not been thus[23] jerked out of the saddle. My forfeit was in my blood; and my life hath answered it. Vengeance on all wild whores, I say!—O, 'tis true—farewell, generation of hackneys!—O! [*Dies.*

Duke. He is dead.
To prison with those monstrous strumpets!

Pet. Stay;
I'll answer for my daughter.

Nib. And I for mine.—
O, well done, girls!

[23] *been thus*] Gifford printed "thus been." D.

Fern. I for yon gentlewoman, sir.

Maur. Good my lord, I am an innocent in the business.

Duke. To prison with him![24] Bear the body hence.

Abbot. Here's fatal sad presages: but 'tis just
He dies by murder that hath liv'd in lust. [*Exeunt.*

ACT IV.

SCENE I. *An apartment in the palace.*

Enter DUKE, FIORMONDA, *and* D'AVOLOS.

Fior. Art thou Caraffa? is there in thy veins
One drop of blood that issu'd from the loins
Of Pavy's ancient dukes? or dost thou sit
On great Lorenzo's seat, our glorious father,
And canst not blush to be so far beneath
The spirit of heroic ancestors?
Canst thou engross[1] a slavish shame, which men
Far, far below the region of thy state.
Not more abhor than study to revenge?
Thou an Italian! I could burst with rage
To think I have a brother so befool'd
In giving patience to a harlot's lust.

D'Av. One, my lord, that doth so palpably, so apparently make her adulteries a trophy, whiles the

[24] Duke. *To prison with* him!] i. e. with Mauruccio, the only innocent person of the party. This good prince seems determined, like the Cardinal in a former play, to have some one to punish. Few third acts can be found so uniformly reprehensible and disgusting as this: the only thing to praise in it is the promptitude with which the author has freed himself, in part, from the loathsome encumbrance of such a worthless rabble.

[1] *engross*] See note, vol. i. p. 270. D.

poting-stick[2] to her unsatiate and more than goatish abomination jeers at and flouts your sleepish,[3] and more than sleepish, security.

Fior. What is she but the sallow-colour'd brat
Of some unlanded bankrupt, taught to catch
The easy fancies[4] of young prodigal bloods
In springes of her stew-instructed art?—
Here's your most virtuous duchess! your rare piece!

D'Av. More base in the infiniteness of her sensuality than corruption can infect:—to clip and inveigle your friend too! O, unsufferable!—a friend! how of all men are you most unfortunate!—to pour out your soul into the bosom of such a creature as holds it religion to make your own trust a key to open the passage to your own wife's womb, to be drunk in the privacies of your bed!—think upon that, sir.

Duke. Be gentle in your tortures, e'en for pity;
For pity's cause I beg it.

Fior. Be a prince!

[2] *poting-stick*] A *poting*, or, as it was more commonly called, a *poking*-stick, was a slender rod of bone or steel, for setting the plaits of ruffs, cuffs, &c. after starching. The *name* of this little implement grievously annoys old Stubbes; it was given to it, he says, by the devil, who brought in the practice of starching. It might, perhaps, have been more elegant; otherwise I do not see much amiss in it. Archdeacon Nares, in his valuable *Glossary*, quotes *poted;* on which he says, "I have seen this word only in the following instance, and do not exactly know its meaning;

'He keepes a starcht gate, weares a formall ruffe,
A nosegay, set face, and a *poted* cuffe.' *Heyw. Brit. Troy*, iv. 50."

The meaning is clear enough: a cuff, of which the plaits had been starched and stiffened, and puffed-out by the *poting*-stick. My old schoolmaster wore a coat with a cuff of this kind; it was large, and turned back very far on the sleeve. The good man had figured in it for half a century on Sundays; but, I grieve to say, it excited in his latter days more mirth than reverence in the ungracious urchins who followed him to church. This note (otherwise of no value) may serve to show that *poted* cuffs came down, at least in the remote provinces, to Queen Anne's days.

[3] *sleepish*] Qy. "sheepish"? (observe the preceding "goatish"). D.

[4] *fancies*] Gifford printed "fancy." D.

Th'adst better, duke, thou hadst, been born a peasant.
Now boys will sing thy scandal in the streets,
Tune ballads to thy infamy, get money
By making pageants of thee, and invent
Some strangely-shap'd man-beast, that may for horns
Resemble thee, and call it Pavy's Duke.

Duke. Endless immortal plague!

D'Av. There's the mischief, sir: in the meantime you shall be sure to have a bastard—of whom you did not so much as beget a little toe, a left ear, or half the further side of an upper lip—inherit both your throne and name: this would kill the soul of very patience itself.

Duke. Forbear; the ashy paleness of my cheek
Is scarleted in ruddy flakes of wrath;
And like some bearded meteor shall suck up,
With swiftest terror, all those dusky mists
That overcloud compassion in our breast.
You've rous'd a sleeping lion, whom no art,
No fawning smoothness shall reclaim, but blood.
And sister thou, thou Roderico, thou,
From whom I take the surfeit of my bane,
Henceforth no more so eagerly pursue
To whet my dulness: you shall see Caraffa
Equal his birth, and matchless in revenge.

Fior. Why, now I hear you speak in majesty.

D'Av. And it becomes my lord most princely.

Duke. Does it?—Come hither, sister. Thou art near
In nature, and as near to me in love:
I love thee, yes, by yon bright firmament,
I love thee dearly. But observe me well:
If any private grudge or female spleen,
Malice or envy, or such woman's frailty,
Have spurr'd thee on to set my soul on fire

Without apparent certainty,—I vow,
And vow again, by all [our] princely blood,
Hadst thou a double soul, or were the lives
Of fathers, mothers, children, or the hearts
Of all our tribe[5] in thine, I would unrip
That womb of bloody mischief with these nails
Where such a cursèd plot as this was hatch'd.—
But, D'Avolos, for thee—no more; to work
A yet more strong impression in my brain,
You must produce an instance to mine eye
Both present and apparent—nay, you shall—or—

Fior. Or what? you will be mad? be rather wise;
Think on Ferentes first, and think by whom
The harmless youth was slaughter'd: had he liv'd,
He would have told you tales: Fernando fear'd it;
And to prevent him,—under show, forsooth,
Of rare device,—most trimly cut him off.
Have you yet eyes, duke?

Duke. Shrewdly urg'd,—'tis piercing.

Fior. For looking on a sight shall split your soul,
You shall not care: I'll undertake myself
To do't some two days hence; for need, to-night,
But that you are in court.

D'Av. Right. Would you desire, my lord, to see them exchange kisses, sucking one another's lips, nay, begetting an heir to the dukedom, or practising more than the very act of adultery itself? Give but a little way by a feigned absence, and you shall find 'em—I blush to speak doing what: I am mad to think on't; you are most shamefully, most sinfully, most scornfully cornuted.

Duke. D'ye play upon me? as I am your prince,
There's some shall roar for this! Why, what was I,
Both to be thought or made so vile a thing?

[5] *tribe*] The 4to has "Tribes;" and so Gifford. D.

Stay, Madam Marquess,—ho, Roderico, you, sir,—
Bear witness that if ever I neglect
One day, one hour, one minute, to wear out
With toil of plot or practice of conceit
My busy skull, till I have found a death
More horrid than the bull of Phalaris,
Or all the fabling poets' dreaming whips;
If ever I take rest, or force a smile
Which is not borrow'd from a royal vengeance,
Before I know which way to satisfy
Fury and wrong,—nay, kneel down [*They kneel*],—let me die
More wretched than despair, reproach, contempt,
Laughter, and poverty itself can make me!
Let's rise on all sides friends [*They rise*]:—now all's agreed:
If the moon serve, some that are safe shall bleed.[6]

Enter BIANCA, FERNANDO, *and* MORONA.

Bian. My lord the duke,—
Duke. Bianca! ha, how is't?
How is't, Bianca?—What, Fernando!—come,
Shall's shake hands, sirs?—'faith, this is kindly done.
Here's three as one: welcome, dear wife, sweet friend!

D'Av. [*aside to Fior.*] I do not like this now; it shows scurvily to me.

Bian. My lord, we have a suit; your friend and I—
Duke. [*aside*] She puts my friend before, most kindly still.
Bian. Must join—

[6] *If the* moon *serve, some that are safe shall bleed.*] In Ford's time, and indeed long before and after it, the days of the *moon* held to be propitious to bleeding were distinguished by particular marks; and such was the absurd reliance on this ignorant medley of quackery and superstition, that few families would have ventured on the operation on one of the *dies nefasti*.

Duke. What, *must?*
Bian. My lord!—
Duke. Must join, you say—
Bian. That you will please to set Mauruccio
At liberty; this gentlewoman here
Hath, by agreement made betwixt them two,
Obtain'd him for her husband: good my lord,
Let me entreat; I dare engage mine honour
He's innocent in any wilful fault.
Duke. Your honour, madam! now beshrew you for't,
T' engage your honour on so slight a ground:
Honour's a precious jewel, I can tell you;
Nay, 'tis, Bianca; go to!—D'Avolos,
Bring us Mauruccio hither.
D'Av. I shall, my lord. [*Exit.*
Mor. I humbly thank your grace.
Fern. And, royal sir, since Julia and Colona,
Chief actors in Ferentes' tragic end,
Were, through their ladies' mediation,
Freed by your gracious pardon; I, in pity,
Tender'd this widow's friendless misery;
For whose reprieve I shall, in humblest duty,
Be ever thankful.

Re-enter D'AVOLOS *with* MAURUCCIO *in rags, and* GIACOPO *weeping.*

Maur. Come you, my learnèd counsel, do not roar;
If I must hang, why, then, lament therefóre:[7]
You may rejoice, and both, no doubt, be great
To serve your prince, when I am turn'd worms'-meat.

[7] *why, then, lament therefóre:*] This in Jonson is a *sneer* at Shakespeare; in Shakespeare, and every other writer, it is a *smile* at Marlowe.

I fear my lands and all I have is begg'd;[8]
Else, woe is me, why should I be so ragg'd?

D'Av. Come on, sir; the duke stays for you.

Maur. O, how my stomach doth begin to puke,
When I do hear that only word, the duke!

Duke. You, sir, look on that woman: are you pleas'd,
If we remit your body from the gaol,
To take her for your wife?

Maur. On that condition, prince, with all my heart.

Mor. Yes, I warrant your grace he is content.

Duke. Why, foolish man, hast thou so soon forgot
The public shame of her abusèd womb,
Her being mother to a bastard's birth?
Or canst thou but imagine she will be
True to thy bed who to herself was false?

Gia. [*to Maur.*] Phew, sir, do not stand upon that; that's a matter of nothing, you know.

Maur. Nay, an't shall please your good grace, an it come to that, I care not; as good men as I have lien in foul sheets, I am sure; the linen has not been much the worse for the wearing a little: I will have her with all my heart.

Duke. And shalt.—Fernando, thou shalt have the grace
To join their hands; put 'em together, friend.

Bian. Yes, do, my lord; bring you the bridegroom hither;
I'll give the bride myself.

D'Av. [*aside*] Here's argument to jealousy as good as drink to the dropsy; she will share any disgrace with him: I could not wish it better.

[8] *my lands and all I have is begg'd;*] As a condemned person: there were greedy courtiers enough in those days to scramble for the property of a falling man, even before the period of legal condemnation.

Duke. Even so: well, do it.

Fern. Here, Mauruccio;
Long live a happy couple!

[*He and Bian. join their hands.*

Duke. 'Tis enough;
Now know our pleasure henceforth. 'Tis our will,
If ever thou, Mauruccio, or thy wife,
Be seen within a dozen miles o' th' court,
We will recal our mercy; no entreat
Shall warrant thee a minute of thy life:
We'll have no servile slavery of lust
Shall breathe near us; dispatch, and get ye hence.—
Bianca, come with me.—[*Aside*] O, my cleft soul!

[*Exeunt Duke and Bian.*

Maur. How's that? must I come no more near the court?

Gia. O, pitiful! not near the court, sir!

D'Av. Not by a dozen miles, indeed, sir. Your only course, I can advise you, is to pass to Naples, and set up a house of carnality: there are very fair and frequent suburbs, and you need not fear the contagion of any pestilent disease, for the worst is very proper to the place.

Fern. 'Tis a strange sentence.

Fior. 'Tis, and sudden too,
And not without some mystery.

D'Av. Will you go, sir?

Maur. Not near the court!

Mor. What matter is it, sweetheart? fear nothing, love; you shall have new change of apparel, good diet, wholesome attendance;—and we will live like pigeons, my lord.

Maur. Wilt thou forsake me, Giacopo?

Gia. I forsake ye! no, not as long as I have a whole ear on my head, come what will come.

Fior. Mauruccio, you did once proffer true love
To me, but since you are more thriftier sped,
For old affection's sake here take this gold;
Spend it for my sake.

Fern. Madam, you do nobly,—
And that's for me, Mauruccio. [*They give him money.*

D'Av. Will ye go, sir?

Maur. Yes, I will go;—and I[9] humbly thank your lordship and ladyship.—Pavy, sweet Pavy, farewell!—
Come, wife,—come, Giacopo:
Now is the time that we away must lag,
And march in pomp with baggage and with bag.
O poor Mauruccio! what hast thou misdone,
To end thy life when life was new begun?
Adieu to all; for lords and ladies see
My woful plight and squires of low degree!

D'Av. Away, away, sirs!

[*Exeunt all but Fior. and Fern.*

Fior. My Lord Fernando,—

Fern. Madam?

Fior. Do you note
My brother's odd distractions? You were wont
To bosom in his counsels: I am sure
You know the ground of it.[10]

Fern. Not I, in troth.

Fior. Is't possible? What would you say, my lord,
If he, out of some melancholy spleen,
Edg'd-on by some thank-picking parasite,
Should now prove jealous? I mistrust it shrewdly.

Fern. What, madam! jealous?

Fior. Yes; for but observe,
A prince whose eye is chooser to his heart
Is seldom steady in the lists of love,

[9] *I*] Omitted by Gifford. D.
[10] *of it.*] The 4to has "on't" (against the metre). D.

Unless the party he affects do match
His rank in equal portion or in friends:
I never yet, out of report, or else
By warranted description, have observ'd
The nature of fantastic jealousy,
If not in him; yet, on my conscience now,
He has no cause.

Fern. Cause, madam! by this light,
I'll pledge my soul against a useless rush.

Fior. I never thought her less; yet, trust me, sir,
No merit can be greater than your praise:
Whereat I strangely wonder, how a man
Vow'd, as you told me, to a single life
Should so much deify the saints from whom
You have disclaim'd devotion.

Fern. Madam, 'tis true;
From them I have, but from their virtues never.

Fior. You are too wise, Fernando. To be plain,
You are in love; nay, shrink not, man, you are;
Bianca is your aim: why do you blush?
She is, I know she is.

Fern. My aim!

Fior. Yes, yours;
I hope I talk no news. Fernando, know
Thou runn'st to thy confusion, if in time
Thou dost not wisely shun that Circe's charm.
Unkindest man! I have too long conceal'd
My hidden flames, when still in silent signs
I courted thee for love, without respect
To youth or state; and yet thou art unkind.
Fernando, leave that sorceress, if not
For love of me, for pity of thyself.

Fern. [*walks aside*] Injurious woman, I defy thy lust.
'Tis not your subtle sifting [that] shall creep

Into the secrets of a heart unsoil'd.—
You are my prince's sister, else your malice
Had rail'd itself to death : but as for me,
Be record all my fate, I do detest
Your fury or affection :—judge the rest. [*Exit.*

Fior. What, gone! well, go thy ways: I see the more
I humble my firm love, the more he shuns
Both it and me. So plain! then 'tis too late
To hope; change, peevish passion, to contempt!
Whatever rages in my blood I feel,
Fool, he shall know I was not born to kneel. [*Exit.*

SCENE II. *Another room in the same.*

Enter D'AVOLOS *and* JULIA.

D'Av. Julia, mine own, speak softly. What, hast thou learned out any thing of this pale widgeon?[11] speak soft; what does she say?

Jul. Foh, more than all; there's not an hour shall pass
But I shall have intelligence, she swears.
Whole nights—you know my mind; I hope you'll give
The gown you promis'd me.

D'Av. Honest Julia, peace; thou'rt a woman worth a kingdom. Let me never be believed now but I think it will be my destiny to be thy husband at last: what though thou have a child,—or perhaps two?

[11] *this pale* widgeon?] Colona, who was the duchess's attendant, as Julia was Fiormonda's. I know not what "whole nights" in the next speech refers to, unless it be part of Colona's intelligence, and mean that the duchess and Fernando have passed such together. D'Avolos finds just such an easy simpleton in Julia as Vasques does in Putana. [See '*Tis Pity she's a Whore.* D.]

Jul. Never but one, I swear.

D'Av. Well, one; is that such a matter? I like thee the better for't; it shows thou hast a good tenantable and fertile womb, worth twenty of your barren, dry, bloodless devourers of youth.—But come, I will talk with thee more privately; the duke has a journey in hand, and will not be long absent: see, he is come already—let's pass away easily. [*Exeunt.*

Enter Duke *and* Bianca.

Duke. Troubled? yes, I have cause.—O, Bianca!
Here was my fate engraven in thy brow,
This smooth, fair, polish'd table; in thy cheeks
Nature summ'd up thy dower: 'twas not wealth,
The miser's god, or royalty of blood,
Advanc'd thee to my bed; but love, and hope
Of virtue that might equal those sweet looks:
If, then, thou shouldst betray my trust, thy faith,
To the pollution of a base desire,
Thou wert a wretched woman.

Bian. Speaks your love
Or fear, my lord?

Duke. Both, both. Bianca, know,
The nightly languish of my dull unrest
Hath stamp'd a strong opinion; for, methought,—
Mark what I say,—as I in glorious pomp
Was sitting on my throne, whiles I had hemm'd
My best-belov'd Bianca in mine arms,
She reach'd my cap of state, and cast it down
Beneath her foot, and spurn'd it in the dust:
Whiles I—O, 'twas a dream too full of fate!—
Was stooping down to reach it, on my head
Fernando, like a traitor to his vows,
Clapt, in disgrace, a coronet of horns.
But, by the honour of anointed kings,

Were both of you hid in a rock of fire,
Guarded by ministers of flaming hell,
I have a sword—'tis here—should make my way
Through fire, through darkness, death, [and hell,] and
all,
To hew your lust-engender'd flesh to shreds,
Pound you to mortar, cut your throats, and mince
Your flesh to mites: I will,—start not,—I will.

Bian. Mercy protect me, will ye murder me?

Duke. Yes.—O, I cry thee mercy!—How the rage
Of my own dream'd-of wrongs[12] made me forget
All sense of sufferance!—Blame me not, Bianca;
One such another dream would quite distract
Reason and self-humanity: yet tell me,
Was't not an ominous vision?

Bian. 'Twas, my lord,
Yet but a vision; for did such a guilt
Hang on mine honour, 'twere no blame in you,
If you did stab me to the heart.

Duke. The heart!
Nay, strumpet, to the soul; and tear it off
From life, to damn it in immortal death.

Bian. Alas! what do you mean, sir?

Duke. I am mad.—
Forgive me, good Bianca; still methinks
I dream and dream anew: now, prithee, chide me.
Sickness and these divisions so distract
My senses, that I take things possible
As if they were; which to remove, I mean
To speed me straight to Lucca, where, perhaps,

[12] *Of my* own *dream'd-of wrongs*] He alludes to the preceding speech. The 4to reads "*undream'd* of wrongs:" but this cannot be right, as the duke has just detailed the pretended *dream* in which he suffered them. A slighter change will give "*e'en* dream'd of," i.e. wrongs endured *merely* in a dream; and this perhaps will be thought the better reading.

Absence and bathing in those healthful springs
May soon recover me; meantime, dear sweet,
Pity my troubled heart; griefs are extreme:
Yet, sweet, when I am gone, think on my dream.—
Who waits without, ho!

Enter PETRUCHIO, NIBRASSA, FIORMONDA, D'AVOLOS, ROSEILLI *disguised as before, and* FERNANDO.

Is provision ready,
To pass to Lucca?

Pet. It attends your highness.

Duke. Friend, hold; take here from me this jewel, this: [*Gives Bian. to Fern.*
Be she your care till my return from Lucca,
Honest Fernando.—Wife, respect my friend.—
Let's go:—but hear ye, wife, think on my dream.
[*Exeunt all but Ros. and Pet.*

Pet. Cousin, one word with you: doth not this cloud
Acquaint you with strange novelties? The duke
Is lately much distemper'd: what he means
By journeying now to Lucca, is to me
A riddle; can you clear my doubt?

Ros. O, sir,
My fears exceed my knowledge, yet I note
No less than you infer; all is not well;
Would 'twere! whosoe'er[13] thrive, I shall be sure
Never to rise to my unhop'd desires.
But, cousin, I shall tell you more anon:
Meantime, pray send my Lord Fernando to me;
I covet much to speak with him.

Pet. And see,
He comes himself; I'll leave you both together. [*Exit.*

[13] *whosoe'er*] Gifford printed "whoever." D.

Re-enter FERNANDO.

Fern. The duke is hors'd for Lucca. How now, coz,
How prosper you in love?
Ros. As still I hop'd.[14]—
My lord, you are undone.
Fern. Undone! in what?
Ros. Lost; and I fear your life is bought and sold;
I'll tell you how. Late in my lady's chamber
As I by chance lay slumbering on the mats,
In comes the Lady Marquess, and with her
Julia and D'Avolos; where sitting down,
Not doubting me, "Madam," quoth D'Avolos,
"We have discover'd now the nest of shame."
In short, my lord,—for you already know
As much as they reported,—there was told
The circumstance of all your private love
And meetings with the duchess; when, at last,
False D'Avolos concluded with an oath,
"We'll make," quoth he, "his heart-strings crack for this."
Fern. Speaking of me?
Ros. Of you: "Ay," quoth the marquess,
"Were not the duke a baby, he would seek
Swift vengeance; for he knew it long ago."
Fern. Let him know it; yet I vow
She is as loyal in her plighted faith
As is the sun in heaven: but put case
She were not, and the duke did know she were not;
This sword lift up, and guided by this arm,
Shall guard her from an armèd troop of fiends
And all the earth beside.[15]

[14] *As still I* hop'd.] i.e. apprehended, expected: see p. 53.

[15] Fernando is a poor wretched creature: he boasts and blusters incessantly of his prowess, and the reader is led to expect that,

Ros. You are too safe
In your destruction.

Fern. Damn him!—he shall feel—
But peace! who comes?

Enter COLONA.

Col. My lord, the duchess craves
A word with you.

Fern. Where is she?

Col. In her chamber.

Ros. Here, have a plum for ie'ee—

Col. Come, fool, I'll give thee plums enow; come, fool.

Fern. Let slaves in mind be servile to their fears;
Our heart is high instarr'd in brighter spheres.
[*Exeunt Fern. and Col.*

Ros. I see him lost already.
If all prevail not, we shall know too late
No toil can shun the violence of fate. [*Exit.*

---

like another Drawcansir, he can upon occasion "control whole armies;" yet he is taken like a rat in a trap, with as little effort as Mauruccio. The Duke too roars and bellows in a similar key, and just as little to the purpose; but his starts are the impotency of dotage raised to frenzy by the machinations of others.

ACT V.

SCENE I. *The palace. The Duchess's bedchamber.*

BIANCA *discovered in her night-attire, leaning on a cushion at a table, holding* FERNANDO *by the hand. Enter above* FIORMONDA.

Fior. [*aside*] Now fly, revenge, and wound the lower earth,
That I, inspher'd above, may cross the race
Of love despis'd, and triumph o'er their graves
Who scorn the low-bent thraldom of my heart!

Bian. Why shouldst thou not be mine? why should the laws,
The iron laws of ceremony, bar
Mutual embraces? what's a vow? a vow?
Can there be sin in unity? could I
As well dispense with conscience as renounce
The outside of my titles, the poor style
Of duchess, I had rather change my life
With any waiting-woman in the land
To purchase one night's rest with thee, Fernando,
Than be Caraffa's spouse a thousand years.

Fior. [*aside*] Treason to wedlock! this would make you sweat.

Fern. Lady, of all[1] * * * * * as before,
* * * what I am, * * *
* * * * * * * *
To survive you, or I will see you first
Or widowèd or buried: if the last,
By all the comfort I can wish to taste,
By your fair eyes, that sepulchre that holds

[1] Fern. *Lady, of all,* &c.] Here occurs one of the greatest lacunæ in all Ford's works. Some lines appear to be quite lost, and the fragments of others that remain cannot be distributed with any certainty. Even the concluding part of Fiormonda's speech should perhaps be transferred elsewhere.

Your coffin shall incoffin me alive;
I sign it with this seal. [*Kisses her.*

Fior. [*aside*] Ignoble strumpet!

Bian. You shall not swear; take off that oath again,
Or thus I will enforce it. [*Kisses him.*

Fern. Use that force,
And make me perjurèd; for whiles your lips
Are made the book, it is a sport to swear,
And glory to forswear.

Fior. [*aside*] Here's fast and loose!
Which, for a ducat, now the game's on foot?

Whilst they are kissing, the Duke *and* D'Avolos, *with their swords drawn, appear at the door, followed by* Petruchio, Nibrassa, *and a* Guard.

Col. [*within*] Help, help! madam, you are betrayed, madam; help, help!

D'Av. [*aside to Duke*] Is there confidence in credit, now, sir? belief in your own eyes? do you see? do you see, sir? can you behold it without lightning?

Col. [*within*] Help, madam, help!

Fern. What noise is that? I heard one cry.

Duke [*comes forward*]. Ha! did you?
Know you who I am?

Fern. Yes; thou'rt Pavy's duke,
Drest like a hangman:[2] see, I am unarm'd,
Yet do not fear thee; though the coward doubt
Of what I could have done hath made thee steal
Th' advantage of this time, yet, duke, I dare
Thy worst, for murder sits upon thy cheeks:
To't, man!

Duke. I am too angry in my rage
To scourge thee unprovided.—Take him hence;

[2] *a hangman*] See note, vol. i. p. 180. D.

Away with him! [*The Guard seize Fern.*

Fern. Unhand me!

D'Av. You must go, sir.

Fern. Duke, do not shame thy manhood to lay hands
On that most innocent lady.[3]

Duke. Yet again!—
Confine him to his chamber.

[*Exeunt D'Av. and the Guard with Fern.*

Leave us all;
None stay, not one; shut up the doors.

[*Exeunt Pet. and Nib.*

Fior. Now show thyself my brother, brave Caraffa.

Duke. Woman, stand forth before me;—wretched whore,
What canst thou hope for?

Bian. Death; I wish no less.
You told me you had dreamt; and, gentle duke,
Unless you be mistook, you're now awak'd.

Duke. Strumpet, I am; and in my hand hold up
The edge that must uncut thy twist of life:
Dost thou not shake?

Bian. For what? to see a weak,
Faint, trembling arm advance a leaden blade?
Alas, good man! put up, put up; thine eyes
Are likelier much to weep than arms to strike:
What would you do now, pray?

Duke. What! shameless harlot!
Rip up the cradle of thy cursèd womb,
In which the mixture of that traitor's lust
Imposthumes for a birth of bastardy.

[3] Our author seems to have very loose notions of female honour. He certainly goes much beyond his age, which was far enough from squeamish on this point, in terming Bianca *innocent*. She is, in fact, a gross and profligate adulteress, and her ridiculous reservations, while they mark her lubricity, only enhance her shame.

Yet come, and if thou think'st thou canst deserve
One mite of mercy, ere the boundless spleen
Of just-consuming wrath o'erswell my reason,
Tell me, bad woman, tell me what could move
Thy heart to crave variety of youth.

Bian. I['ll] tell ye, if you needs would be resolv'd;
I held Fernando much the properer man.

Duke. Shameless, intolerable whore!

Bian. What ails you?
Can you imagine, sir, the name of duke
Could make a crookèd leg, a scambling foot,[4]
A tolerable face, a wearish hand,
A bloodless lip, or such an untrimm'd beard
As yours, fit for a lady's pleasure? no:
I wonder you could think 'twere possible,
When I had once but look'd on your Fernando,
I ever could love you again; fie, fie!
Now, by my life, I thought that long ago
Y' had known it, and been glad you had a friend
Your wife did think so well of.

Duke. O my stars!
Here's impudence above all history.
Why, thou detested reprobate in virtue,
Dar'st thou, without a blush, before mine eyes
Speak such immodest language?

Bian. Dare! yes, 'faith,
You see I dare: I know what you would say now;
You would fain tell me how exceeding much

[4] *a* scambling *foot,*] i.e. a *sprawling, shuffling* foot: *wearish* is used by our old writers for wizened, withered, decayed, &c. I have already remarked the similarity between this abandoned woman and Annabella: the same wantonness of abuse, the same audacious avowal of infamy, the same taunting provocation; and all delivered in such a style of Pict-hatch eloquence as the veriest waistcoater of Ford's days would have shrunk from;

"verbis olido stans
Fornice mancipium quibus abstinet."

I am beholding to you, that vouchsaf'd
Me, from a simple gentlewoman's place,
The honour of your bed : 'tis true, you did ;
But why? 'twas but because you thought I had
A spark of beauty more than you had seen.
To answer this, my reason is the like ;
The self-same appetite which led you on
To marry me led me to love your friend :
O, he's a gallant man ! if ever yet
Mine eyes beheld a miracle compos'd
Of flesh and blood, Fernando has my voice.
I must confess, my lord, that for a prince
Handsome enough you are, [and—] and no more ;
But to compare yourself with him ! trust me,
You are too much in fault. Shall I advise you ?
Hark in your ear ; thank heaven he was so slow
As not to wrong your sheets ; for, as I live,
The fault was his, not mine.

Fior. Take this, take all.

Duke. Excellent, excellent ! the pangs of death
Are music to this.—
Forgive me, my good Genius ; I had thought
I match'd a woman, but I find she is
A devil, worser than the worst in hell.—
Nay, nay, since we are in, e'en come, say on ;
I mark you to a syllable : you say
The fault was his, not yours ; why, virtuous mistress,
Can you imagine you have so much art
Which may persuade me you and your close markman
Did not a little traffic in my right ?

Bian. Look, what I said, 'tis true ; for, know it now,—
I must confess I miss'd no means, no time,
To win him to my bosom ; but so much,
So holily, with such religion,

He kept the laws of friendship, that my suit
Was held but, in comparison, a jest;
Nor did I ofter urge the violence
Of my affection, but as oft he urg'd
The sacred vows of faith 'twixt friend and friend:
Yet be assur'd, my lord, if ever language
Of cunning servile flatteries, entreaties,
Or what in me is, could procure his love,
I would not blush to speak it.

Duke. Such another
As thou art, miserable creature, would
Sink the whole sex of women: yet confess
What witchcraft us'd the wretch to charm the heart[5]
Of the once spotless temple of thy mind?
For without witchcraft it could ne'er be done.

Bian. Phew!—an you be in these tunes, sir, I'll leave;[6]
You know the best and worst and all.

Duke. Nay, then,
Thou tempt'st me to thy ruin. Come, black angel,
Fair devil, in thy prayers reckon up
The sum in gross of all thy veinèd follies;[7]
There, amongst other, weep in tears of blood
For one above the rest, adultery!
Adultery, Bianca! such a guilt
As, were the sluices of thine eyes let up,
Tears cannot wash it off: 'tis not the tide

[5] *to charm the heart*] This reading has been made out of the old copy, which has "the *art*." I can think of no word nearer the traces of the original; and yet to "charm the *heart* of the temple of the mind" is an expression which will be as little admired as comprehended. [Is "art" a mistake for "*altar*"? Afterwards we have "The *altar* of her purity," p. 99. D.]

[6] *I'll leave;*] i.e. I'll leave off, say no more.—Gifford, misunderstanding the expression, printed "I'll leave [you]." D.

[7] *veinèd follies;*] i.e. ingrained, as we say; follies that run in the blood.

Of trivial wantonness from youth to youth,
But thy abusing of thy lawful bed,
Thy husband's bed; his in whose breast thou slept'st,[8]
His that did prize thee more than all the trash
Which hoarding worldlings make an idol of.
When thou shalt find the catalogue enroll'd
Of thy misdeeds, there shall be writ in text
Thy bastarding the issues of a prince.
Now turn thine eyes into thy hovering soul,
And do not hope for life; would angels sing
A requiem at my hearse but to dispense[9]
With my revenge on thee, 'twere all in vain:
Prepare to die!

Bian. [*opens her bosom*] I do; and to the point
Of thy sharp sword with open breast I'll run
Half way thus naked; do not shrink, Caraffa;
This daunts not me: but in the latter act
Of thy revenge, 'tis all the suit I ask
At my last gasp, to spare thy noble friend;
For life to me without him were a death.

Duke. Not this; I'll none of this; 'tis not so fit.—
Why should I kill her? she may live and change,
Or— [*Throws down his sword.*

Fior. Dost thou halt? faint coward, dost thou wish
To blemish all thy glorious ancestors?
Is this thy courage?

Duke. Ha! say you so too?—
Give me thy hand, Bianca.

Bian. Here.

Duke. Farewell;

[8] *slept'st,*] The 4to has "sleep'st;" and so Gifford. D.

[9] *would angels sing*
A requiem at my hearse but to dispense, &c.] i.e.—if so plain a passage needs explanation—Could I secure a happy immortality by sparing thy life, I would not forgo my revenge.

Thus go in everlasting sleep to dwell!
[*Draws his dagger and stabs her.*
Here's blood for lust, and sacrifice for wrong.
Bian. 'Tis bravely done; thou hast struck home at once:
Live to repent too late. Commend my love
To thy true friend, my love to him that owes it;
My tragedy to thee;[10] my heart to—to—Fernando.
O—O! [*Dies.*
Duke. Sister, she's dead.
Fior. Then, whiles thy rage is warm
Pursue the causer of her trespass.[11]
Duke. Good:
I'll slack no time[12] whiles I am hot in blood.
[*Takes up his sword and exit.*
Fior. Here's royal vengeance! this becomes the state
Of his disgrace and my unbounded hate.[13] [*Exit above.*

SCENE II. *An apartment in the palace.*

Enter FERNANDO, NIBRASSA, *and* PETRUCHIO.

Pet. May we give credit to your words, my lord?
Speak, on your honour.
Fern. Let me die accurs'd,
If ever, through the progress of my life,
I did as much as reap the benefit

[10] *My tragedy to thee;*] I have supposed that Bianca alludes to her husband; but it is also possible that she may direct herself to Fiormonda, who from the gallery had urged-on her murder with such violence. "*Owes*" is used in this speech in the sense of *owns, possesses.*

[11] *trespass.*] The 4to has "trespasses;" and so Gifford. D.

[12] *I'll slack no time*] i.e. I'll hasten.

[13] *my unbounded* hate.] So I venture to read. The 4to has "unbounded *fate,*" which conveys no meaning.

Of any favour from her save a kiss:
A better woman never bless'd the earth.

Nib. Beshrew my heart, young lord, but I believe thee: alas, kind lady, 'tis a lordship to a dozen of points[14] but the jealous madman will in his fury offer her some violence.

Pet. If it be thus, 'twere fit you rather kept
A guard about you for your own defence
Than to be guarded for security
Of his revenge; he is extremely mov'd.

Nib. Passion of my body, my lord, if he come in his odd fits to you, in the case you are, he might cut your throat ere you could provide a weapon of defence: nay, rather than it shall be so, hold, take my sword in your hand; 'tis none of the sprucest, but 'tis a tough fox[15] will not fail his master, come what will come. Take it; I'll answer't, I: in the mean time Petruchio and I will back to the duchess' lodging.

[*Gives Fern. his sword.*

Pet. Well thought on;—and, despite[16] of all his rage,
Rescue the virtuous lady.

Nib. Look to yourself, my lord! the duke comes.

Enter the Duke, *a sword in one hand, and a bloody dagger in the other.*

Duke. Stand, and behold thy executioner,
Thou glorious traitor! I will keep no form
Of ceremonious law to try thy guilt:

[14] *points*] See note, vol. i. p. 292. D.

[15] *'tis a tough* fox] A cant term for a *sword*. So in Beaumont and Fletcher;

"*Fab.* Put up your *sword*;
I've seen it often; 'tis a *fox*.
Jac. It is so." *The Captain*.

[16] *and, despite*] The 4to has "*and in despight*;" and so Gifford. D.

Look here, 'tis written on my poniard's point,
The bloody evidence of thy untruth,
Wherein thy conscience and the wrathful rod
Of heaven's scourge for lust at once give up
The verdict of thy crying villanies.
I see thou'rt arm'd: prepare, I crave no odds
Greater than is the justice of my cause;
Fight, or I'll kill thee.

Fern. Duke, I fear thee not:
But first I charge thee, as thou art a prince,
Tell me how hast thou us'd thy duchess?

Duke. How!
To add affliction to thy trembling ghost,
Look on my dagger's crimson dye, and judge.

Fern. Not dead?

Duke. Not dead! yes, by my honour's truth: why, fool,
Dost think I'll hug my injuries? no, traitor!
I'll mix your souls together in your deaths,
As you did both your bodies in her life.—
Have at thee!

Fern. Stay; I yield my weapon up.

[*He drops his sword.*

Here, here's my bosom: as thou art a duke,
Dost honour goodness, if the chaste Bianca
Be murder'd, murder me.

Duke. Faint-hearted coward,
Art thou so poor in spirit! Rise and fight;
Or, by the glories of my house and name,
I'll kill thee basely.

Fern. Do but hear me first:
Unfortunate Caraffa, thou hast butcher'd
An innocent, a wife as free from lust
As any terms of art can deify.

Duke. Pish, this is stale dissimulation;

I'll hear no more.

Fern. If ever I unshrin'd
The altar of her purity, or tasted
More of her love than what without control
Or blame a brother from a sister might,
Rack me to atomies. I must confess
I have too much abus'd thee; did exceed
In lawless courtship; 'tis too true, I did:
But, by the honour which I owe to goodness,
For any actual folly I am free.

Duke. 'Tis false: as much in death for thee she spake.

Fern. By yonder starry roof, 'tis true. O duke!
Couldst thou rear up another world like this,
Another like to that, and more, or more,
Herein thou art most wretched; all the wealth
Of all those worlds could not redeem the loss
Of such a spotless wife. Glorious Bianca,
Reign in the triumph of thy martyrdom;
Earth was unworthy of thee!

Nib. Pet. Now, on our lives, we both believe him.

Duke. Fernando, dar'st thou swear upon my sword
To justify thy words?

Fern. I dare; look here. [*Kisses the sword.*
'Tis not the fear of death doth prompt my tongue,
For I would wish to die; and thou shalt know,
Poor miserable duke, since she is dead,
I'll hold all life a hell.

Duke. Bianca chaste!

Fern. As virtue's self is good.

Duke.[17] Chaste, chaste, and kill'd by me! to her
I offer up this remnant of my—

[*Offers to stab himself, and is stayed by Fern.*

[17] *Duke.*] From the first line of this speech (which is arranged as above in the 4to) something appears to have dropt out. D.

Fern. Hold!
Be gentler to thyself.
Pet. Alas, my lord,
Is this[18] a wise man's carriage?
Duke. Whither now
Shall I run from the day, where never man,
Nor eye, nor eye of heaven may see a dog
So hateful as I am? Bianca chaste!
Had not the fury of some hellish rage
Blinded all reason's sight, I must have seen
Her clearness in her confidence to die.
Your leave—
[*Kneels, holds up his hands, and, after speaking to himself a little, rises.*
'Tis done: come, friend, now for her love,
Her love that prais'd thee in the pangs of death,
I'll hold thee dear.—Lords, do not care for me,
I am too wise to die yet.—O, Bianca!

Enter D'AVOLOS.

D'Av. The Lord Abbot of Monaco, sir, is, in his return from Rome, lodged last night late in the city very privately; and hearing the report of your journey, only intends to visit your duchess to-morrow.

Duke. Slave, torture me no more!—Note him, my lords;
If you would choose a devil in the shape
Of man, an arch-arch-devil, there stands one.—
We'll meet our uncle.—Order straight, Petruchio,
Our duchess may be coffin'd; 'tis our will
She forthwith be interr'd, with all the speed
And privacy you may, i' th' college-church
Amongst Caraffa's ancient monuments:

18 *Is this*] The 4to has "this is." D.

Some three days hence we'll keep her funeral.—
Damn'd villain! bloody villain!—O, Bianca!—
No counsel from our cruel wills can win us;
But ills once done, we bear our guilt within us.

[*Exeunt all but D'Av.*

D'Av. Good b'wi'ye! *Arch-arch-devil!* why, I am paid. Here's bounty for good service! beshrew my heart, it is a right princely reward. Now must I say my prayers, that I have lived to so ripe an age to have my head stricken off. I cannot tell;[19] 't may be my Lady Fiormonda will stand on my behalf to the duke: that's but a single hope;[20] a disgraced courtier oftener finds enemies to sink him when he is falling than friends to relieve him. I must resolve to stand to the hazard of all brunts now. Come what may, I will not die like a coward;[21] and the world shall know it.

[*Exit.*

SCENE III. *Another apartment in the same.*

Enter FIORMONDA, *and* ROSEILLI *discovering himself.*

Ros. Wonder not, madam; here behold the man
Whom your disdain hath metamorphosèd.
Thus long have I been clouded in this shape,
Led on by love; and in that love, despair:
If not the sight of our distracted court,
Nor pity of my bondage, can reclaim
The greatness of your scorn, yet let me know
My latest doom from you.

[19] *I cannot tell;*] i.e. I know not what to think. For more examples of this mode of expression, which has been grossly misunderstood, see *Jonson*, vol. i. p. 125.

[20] *that's but a single hope;*] Weak, feeble: see vol. i. p. 173.

[21] *coward;*] The 4to has "Cow;" nor did Gifford alter it. D.

Fior. Strange miracle!
Roseilli, I must honour thee: thy truth,
Like a transparent mirror, represents
My reason with my errors. Noble lord,
That better dost deserve a better fate,
Forgive me: if my heart can entertain
Another thought of love, it shall be thine.
Ros. Blessèd, for ever blessèd be the words!
In death you have reviv'd me.

Enter D'AVOLOS.

D'Av. [*aside*] Whom have we here? Roseilli, the supposed fool? 'tis he; nay, then, help me a brazen face!—My honourable lord!—

Ros. Bear off, bloodthirsty man! come not [thou] near me.
D'Av. Madam, I trust the service—
Fior. Fellow, learn to new-live: the way to thrift
For thee in grace[22] is a repentant shrift.
Ros. Ill has thy life been, worse will be thy end:
Men flesh'd in blood know seldom to amend.

Enter Servant.

Ser. His highness commends his love to you, and expects your presence; he is ready to pass to the church, only staying for my lord abbot to associate him.—Withal, his pleasure is, that you, D'Avolos, forbear to rank in this solemnity in the place of secretary; else to be there as a private man.—Pleaseth you to go? [*Exeunt all but D'Av.*

D'Av. As a private man! what remedy? This way

[22] *the way to thrift
For thee in grace*, &c.] i. e. the way for thee to thrive in grace is, &c.

they must come; and here I will stand, to fall amongst 'em in the rear.

A solemn strain of soft music. The scene opens, and discovers the church, with a tomb in the background.

Enter Attendants *with torches, after them two* Friars; *then the* Duke *in mourning manner; after him the* Abbot, FIORMONDA, COLONA, JULIA, ROSEILLI, PETRUCHIO, NIBRASSA, *and a* Guard.—D'AVOLOS *follows. When the procession approaches the tomb they all kneel. The* Duke *goes to the tomb, and lays his hand on it. The music ceases.*

Duke. Peace and sweet rest sleep here! Let not the touch
Of this my impious hand profane the shrine
Of fairest purity, which hovers yet
About those[23] blessèd bones inhears'd within.
If in the bosom of this sacred tomb,
Bianca, thy disturbèd ghost doth range,
Behold, I offer up the sacrifice
Of bleeding tears, shed from a faithful spring,
Pouring[24] oblations of a mourning heart
To thee, offended spirit! I confess
I am Caraffa, he, that wretched man,
That butcher, who, in my enragèd spleen,
Slaughter'd the life of innocence and beauty.
Now come I to pay tribute to those wounds
Which I digg'd up, and reconcile the wrongs
My fury wrought and my contrition mourns.
So chaste, so dear a wife was never man
But I enjoy'd; yet in the bloom and pride
Of all her years untimely took her life.—

[23] *those*] Gifford printed "these." D.
[24] *Pouring*] The 4to has "Roaring." D.

Enough: set ope the tomb, that I may take
My last farewell, and bury griefs with her.

[*The tomb is opened, out of which rises Fernando in his winding-sheet, only his face discovered, and as the Duke is going in, puts him back.*

Fern. Forbear! what art thou that dost rudely press
Into the confines of forsaken graves?
Has[25] death no privilege? Com'st thou, Caraffa,
To practise yet a rape upon the dead?
Inhuman tyrant!—
Whats'ever thou intendest, know this place
Is pointed out for my inheritance;
Here lies the monument of all my hopes:
Had eager lust intrunk'd my conquer'd soul,
I had not buried living joys in death.
Go, revel in thy palace, and be proud
To boast thy famous murders; let thy smooth,
Low-fawning parasites renown thy act:
Thou com'st not here.

Duke. Fernando, man of darkness,
Never till now, before these dreadful sights,
Did I abhor thy friendship: thou hast robb'd
My resolution of a glorious name.
Come out, or, by the thunder of my rage,
Thou diest a death more fearful than the scourge
Of death can whip thee with.

Fern. Of death!—poor duke!
Why, that's the aim I shoot at; 'tis not threats—
Maugre thy power, or[26] the spite of hell—
Shall rent[27] that honour: let life-hugging slaves,

[25] *Has*] Gifford printed "Hath." D.
[26] *or*] The 4to has "of." D.
[27] *rent*] Gifford printed "rend." See note, vol. i. p. 194. D.

Whose hands imbru'd in butcheries like thine
Shake terror to their souls, be loth to die!
See, I am cloth'd in robes that fit the grave:
I pity thy defiance.

Duke. Guard, lay hands,
And drag him out.

Fern. Yes, let 'em; here's my shield;
Here's health to victory!—

[*As the Guard go to seize him, he drinks-off a phial of poison.*

Now do thy worst.—
Farewell, duke! once I have outstripp'd thy plots;[28]
Not all the cunning antidotes of art
Can warrant me twelve minutes of my life:
It works, it works already, bravely! bravely!—
Now, now I feel it tear each several joint.
O royal poison! trusty friend! split, split
Both heart and gall asunder, excellent bane!—
Roseilli, love my memory.—Well search'd out,
Swift, nimble venom! torture every vein.—
I come, Bianca—cruel torment, feast,
Feast on, do!—Duke, farewell.—Thus I—hot flames!—
Conclude my love,—and seal it in my bosom!—
O! [*Dies.*

Abbot. Most desperate end!

Duke. None stir;
Who steps a foot steps to his utter ruin.—
And art thou gone, Fernando? art thou gone?
Thou wert a friend unmatch'd; rest in thy fame.—
Sister, when I have finish'd my last days,
Lodge me, my wife, and this unequall'd friend,

[28] once *I have outstripp'd thy plots;*] i.e. *once for all*, finally, effectually; a sense which the word frequently bears in our old writers.

All in one monument.—Now to my vows.
Never henceforth let any passionate tongue
Mention Bianca's and Caraffa's name,
But let each letter in that tragic sound
Beget a sigh, and every sigh a tear:
Children unborn, and widows whose lean cheeks
Are furrow'd-up by age, shall weep whole nights,
Repeating but the story of our fates;
Whiles in the period, closing up their tale,
They must conclude how for Bianca's love
Caraffa, in revenge of wrongs to her,
Thus on her altar sacrific'd his life. [*Stabs himself.*

Abbot. O, hold the duke's hand!

Fior. Save my brother, save him!

Duke. Do, do; I was too willing to strike home
To be prevented. Fools, why, could you dream
I would outlive my outrage?—Sprightful flood,
Run out in rivers! O, that these thick streams
Could gather head, and make a standing pool,
That jealous husbands here might bathe in blood!
So! I grow sweetly empty; all the pipes
Of life unvessel life.—Now, heavens, wipe out
The writing of my sin!—Bianca, thus
I creep to thee—to thee—to thee, Bi—an—ca.
[*Dies.*

Ros. He's dead already, madam.

D'Av. [*aside*] Above hope! here's labour saved; I could bless the Destinies.

Abbot. 'Would I had never seen it!

Fior. Since 'tis thus,
My Lord Roseilli, in the true requital
Of your continu'd love, I here possess
You of the dukedom, and with it of me,
In presence of this holy abbot.

Abbot. Lady, then,

From my hand take your husband; long enjoy
[*Joins their hands.*
Each to each other's comfort and content!

All. Long live Roseilli!

Ros. First, thanks[29] to heaven; next, lady, to your love;
Lastly, my lords, to all: and that the entrance
Into this principality may give
Fair hopes of being worthy of our place,
Our first work shall be justice.—D'Avolos,
Stand forth.

D'Av. My gracious lord!—

Ros. No, graceless villain!
I am no lord of thine.—Guard, take him hence,
Convey him to the prison's top; in chains
Hang him alive; whosoe'er[30] lends a bit
Of bread to feed him dies.—Speak not against it,
I will be deaf to mercy.—Bear him hence!

D'Av. Mercy, new duke! here's my comfort, I make but one in the number of the tragedy of princes.
[*He is led off.*

Ros. Madam, a second charge is to perform
Your brother's testament; we'll rear a tomb
To those unhappy lovers, which shall tell
Their fatal loves to all posterity.—
Thus, then, for you; henceforth I here dismiss
The mutual comforts of our marriage-bed:
Learn to new-live, my vows unmov'd shall stand;
And since your life hath been so much uneven,
Bethink in time to make your peace with heaven.

Fior. O, me! is this your love?

Ros. 'Tis your desert;
Which no persuasion shall remove.

[29] *thanks*] The 4to has "thanke." D.
[30] *whosoe'er*] Gifford printed "whoever." D.

Abbot. 'Tis fit;
Purge frailty with repentance.
Fior. I embrace it:
Happy too late, since lust hath made me foul,
Henceforth I'll dress my bride-bed in my soul.
Ros. Please you to walk, Lord Abbot?
Abbot. Yes, set on.
No age hath heard, nor[31] chronicle can say,
That ever here befell a sadder day. [*Exeunt.*

[31] *nor*] Gifford printed "or." D.

The catastrophe of this drama does not shame its progress. Enough, indeed, are left to bury the dead, but the mortality is nearly as widely spread as in *'Tis Pity she's a Whore;* and, to confess the truth, had all the survivors, with the exception of the Abbot, been involved in the same fate, no one would have "raised the waters" for them. Roseilli had hitherto preserved some of our esteem; but his treatment of Fiormonda, who had done nothing to excite his displeasure, except giving him the dukedom, with herself, since he exclaimed, upon her promise of kindness,

> "Blessèd, for ever blessèd be the words!
> In death you have reviv'd me,"

reduces him to a level with the rest. It is useless to observe on the other characters; the duchess dying in *odour of chastity*, after confessing and triumphing in her lascivious passion; the poor duke, in defiance of it, affirming that "no man was ever blest with so good and loving a wife," and falling upon his sword, that he may the sooner share her tomb, together with his "unequalled friend," who so zealously had laboured to dishonour him; with other anomalies of a similar kind,—render this one of the least attractive of Ford's pieces. It is not, however, without its beauties: many scenes are charmingly written for the greater part; and few of our author's works contain more striking examples of his characteristic merits and defects. It was received, the title-page says, *generally well;* an expression of which it would be hazardous to fix the precise import; but the author and his friends appear to have regarded it with complacency.

PERKIN WARBECK.

The title of the old 4to is "The Chronicle Historie of Perkin Warbeck. A Strange Truth. Acted (some-times) by the Queenes Maiesties Servants at the Phœnix in Drurie lane. Fide Honor. London, Printed by T. P. for Hugh Beeston, and are to be sold at his Shop, neere the Castle in Cornehill, 1634." Here again we have the poet's anagram, *Fide Honor*.

It was reprinted in 1714 in 12mo, when the nation was in a state of disquietude from insurgent movements in Scotland. In 1745 it appears to have been brought out at Goodman's Fields, on occasion, Oldys says, of the present rebellion under the Pretender's eldest son. Nothing is said of its reception: it could scarcely be very favourable at such a period; for, to the reproach of the judgment of those who brought it forward, it is calculated to defeat the very object which they had in view, and to excite a compassionate feeling—not for the king upon the throne, but for his youthful competitor.[1]

[1] "There are now, in December 1745, on occasion of the present rebellion under the Pretender's eldest son, two plays, near finished, on this story of Perkin Warbeck; one by Charles Macklin the player, the other by Mr. Joseph Elderton, a young attorney; the former for Drury Lane, the latter at Covent Garden; but this play of John Ford's has got the start of them at Goodman's Fields. Macklin's was a silly performance, and was soon dismissed, he being twenty pounds out of pocket by acting it, yet got it printed. Elderton's was not finished before it was too late in the season to act it; and when the rebellion was suppressed in the field, it was thought unreasonable to revive it on the stage. Macklin's was called by the foolish title of 'King Henry VII., or the Popish Impostor;' popery being looked on as no objection in that reign. Elderton's was called 'The Pretender.'" *Ms. Notes to Langbaine, by Oldys.*

My kind old friend Mr. Waldron, with whom perished more interesting and amusing theatrical history than can perhaps now be found on the stage, told me that Badeley the actor gave him the following anecdote; "I was sitting one evening at the Cider-Cellar with Macklin, and incidentally observed (for I was not very deeply read in theatrical history), that I wondered there had not been a play written on the story of Perkin Warbeck. 'There has, sir,' gruffly replied Macklin. 'Indeed! and how did it succeed?' 'It was damned, sir.' 'Bless me! it must have been very ill written, then—such a story! Pray, Mr. Macklin, who was the stupid author?' 'I, sir!' roared the veteran, in a tone that took away, continued Badeley, all desire to continue the conversation."

TO

THE RIGHTLY[2] HONOURABLE

WILLIAM CAVENDISH,

EARL OF NEWCASTLE, VISCOUNT MANSFIELD, LORD BOLSOVER AND OGLE.[3]

MY LORD,

OUT of the darkness of a former age,—enlightened by a late both learned and an honourable pen,[4]—I have endeavoured to personate a great attempt, and in it a greater danger. In *other labours* you may read actions of antiquity discoursed; in *this abridgment* find the actors themselves discoursing, in some kind prac-

[2] *rightly*] Gifford printed "right." D.

[3] "William Cavendish (nephew to the first Earl of Devonshire), Lord Ogle," Collins says, "*jure materno*, was born in the year 1592, and was early in favour with James I., by whom he was made a Knight of the Bath in 1610, and created a peer by the title of Viscount Mansfield in 1623. He continued in favour with Charles I., who created him Earl of Newcastle-upon-Tyne, 1628, and Marquis six [sixteen?] years afterwards. In 1638 the king assigned him the office of governor to the Prince of Wales. His exertions in favour of the royal cause during the rebellion are too well known to require any notice in this place. He was created Duke of Newcastle in 1665, and died in 1676, at the advanced age of 84." So much is said of the Duke of Newcastle in the Introduction to the *Works of Ben Jonson*, that it may suffice to refer the reader who is desirous of learning more of so distinguished a nobleman to that collection. See vols. i. and ix.

[4] *learned and an honourable pen,*] That of the great Lord Bacon. He alludes to his *History of King Henry VII.*

tised as well *what* to speak as speaking *why* to do. Your lordship is a most competent judge in expressions of such credit; commissioned by your known ability in examining, and enabled by your knowledge in determining, the monuments of time.[5] Eminent titles may, indeed, inform *who* their owners are, not often *what*. To yours the addition of that information in both cannot in any application be observed flattery, the authority being established by truth. I can only acknowledge the errors in writing mine own; the worthiness of the subject written being a perfection in the story and of it. The custom of your lordship's entertainments—even to strangers—is rather an example than a fashion: in which consideration I dare not profess a curiosity; but am only studious that your lordship will please, amongst such as best honour your goodness, to admit into your noble construction

JOHN FORD.

[5] *the monuments of* time.] i.e. such as are destined to live to future ages; a compliment somewhat too high even for this great and good man, whose judgment in matters of mere literature never possessed that commanding influence which the grateful poet seems inclined to endow him with.

DRAMATIS PERSONÆ.

HENRY VII.
LORD DAWBENEY.
SIR WILLIAM STANLEY, lord chamberlain.
EARL OF OXFORD.
EARL OF SURREY.
FOX, bishop of Durham.
URSWICK, chaplain to the king.
SIR ROBERT CLIFFORD.
LAMBERT SIMNEL.
HIALAS, a Spanish agent.

JAMES IV., king of Scotland.
EARL OF HUNTLEY.
EARL OF CRAWFORD.
LORD DALYELL.
MARCHMONT, a herald.

PERKIN WARBECK.
STEPHEN FRION, his secretary.
JOHN A-WATER, mayor of Cork.
HERON, a mercer.
SKELTON, a tailor.
ASTLEY, a scrivener.

LADY KATHERINE GORDON.
COUNTESS OF CRAWFORD.
JANE DOUGLAS, Lady Katherine's attendant.

Sheriff, Constables, Officers, Guards, Servingmen, Masquers, and Soldiers.

SCENE—*Partly in England, partly in Scotland.*

PROLOGUE.

STUDIES have of this nature been of late
So out of fashion, so unfollow'd, that
It is become more justice to revive
The antic follies of the times than strive
To countenance wise industry: no want
Of art doth render wit or lame or scant
Or slothful in the purchase of fresh bays;
But want of truth in them who give the praise
To their self-love, presuming to out-do
The writer, or—for need—the actors too.
But such this[6] author's silence best befits,
Who bids them be in love with their own wits.
From him to clearer judgments we can say
He shows a history couch'd in a play;
A history of noble mention, known,
Famous, and true; most noble, 'cause our own;
Not forg'd from Italy, from France, from Spain,
But chronicled at home; as rich in strain
Of brave attempts as ever fertile rage
In action could beget to grace the stage.
We cannot limit scenes, for the whole land
Itself appear'd too narrow to withstand
Competitors for kingdoms; nor is here
Unnecessary mirth forc'd to endear
A multitude: on these two rests the fate
Of worthy expectation,—truth and state.

[6] *this*] Gifford printed "the." D.

PERKIN WARBECK.

ACT I.

SCENE I. *Westminster. The royal presence-chamber.*

Enter King HENRY, *supported to the throne by the* Bishop of Durham *and* Sir WILLIAM STANLEY; Earl of Oxford, Earl of Surrey, *and* Lord DAWBENEY. *A Guard.*

K. Hen. Still to be haunted, still to be pursu'd,
Still to be frighted with false apparitions
Of pageant majesty and new-coin'd greatness,
As if we were a mockery king in state,
Only ordain'd to lavish sweat and blood,
In scorn and laughter, to the ghosts of York,
Is all below our merits:[1] yet, my lords,
My friends and counsellors, yet we sit fast
In our own royal birthright; the rent face
And bleeding wounds of England's slaughter'd people
Have been by us, as by the best physician,
At last both throughly cur'd and set in safety;
And yet, for all this glorious work of peace,

[1] Ford has closely followed Lord Bacon: here we have almost his very words; "At this time the king began again to be *haunted with sprites* by the magic and curious arts of the Lady Margaret, who raised up *the ghost of Richard duke of York*, second son to King Edward the Fourth, to walk and vex the king," &c.

Ourself is scarce secure.
Dur. The rage of malice
Conjures fresh spirits with the spells of York.
For ninety years ten English kings and princes,
Threescore great dukes and earls, a thousand lords
And valiant knights, two hundred fifty thousand
Of English subjects have in civil wars
Been sacrific'd to an uncivil thirst
Of discord and ambition: this hot vengeance
Of the just powers above to utter ruin
And desolation had rain'd[2] on, but that
Mercy did gently sheathe the sword of justice,
In lending to this blood-shrunk commonwealth
A new soul, new birth, in your sacred person.
Daw. Edward the Fourth, after a doubtful fortune,
Yielded to nature, leaving to his sons,
Edward and Richard, the inheritance
Of a most bloody purchase: these young princes,
Richard the tyrant, their unnatural uncle,
Forc'd to a violent grave:—so just is Heaven,
Him hath your majesty by your own arm,
Divinely strengthen'd, pull'd from his boar's sty,[3]
And struck the black usurper to a carcass.
Nor doth the house of York decay in honours,
Though Lancaster doth repossess his right;
For Edward's daughter is King Henry's queen,—
A blessèd union, and a lasting blessing
For this poor panting island, if some shreds,
Some useless remnant of the house of York
Grudge not at this content.
Oxf. Margaret of Burgundy

[2] *rain'd*] The 4to has "reign'd;" which Gifford retained. D.

[3] *pull'd from his* boar's sty,] This contemptuous allusion to the armorial bearings of Richard III. is very common in our old writers. Shakespeare has it frequently in his tragedy of this usurper.

Blows fresh coals of division.
Sur. Painted fires,
Without or heat to scorch[4] or light to cherish.
Daw. York's headless trunk, her father; Edward's fate,
Her brother, king; the smothering of her nephews
By tyrant Gloster, brother to her nature;
Nor Gloster's own confusion,—all decrees
Sacred in heaven,—can move this woman-monster,
But that she still, from the unbottom'd mine
Of devilish policies, doth vent the ore
Of troubles and sedition.
Oxf. In her age—
Great sir, observe the wonder[5]—she grows fruitful,
Who in her strength of youth was always barren:
Nor are her births as other mothers' are,
At nine or ten months' end; she has been with child
Eight, or seven years at least; whose twins being born,—
A prodigy in nature,—even the youngest
Is fifteen years of age at his first entrance,
As soon as known i' th' world; tall striplings, strong
And able to give battle unto kings,
Idols of Yorkish malice.
Daw. And but idols;[6]
A steely hammer crushes 'em to pieces.

[4] *or heat to scorch*] The 4to has "to *heate* or *scortch*." D.

[5] Oxford's speech is principally taken from that of Henry's ambassador (Sir W. Warham) to the Archduke; "It is the strangest thing in the world, that the Lady Margaret (excuse us if we name her, whose malice to the king is both causeless and endless) should now, when she is old, at the time when other women give-over child-bearing, bring forth *two such monsters, being not the births of nine or ten months, but of many years. And whereas other natural mothers bring forth children weak and not able to help themselves, she bringeth forth tall striplings, able soon after their coming into the world to bid battle to mighty kings.*"

[6] Daw. *And but idols;* &c.] The 4to, by mistake, gives this short speech also to Oxford. It is much in Dawbeney's manner.

K. Hen. Lambert, the eldest, lords, is in our service,
Preferr'd by an officious care of duty
From the scullery to a falconer; strange example!
Which shows the difference between noble natures
And the base-born: but for the upstart duke,
The new-reviv'd York, Edward's second son,
Murder'd long since i' th' Tower,—he lives again,
And vows to be your king.

Stan. The throne is fill'd, sir.

K. Hen. True, Stanley; and the lawful heir sits on it:
A guard of angels and the holy prayers
Of loyal subjects are a sure defence
Against all force and counsel of intrusion.—
But now, my lords, put case, some of our nobles,
Our great ones, should give countenance and courage
To trim Duke Perkin; you will all confess
Our bounties have unthriftily been scatter'd
Amongst unthankful men.

Daw. Unthankful beasts,
Dogs, villains, traitors!

K. Hen. Dawbeney, let the guilty
Keep silence; I accuse none, though I know
Foreign attempts against a state and kingdom
Are seldom without some great friends at home.

Stan. Sir, if no other abler reasons else
Of duty or allegiance could divert
A headstrong resolution, yet the dangers
So lately pass'd by men of blood and fortunes
In Lambert Simnel's party[7] must command

[7] *Simnel's party*] Simnel's party (for he himself was a mere puppet in the hands of the Earl of Lincoln) was utterly defeated in the battle of Newark. "Bold Martin Swart," one of the most celebrated of those soldiers of fortune who in that age traversed Europe with a band of mercenaries, ready to fight for the first person that

More than a fear, a terror to conspiracy.
The high-born Lincoln, son to De la Pole,
The Earl of Kildare,—[the] Lord Geraldine,—
Francis Lord Lovell, and the German baron
Bold Martin Swart, with Broughton and the rest,—
Most spectacles of ruin, some of mercy,—
Are precedents sufficient to forewarn
The present times, or any that live in them,
What folly, nay, what madness, 'twere to lift
A finger up in all defence but yours,
Which can be but imposturous in a title.

K. Hen. Stanley, we know thou lov'st us, and thy heart
Is figur'd on thy tongue; nor think we less
Of any's here.—How closely we have hunted
This cub, since he unlodg'd, from hole to hole,
Your knowledge is our chronicle: first Ireland,
The common stage of novelty, presented
This gewgaw to oppose us; there the Geraldines
And Butlers once again stood in support
Of this colossic statue: Charles of France
Thence call'd him into his protection,
Dissembled him the lawful heir of England;
Yet this was all[8] but French dissimulation,
Aiming at peace with us; which being granted
On honourable terms on our part, suddenly
This smoke of straw was pack'd from France again,
T' infect some grosser air: and now we learn—

---

would pay them, fell in this action, after "performing bravely," as the noble historian says, "with his Germans." Lambert was taken prisoner. Henry saved his life,—for which Bacon produces many good reasons,—and advanced him first to the dignity of a turnspit in his own kitchen, and subsequently to that of an under-falconer.

[8] *Yet this was all*, &c.] "When he [Perkin] was comen to the court of France, the king received him with great honour.—At the same time there repaired unto Perkin divers Englishmen of quality, Sir George Nevill, Sir John Taylor, and about one hundred more.—

Maugre the malice of the bastard Nevill,
Sir Taylor, and a hundred English rebels—
They're all retir'd to Flanders, to the dam
That nurs'd this eager whelp, Margaret of Burgundy.
But we will hunt him there too; we will hunt him,
Hunt him to death, even in the beldam's closet,
Though th' archduke were his buckler!

Sur. She has styl'd him
"The fair white rose of England."

Daw. Jolly gentleman!
More fit to be a swabber to the Flemish
After a drunken surfeit.

Enter URSWICK *with a paper.*

Urs. Gracious sovereign,
Please you peruse this paper. [*The king reads.*

Dur. The king's countenance
Gathers a sprightly blood.

Daw. Good news; believe it.

K. Hen. Urswick, thine ear.[9] Thou'st lodg'd him?

But *all this, on the French king's part, was but a trick, the better to bow King Henry to peace;* and therefore upon the first grain of incense that was sacrificed upon the altar of peace at Bulloigne, Perkin *was smoked away.*" Sir Taylor is a very unusual mode of designating a knight; but perhaps the king does it in scorn.

[9] *Urswick, thine ear.*] Christopher Urswick was at this time almoner to the king. He had been chaplain to the Countess of Richmond, who afterwards married Thomas Lord Stanley, the elder brother of Sir W. Stanley, the person here implicated, and was trusted by this nobleman with the correspondence between him and Richmond (Henry VII.), and therefore, perhaps, much in his confidence and esteem. His eager importunity to betray the brother of his former patron argues but little for his character; but in those days much consistency is rarely to be found. Weaver, who gives his epitaph,—by which it appears that he possessed and resigned several high stations in the church,—concludes thus; "Here let him rest, as an example for all unjust prelates to admire, and for few or none to imitate." The news which Urswick now communicated was evidently that of his having privately brought the double traitor Clifford, the confidential agent of Warbeck's party, to England.

Lord Bacon says, "none engaged their fortunes in this business openly but two, Sir Robert Clifford and Master William Barley,—

Urs. Strongly safe, sir.
K. Hen. Enough :—is Barley come too?
Urs. No, my lord.
K. Hen. No matter—phew! he's but a running weed,
At pleasure to be pluck'd-up by the roots :
But more of this anon.—I have bethought me.
My lords, for reasons which you shall partake,
It is our pleasure to remove our court
From Westminster to the Tower :[10] we will lodge
This very night there; give, Lord Chamberlain,
A present order for 't.
Stan. [*aside*] The Tower!—I shall, sir.
K. Hen. Come, my true, best, fast friends: these clouds will vanish,
The sun will shine at full; the heavens are clearing.
[*Flourish. Exeunt.*

SCENE II. *Edinburgh. An apartment in* Lord HUNTLEY'S *house.*

Enter HUNTLEY *and* DALYELL.

Hunt. You trifle time, sir.
Dal. O, my noble lord,

---

sent, indeed, from the party of the conspirators here to understand the truth of those things that passed there [i.e. in Flanders], and not without some help of moneys from hence, provisionally to be delivered, if they found and were satisfied that there was truth in these pretences."

Clifford, it appears, was soon won to give-up his employers. Master Barley, for whom Henry next inquires, did not betray his cause quite so speedily, nor trust quite so readily to the king's clemency as Clifford: in the end, however, he also returned to England, and was pardoned.

[10] Lord Bacon well accounts for this sudden resolution of the king; "The place of the Tower was chosen to that end, that if Clifford should accuse any of the great ones, they might without suspicion or noise, or sending abroad of warrants, be presently attached; the court and prison being within the cincture of one wall."

You construe my griefs to so hard a sense,
That where the text is argument of pity,
Matter of earnest love, your gloss corrupts it
With too much ill-plac'd mirth.

Hunt. Much mirth! Lord Dalyell;
Not so, I vow. Observe me, sprightly gallant.
I know thou art a noble lad, a handsome,
Descended from an honourable ancestry,
Forward and active, dost resolve to wrestle
And ruffle in the world by noble actions
For a brave mention to posterity:
I scorn not thy affection to my daughter,
Not I, by good Saint Andrew; but this bugbear,
This whoreson[11] tale of honour,—honour, Dalyell!—
So hourly chats and tattles in mine ear
The piece of royalty that is stitch'd-up
In my Kate's blood, that 'tis as dangerous
For thee, young lord, to perch so near an eaglet
As foolish for my gravity to admit it:
I have spoke all at once.

Dal. Sir, with this truth
You mix such wormwood, that you leave no hope
For my disorder'd palate e'er to relish
A wholesome taste again: alas, I know, sir,
What an unequal distance lies between
Great Huntley's daughter's birth and Dalyell's fortunes;
She's the king's kinswoman, plac'd near the crown,
A princess of the blood, and I a subject.

Hunt. Right; but a noble subject; put in that too.

Dal. I could add more; and in the rightest line
Derive my pedigree from Adam Mure,
A Scottish knight; whose daughter was the mother
To him who first begot the race of Jameses,
That sway the sceptre to this very day.

[11] *whoreson*] The 4to has "whoresome." D.

But kindreds are not ours when once the date
Of many years have swallow'd up the memory
Of their originals; so pasture-fields
Neighbouring too near the ocean are swoop'd-up,
And known no more: for stood I in my first
And native greatness, if my princely mistress
Vouchsaf'd me not her servant, 'twere as good
I were reduc'd to clownery, to nothing,
As to a throne of wonder.

Hunt. [*aside*] Now, by Saint Andrew,
A spark of mettle! he has a brave fire in him:
I would he had my daughter, so I knew 't not.
But ['t] must not be so, must not.—Well, young lord,
This will not do yet: if the girl be headstrong,
And will not hearken to good counsel, steal her,
And run away with her; dance galliards, do,
And frisk about the world to learn the languages:
'Twill be a thriving trade; you may set up by't.

Dal. With pardon, noble Gordon, this disdain
Suits not your daughter's virtue or my constancy.

Hunt. You're angry.—[*Aside*] Would he would beat me, I deserve it.—
Dalyell, thy hand; we're friends: follow thy courtship,
Take thine own time and speak; if thou prevail'st
With passion more than I can with my counsel,
She's thine; nay, she is thine: 'tis a fair match,
Free and allow'd. I'll only use my tongue,
Without a father's power; use thou thine:
Self do, self have: no more words; win and wear her.

Dal. You bless me; I am now too poor in thanks
To pay the debt I owe you.

Hunt. Nay, thou'rt poor
Enough.—[*Aside*] I love his spirit infinitely.—
Look ye, she comes: to her now, to her, to her!

Enter KATHERINE *and* JANE.

Kath. The king commands your presence, sir.
Hunt. The gallant—
This, this, this lord, this servant, Kate, of yours,
Desires to be your master.
Kath. I acknowledge him
A worthy friend of mine.
Dal. Your humblest creature.
Hunt. [*aside*] So, so! the game's a-foot; I'm in cold hunting;
The hare and hounds are parties.
Dal. Princely lady,
How most unworthy I am to employ
My services in honour of your virtues,
How hopeless my desires are to enjoy
Your fair opinion, and much more your love,—
Are only matter of despair, unless
Your goodness give large warrant[12] to my boldness,
My feeble-wing'd ambition.
Hunt. [*aside*] This is scurvy.
Kath. My lord, I interrupt you not.
Hunt. [*aside*] Indeed!
Now, on my life, she'll court him.—Nay, nay, on, sir.
Dal. Oft have I tun'd the lesson of my sorrows
To sweeten discord and enrich your pity;
But all in vain: here had my comforts sunk,
And never risen again to tell a story
Of the despairing lover, had not now,
Even now, the earl your father—
Hunt. [*aside*] He means me, sure.

12 *matter of despair, unless*
Your goodness give large warrant] Gifford printed
"matters *of despair, unless*
Your goodness gives *large* warrants." D.

Dal. After some fit disputes of your condition,
Your highness and my lowness, given a license
Which did not more embolden than encourage
My faulting tongue.
Hunt. How, how? how's that? embolden!
Encourage! I encourage ye! d'ye hear, sir?—
A subtle trick, a quaint one:—will you hear, man?
What did I say to you? come, come, to th' point.
Kath. It shall not need, my lord.
Hunt. Then hear me, Kate.—
Keep you on that hand of her, I on this.—
Thou stand'st between a father and a suitor,
Both striving for an interest in thy heart:
He courts thee for affection, I for duty;
He as a servant pleads, but by the privilege
Of nature though I might command, my care
Shall only counsel what it shall not force.
Thou canst but make one choice; the ties of marriage
Are tenures not at will, but during life.
Consider whose thou art, and who; a princess,
A princess of the royal blood of Scotland,
In the full spring of youth and fresh in beauty.
The king that sits upon the throne is young,
And yet unmarried, forward in attempts
On any least occasion to endanger
His person: wherefore, Kate, as I am confident
Thou dar'st not wrong thy birth and education
By yielding to a common servile rage
Of female wantonness, so I am confident
Thou wilt proportion all thy thoughts to side
Thy equals,[13] if not equal thy superiors.
My Lord of Dalyell, young in years, is old

[13] *to side Thy equals,*] "*Side*" in Ford is used in the familiar and proper sense, to keep pace with, to be equally forward.

In honours, but nor eminent in titles
[N]or in estate, that may support or add to
The expectation of thy fortunes. Settle
Thy will and reason by a strength of judgment;
For, in a word, I give thee freedom; take it.
If equal fates have not ordain'd to pitch
Thy hopes above my height, let not thy passion
Lead thee to shrink mine honour[14] in oblivion:
Thou art thine own; I have done.[15]

Dal. O, you're all oracle,
The living stock and root of truth and wisdom!

Kath. My worthiest lord and father, the indulgence
Of your sweet composition thus commands
The lowest of obedience; you have granted
A liberty so large, that I want skill
To choose without direction of example:
From which I daily learn, by how much more
You take off from the roughness of a father,
By so much more I am engag'd to tender
The duty of a daughter. For respects
Of birth, degrees of title, and advancement,

[14] *Lead thee to* shrink *mine honour*, &c.] This is the reading of the 4to, and makes very good sense; but from the general tenor of the sentence I am inclined to believe that the poet's word was "*sink.*"

[15] *I have done.*] And done well too! The person here meant is George, the eldest son of Alexander Seton, and second Earl of Huntley. He married Anabella, daughter of James I.: hence it is that he talks in his opening speech of "the piece of royalty that is stitched-up in his Kate's blood." What authority the poet had for the histrionic character of this nobleman I know not; but if the princely family of the Gordons ever numbered such a personage as this among their ancestors, let them be justly proud of him; for neither on the stage nor in the great drama of life will there be easily found a character to put in competition with him.

Daliell (for so Ford writes it) is also a noble fellow. There are two persons of that name, William and Robert Dalzell, grandsons of Sir John Dalzell, either of whom, from the date, might be meant for the character here introduced. Of the former nothing is recorded: the latter, Douglas says, "was killed at Dumfries in a skirmish between Maxwell and Crichton, July 1508."

I nor admire nor slight them; all my studies
Shall ever aim at this perfection only,
To live and die so, that you may not blush
In any course of mine to own me yours.

Hunt. Kate, Kate, thou grow'st upon my heart like peace,
Creating every other hour a jubilee.

Kath. To you, my Lord of Dalyell, I address
Some few remaining words: the general fame
That speaks your merit, even in vulgar tongues
Proclaims it clear; but in the best, a precedent.

Hunt. Good wench, good girl, i' faith!

Kath. For my part, trust me,
I value mine own worth at higher rate
'Cause you are pleas'd to prize it: if the stream
Of your protested service—as you term it—
Run in a constancy more than a compliment,
It shall be my delight that worthy love
Leads you to worthy actions, and these guide ye
Richly to wed an honourable name:
So every virtuous praise in after-ages
Shall be your heir, and I in your brave mention
Be chronicled the mother of that issue,
That glorious issue.

Hunt. O, that I were young again!
She'd make me court proud danger, and suck spirit
From reputation.

Kath. To the present motion
Here's all that I dare answer: when a ripeness
Of more experience, and some use of time,
Resolves to treat the freedom of my youth
Upon exchange of troths, I shall desire
No surer credit of a match with virtue
Than such as lives in you; mean time my hopes are
Preser[v]'d secure in having you a friend.

Dal. You are a blessèd lady, and instruct
Ambition not to soar a farther flight
Than in the perfum'd air of your soft voice.—
My noble Lord of Huntley, you have lent
A full extent of bounty to this parley;
And for it shall command your humblest servant.

Hunt. Enough: we are still friends, and will continue
A hearty love.—O, Kate, thou art mine own!—
No more:—my Lord of Crawford.

Enter CRAWFORD.[16]

Craw. From the king
I come, my Lord of Huntley, who in council
Requires your present aid.

Hunt. Some weighty business?

Craw. A secretary from a Duke of York,
The second son to the late English Edward,
Conceal'd, I know not where, these fourteen years,
Craves audience from our master; and 'tis said
The duke himself is following to the court.

Hunt. Duke upon duke! 'tis well, 'tis well; here's bustling
For majesty.—My lord, I will along with ye.

Craw. My service, noble lady!

Kath. Please ye walk, sir?

Dal. [*aside*] Times have their changes;[17] sorrow makes men wise;

[16] *Enter* Crawford.] This is probably (for I speak with great hesitation on the subject) John, second son of David, fourth Earl Crawford. If I am right in this conjecture, he stood in some kind of relationship to Huntley; his elder brother Alexander (dead at this period) having married Lady Jane Gordon, the earl's second daughter.

[17] *Times have their changes*, &c.] In the 4to this couplet is marked with inverted commas, as if it were a quotation; and so Gifford. But in early books the gnomic portions are frequently so distinguished: see my *Remarks on Mr. Collier's and Mr. Knight's eds. of Shakespeare*, p. 207. D.

The sun itself must set as well as rise;
Then, why not I?—Fair madam, I wait on ye.
[*Exeunt.*

SCENE III. *London. An apartment in the Tower.*

Enter the Bishop of Durham, Sir ROBERT CLIFFORD, *and* URSWICK. *Lights.*

Dur. You find, Sir Robert Clifford, how securely
King Henry, our great master, doth commit
His person to your loyalty; you taste
His bounty and his mercy even in this,
That at a time of night so late, a place
So private as his closet, he is pleas'd
T' admit you to his favour. Do not falter
In your discovery; but as you covet
A liberal grace, and pardon for your follies,
So labour to deserve 't by laying open
All plots, all persons that contrive against it.

Urs. Remember not the witchcraft or the magic,
The charms and incantations, which the sorceress
Of Burgundy hath cast upon your reason:
Sir Robert, be your own friend now, discharge
Your conscience freely; all of such as love you
Stand sureties for your honesty and truth.
Take heed you do not dally with the king;
He's wise as he is gentle.

Clif. I am miserable,
If Henry be not merciful.

Urs. The king comes.

Enter King HENRY.

K. Hen. Clifford!

Clif. [*kneels*] Let my weak knees root[18] on the earth,

[18] *root*] The 4to has "rot;" and so Gifford. D.

If I appear as leperous in my treacheries
Before your royal eyes, as to mine[19] own
I seem a monster by my breach of truth.

K. Hen. Clifford, stand up; for instance of thy safety,
I offer thee my hand.

Clif. A sovereign balm
For my bruis'd soul, I kiss it with a greediness.
[*Kisses the King's hand, and rises.*
Sir, you're a just master, but I—

K. Hen. Tell me,
Is every circumstance thou hast set down
With thine own hand within this paper true?
Is it a sure intelligence of all
The progress of our enemies' intents
Without corruption?

Clif. True, as I wish heaven,
Or my infected honour white again.

K. Hen. We know all, Clifford, fully, since this meteor,
This airy apparition first discradled
From Tournay into Portugal, and thence
Advanc'd his fiery blaze for adoration
To th' superstitious Irish; since the beard
Of this wild comet, conjur'd into France,
Sparkled in antic flames in Charles his court;
But shrunk again from thence, and, hid in darkness,
Stole into Flanders * * * * *
* * * * * flourishing the rags[20]

[19] *mine*] Gifford printed "my." D.

[20] *Stole into Flanders, flourishing the rags,* &c.] Something is apparently lost here, perhaps the end of this line and the beginning of the next, as I have marked them in the text. The import is clear enough;

"there embark'd his followers,
And made for England, flourishing the rags," &c.

In this expedition Perkin did not land; and those of his followers

Of painted power on the shore of Kent,
Whence he was beaten back with shame and scorn,
Contempt, and slaughter of some naked outlaws:
But tell me what new course now shapes Duke Perkin?

Clif. For Ireland, mighty Henry; so instructed
By Stephen Frion,[21] sometimes[22] secretary
In the French tongue unto your sacred excellence,
But Perkin's tutor now.

K. Hen. A subtle villain,
That Frion, Frion,—You, my Lord of Durham,
Knew well the man.

Dur. French both in heart and actions.

K. Hen. Some Irish heads work in this mine of treason;
Speak 'em.

Clif. Not any of the best; your fortune
Hath dull'd their spleens. Never had counterfeit
Such a confusèd rabble of lost bankrupts
For counsellors: first Heron, a broken mercer,
Then John a-Water, sometimes[22] Mayor of Cork,
Skelton a tailor, and a scrivener
Call'd Astley: and whate'er these list to treat of,
Perkin must harken to; but Frion, cunning
Above these dull capacities, still prompts him
To fly to Scotland to young James the Fourth,

---

whom he sent on shore at Sandwich were defeated by the Kentish men. The prisoners, to the amount of 150 (mostly foreigners), were executed; "hanged," as Lord Bacon says, "some of them at London and Wapping, and the rest at divers places upon the seacoast of Kent, Sussex, and Norfolk, for sea-marks or lighthouses to teach Perkin's people to avoid the coast."

[21] *Stephen Frion,*] Frion had been seduced from Henry's service by the Duchess of Burgundy, and was a very active agent in the great drama which she was now preparing to bring forward. "He followed his [Perkin's] fortune both then and for a long time after," Bacon says, "and was indeed his principal counsellor and instrument in all his proceedings."

[22] *sometimes*] See note, vol. i. p. 206. D.

And sue for aid to him: this is the latest
Of all their resolutions.

K. Hen. Still more Frion!
Pestilent adder, he will hiss-out poison
As dangerous as infectious: we must match him.[23]
Clifford, thou hast spoke home; we give thee life:
But, Clifford, there are people of our own
Remain behind untold; who are they, Clifford?
Name those, and we are friends, and will to rest;
'Tis thy last task.

Clif. O, sir, here I must break
A most unlawful oath to keep a just one.

K. Hen. Well, well, be brief, be brief.

Clif. The first in rank
Shall be John Ratcliffe, Lord Fitzwater, then
Sir Simon Mountford and Sir Thomas Thwaites,
With William Dawbeney, Chessoner, Astwood,
Worseley the Dean of Paul's, two other friars,
And Robert Ratcliffe.[24]

K. Hen. Churchmen are turn'd devils.
These are the principal?

Clif. One more remains
Unnam'd, whom I could willingly forget.

K. Hen. Ha, Clifford! one more?

Clif. Great sir, do not hear him;
For when Sir William Stanley, your lord chamberlain,
Shall come into the list, as he is chief,
I shall lose credit with ye; yet this lord
Last nam'd is first against you.

K. Hen. Urswick, the light!—
View well my face, sirs; is there blood left in it?

Dur. You alter strangely, sir.

[23] *him.*] The 4to has "'em;" and so Gifford. See note, p. 143. D.

[24] All these were seized, tried, and condemned for high-treason: most of them perished upon the scaffold. Worseley and the two Dominicans were spared.

K. Hen. Alter, lord bishop!
Why, Clifford stabb'd me, or I dream'd he stabb'd me.—
Sirrah, it is a custom with the guilty
To think they set their own stains off by laying
Aspersions on some nobler than themselves;
Lies wait on treasons, as I find it here.
Thy life again is forfeit; I recall
My word of mercy, for I know thou dar'st
Repeat the name no more.

Clif. I dare, and once more,
Upon my knowledge, name Sir William Stanley
Both in his counsel and his purse the chief
Assistant to the feignèd Duke of York.

Dur. Most strange!

Urs. Most wicked!

K. Hen. Yet again, once more.

Clif. Sir William Stanley is your secret enemy,
And, if time fit, will openly profess it.

K. Hen. Sir William Stanley! Who? Sir William Stanley!
My chamberlain, my counsellor, the love,
The pleasure of my court, my bosom-friend,
The charge and the controlment of my person,
The keys and secrets of my treasury,
The all of all I am! I am unhappy.
Misery of confidence,—let me turn traitor
To mine[25] own person, yield my sceptre up
To Edward's sister and her bastard duke!

Dur. You lose your constant temper.

K. Hen. Sir William Stanley!
O, do not blame me; he, 'twas only he,
Who, having rescu'd me in Bosworth-field
From Richard's bloody sword, snatch'd from his head

[25] *mine*] Gifford printed "my." D.

The kingly crown, and plac'd it first on mine.[26]
He never fail'd me: what have I deserv'd
To lose this good man's heart, or he his own?

Urs. The night doth waste; this passion ill becomes ye;
Provide against your danger.

K. Hen. Let it be so.
Urswick, command straight Stanley to his chamber;—
'Tis well we are i' th' Tower;—set a guard on him.—
Clifford, to bed; you must lodge here to-night;
We'll talk with you to-morrow.—My sad soul
Divines strange troubles.

Daw. [*within*] Ho! the king, the king!
I must have entrance.

K. Hen. Dawbeney's voice; admit him.
What new combustions huddle next, to keep
Our eyes from rest?

Enter DAWBENEY.

The news?

Daw. Ten thousand Cornish,
Grudging to pay your subsidies, have gather'd
A head; led by a blacksmith and a lawyer,
They make for London, and to them is join'd
Lord Audley: as they march, their number daily
Increases; they are—

K. Hen. Rascals!—talk no more;
Such are not worthy of my thoughts to-night.

[26] Shakespeare thus notices the circumstance;

"*Enter* STANLEY *bearing the crown.*

Stanley. Courageous Richmond, well hast thou acquit thee!
Lo, here, this long-usurpèd royalty
From the dead temples of this bloody wretch
Have I pluck'd off, to grace thy brows withal:
Wear it, enjoy it, and make much of it." *Richard III.*

To bed; and if I cannot sleep, I'll wake.[27]—
When counsels fail, and there's in man no trust,
Even then an arm from heaven fights for the just.
[*Exeunt.*

ACT II.

SCENE I. *Edinburgh. The presence-chamber in the palace.*

Enter above the Countess of Crawford, Lady KATHERINE, JANE, *and other Ladies.*

Countess of C. Come, ladies, here's a solemn preparation
For entertainment of this English prince;
The king intends grace more than ordinary:
'Twere pity now if he should prove a counterfeit.
Kath. Bless the young man, our nation would be laugh'd at
For honest souls through Christendom! My father
Hath a weak stomach to the business, madam,
But that the king must not be cross'd.
Countess of C. He brings
A goodly troop, they say, of gallants with him;
But very modest people, for they strive not
To fame their names too much; their godfathers
May be beholding to them, but their fathers
Scarce owe them thanks: they are disguisèd princes,[1]

[27] *To bed; and if I cannot sleep, I'll wake.*] The 4to has "And if I cannot sleepe, Ile wake:—to bed." D.

[1] *they are disguisèd princes,* &c.] The Countess is pleased to be facetious. It appears, however, from better authorities than those before us, that Perkin was very respectably, not to say honourably, attended on this occasion.

Brought up, it seems, to honest trades; no matter,
They will break forth in season.
Jane. Or break out;
For most of 'em are broken by report.— [*A flourish.*
The king!
Kath. Let us observe 'em and be silent.

Enter King JAMES, HUNTLEY, CRAWFORD, DALYELL, *and other Noblemen.*

K. Ja. The right of kings, my lords, extends not only
To the safe conservation of their own,
But also to the aid of such allies
As change of time and state hath oftentimes
Hurl'd down from careful crowns to undergo
An exercise of sufferance in both fortunes:
So English Richard, surnam'd Cœur-de-Lion,
So Robert Bruce, our royal ancestor,
Forc'd by the trial of the wrongs they felt,
Both sought and found supplies from foreign kings,
To repossess their own. Then grudge not, lords,
A much-distressèd prince: King Charles of France
And Maximilian of Bohemia both
Have ratified his credit by their letters;
Shall we, then, be distrustful? No; compassion
Is one rich jewel that shines in our crown,
And we will have it shine there.
Hunt. Do your will, sir.
K. Ja. The young duke is at hand: Dalyell, from us
First greet him, and conduct him on; then Crawford
Shall meet him next; and Huntley, last of all,
Present him to our arms. [*Exit Dal.*]—Sound sprightly music,
Whilst majesty encounters majesty. [*Hautboys.*

Re-enter DALYELL *with* PERKIN WARBECK, *followed at a distance by* FRION, HERON, SKELTON, ASTLEY, *and* JOHN A-WATER. CRAWFORD *advances, and salutes* PERKIN *at the door, and afterwards* HUNTLEY, *who presents him to the King: they embrace; the Noblemen slightly salute his Followers.*

War. Most high, most mighty king![2] that now
there stands
Before your eyes, in presence of your peers,
A subject of the rarest kind of pity
That hath in any age touch'd noble hearts,
The vulgar story of a prince's ruin
Hath made it too apparent: Europe knows,
And all the western world, what persecution
Hath rag'd in malice against us, sole heir
To the great throne of old[3] Plantagenets.
How from our nursery we have been hurried
Unto the sanctuary, from the sanctuary
Forc'd to the prison, from the prison hal'd
By cruel hands to the tormentor's fury,
Is register'd already in the volume
Of all men's tongues; whose true relation draws
Compassion, melted into weeping eyes
And bleeding souls: but our misfortunes since

[2] War. *Most high, most mighty king!* &c.] This speech is skilfully abridged from the historian. When it could be done with proper effect, the words are taken with no greater change than was necessary for the metrical arrangement; in other places the poet is content with clothing the sentiments in his own language, but always with the original in view. The speech before us opens thus in Bacon; "*High and mighty king!* your grace, and these your nobles here present, may be pleased benignly to bow your ears to hear the tragedy of a young man . . . . tossed from misery to misery. . . . . You see here before you the spectacle of a Plantagenet, *who hath been carried from the nursery to the sanctuary, from the sanctuary to the direful prison, from the prison to the hand of the cruel tormentor,*" &c.

[3] *old*] Gifford printed "th' *old*." D.

Have rang'd a larger progress through strange lands,
Protected in our innocence by heaven.
Edward the Fifth, our brother, in his tragedy
Quench'd their hot thirst of blood, whose hire to murder
Paid them their wages of despair and horror;
The softness of my childhood smil'd upon
The roughness of their task, and robb'd them farther
Of hearts to dare, or hands to execute.
Great king, they spar'd my life, the butchers spar'd it;
Return'd the tyrant, my unnatural uncle,
A truth of my dispatch: I was convey'd
With secrecy and speed to Tournay; foster'd
By obscure means, taught to unlearn myself:
But as I grew in years, I grew in sense
Of fear and of disdain; fear of the tyrant
Whose power sway'd the throne then: when disdain
Of living so unknown, in such a servile
And abject lowness, prompted me to thoughts
Of recollecting who I was, I shook off
My bondage, and made haste to let my aunt
Of Burgundy acknowledge me her kinsman,
Heir to the crown of England, snatch'd by Henry
From Richard's head; a thing scarce known i' th'
world.

K. Ja. My lord, it stands not with your counsel
now
To fly upon invectives: if you can
Make this apparent what you have discours'd
In every circumstance, we will not study
An answer, but are ready in your cause.

War. You are a wise and just king, by the powers
Above reserv'd, beyond all other aids,
To plant me in mine own inheritance,
To marry these two kingdoms in a love
Never to be divorc'd while time is time.

As for the manner, first of my escape,
Of my conveyance next, of my life since,
The means and persons who were instruments,
Great sir, 'tis fit I over-pass in silence;
Reserving the relation to the secrecy
Of your own princely ear, since it concerns
Some great ones living yet, and others dead,
Whose issue might be question'd. For your bounty,
Royal magnificence to him that seeks it,
We vow hereafter to demean ourself
As if we were your own and natural brother,
Omitting no occasion in our person
T' express a gratitude beyond example.

K. Ja. He must be more than subject who can utter
The language of a king, and such is thine.
Take this for answer: be whate'er thou art,
Thou never shalt repent that thou hast put
Thy cause and person into my protection.
Cousin of York, thus once more we embrace thee;
Welcome to James of Scotland! for thy safety,
Know, such as love thee not shall never wrong thee.
Come, we will taste a while our court-delights,
Dream hence afflictions past, and then proceed
To high attempts of honour. On, lead on!—
Both thou and thine are ours, and we will guard ye.—
Lead on! [*Exeunt all but the Ladies above.*

Countess of C. I have not seen a gentleman
Of a more brave aspéct or goodlier carriage;
His fortunes move not him.—Madam, you're passionate.[4]

Kath. Beshrew me, but his words have touch'd me home,

[4] *Madam, you're* passionate.] i.e. *distressed, deeply affected:* the Countess had observed Katherine weeping.

As if his cause concern'd me: I should pity him,
If he should prove another than he seems.

Re-enter CRAWFORD.

Craw. Ladies, the king commands your presence instantly
For entertainment of the duke.
Kath. The duke
Must, then, be entertain'd, the king obey'd;
It is our duty.
Countess of C. We will all wait on him.
[*Exeunt the Ladies above. Exit Crawford.*

SCENE II. *London. The Tower.*

A flourish. Enter King HENRY, Oxford, Durham, Surrey.

K. Hen. Have ye condemn'd my chamberlain?
Dur. His treasons
Condemn'd him, sir; which were as clear and manifest
As foul and dangerous: besides, the guilt
Of his conspiracy press'd him so nearly,
That it drew from him free confession
Without an importunity.
K. Hen. O, lord bishop,
This argu'd shame and sorrow for his folly,
And must not stand in evidence against
Our mercy and the softness of our nature:
The rigour and extremity of law
Is sometimes too-too bitter; but we carry
A chancery of pity in our bosom.
I hope we may reprieve him from the sentence
Of death; I hope we may.
Dur. You may, you may;

And so persuade your subjects that the title
Of York is better, nay, more just and lawful,
Than yours of Lancaster! so Stanley holds:
Which if it be not treason in the highest,
Then we are traitors all, perjur'd and false,
Who have took oath to Henry and the justice
Of Henry's title; Oxford, Surrey, Dawbeney,
With all your other peers of state and church,
Forsworn, and Stanley true alone to heaven
And England's lawful heir!

Oxf. By Vere's old honours,
I'll cut his throat dares speak it.

Sur. 'Tis a quarrel
T' engage a soul in.

K. Hen. What a coil is here
To keep my gratitude sincere and perfect!
Stanley was once my friend,[5] and came in time
To save my life; yet, to say truth, my lords,
The man stay'd long enough t' endanger it:—
But I could see no more into his heart
Than what his outward actions did present;
And for 'em have rewarded him[6] so fully,
As that there wanted nothing in our gift
To gratify his merit, as I thought,
Unless I should divide my crown with him,
And give him half; though now I well perceive
'Twould scarce have serv'd his turn without the whole.

[5] *Stanley was once my friend,* &c.] Much of this is from the noble historian. The king certainly holds a very different language from that which we had in a former page; but it is characteristic of his close, cold, and selfish nature. "As a little leaven," Bacon says, "of new distaste doth commonly sour the whole lump of former merits, the king's wit began now to suggest unto his passion that Stanley at Bosworth-field, *though he came time enough to save his life, yet he stayed long enough to endanger it.*" After all, the writer hints, as broadly as he dared, that Stanley's main guilt lay in his vast accumulations, which Henry viewed with too greedy an eye.

[6] *him*] The 4to has "'em." D.

But I am charitable, lords; let justice
Proceed in execution, whiles I mourn
The loss of one whom I esteem'd a friend.

Dur. Sir, he is coming this way.

K. Hen. If he speak to me,
I could deny him nothing; to prevent it,
I must withdraw. Pray, lords, commend my favours
To his last peace, which I with him[7] will pray for:
That done, it doth concern us to consult
Of other following troubles. [*Exit.*

Oxf. I am glad
He's gone: upon my life, he would have pardon'd
The traitor, had he seen him.

Sur. 'Tis a king
Compos'd of gentleness.

Dur. Rare and unheard of:
But every man is nearest to himself;
And that the king observes; 'tis fit he should.

Enter STANLEY, Executioner, Confessor, URSWICK, *and* DAWBENEY.

Stan. May I not speak with Clifford ere I shake
This piece of frailty off?

Daw. You shall; he's sent for.

Stan. I must not see the king?

Dur. From him, Sir William,
These lords and I am sent; he bade us say
That he commends his mercy to your thoughts;
Wishing the laws of England could remit
The forfeit of your life as willingly
As he would in the sweetness of his nature
Forget your trespass: but howe'er your body
Fall into dust, he vows, the king himself

[7] *I with him*] Gifford printed "with him, I." D.

Doth vow, to keep a requiem for your soul,
As for a friend close treasur'd in his bosom.

Oxf. Without remembrance of your errors past,
I come to take my leave, and wish you heaven.

Sur. And I; good angels guard ye!

Stan. O, the king,
Next to my soul, shall be the nearest subject
Of my last prayers. My grave Lord of Durham,
My Lords of Oxford, Surrey, Dawbeney, all,
Accept from a poor dying man a farewell.
I was as you are once,—great, and stood hopeful
Of many flourishing years; but fate and time
Have wheel'd about, to turn me into nothing.

Daw. Sir Robert Clifford comes,—the man, Sir William,
You so desire to speak with.

Dur. Mark their meeting.

Enter CLIFFORD.

Clif. Sir William Stanley, I am glad your conscience
Before your end hath emptied every burthen
Which charg'd it, as that you can clearly witness
How far I have proceeded in a duty
That both concern'd my truth and the state's safety.

Stan. Mercy, how dear is life to such as hug it!
Come hither; by this token think on me!

[*Makes a cross on Clifford's face with his finger.*

Clif. This token! What! I am[8] abus'd?

Stan. You are not.
I wet upon your cheeks a holy sign,—
The cross, the Christian's badge, the traitor's infamy:
Wear, Clifford, to thy grave this painted emblem;
Water shall never wash it off; all eyes

[8] *I am*] Gifford unnecessarily printed "am I." D.

That gaze upon thy face shall read there written
A state-informer's character; more ugly
Stamp'd on a noble name than on a base.
The heavens forgive thee!—Pray, my lords, no change
Of words; this man and I have us'd too many.

Clif. Shall I be disgrac'd
Without reply?

Dur. Give losers leave to talk;
His loss is irrecoverable.

Stan. Once more,
To all a long farewell! The best of greatness
Preserve the king! My next suit is, my lords,
To be remember'd to my noble brother,
Derby, my much-griev'd brother:[9] O, persuade him
That I shall stand no blemish to his house
In chronicles writ in another age.
My heart doth bleed for him and for his sighs:
Tell him, he must not think the style of Derby,
Nor being husband to King Henry's mother,
The league with peers, the smiles of fortune, can
Secure his peace above the state of man.
I take my leave, to travel to my dust:
Subjects deserve their deaths whose kings are just.—
Come, confessor.—On with thy axe, friend, on!
[*He is led off to execution.*

Clif. Was I call'd hither by a traitor's breath
To be upbraided? Lords, the king shall know it.

Re-enter King HENRY *with a white staff.*

K. Hen. The king doth know it, sir; the king hath heard

[9] *Derby, my much-griev'd brother:*] See note p. 122. Lord Stanley had been raised to the dignity of an earl in October 1485, a few weeks after the battle of Bosworth.

What he or you could say. We have given credit
To every point of Clifford's information,
The only evidence 'gainst Stanley's head:
He dies for't; are you pleas'd?

Clif. I pleas'd, my lord!

K. Hen. No echos: for your service, we dismiss
Your more attendance on the court; take ease,
And live at home; but, as you love your life,
Stir not from London without leave from us.
We'll think on your reward: away!

Clif. I go, sir. [*Exit.*

K. Hen. Die all our griefs with Stanley! Take this staff
Of office, Dawbeney;[10] henceforth be our chamberlain.

Daw. I am your humblest servant.

K. Hen. We are follow'd
By enemies at home, that will not cease
To seek their own confusion: 'tis most true
The Cornish under Audley are march'd on
As far as Winchester;—but let them come,
Our forces are in readiness; we'll catch 'em
In their own toils.

Daw. Your army, being muster'd,
Consists in all, of horse and foot, at least
In number six-and-twenty thousand; men
Daring and able, resolute to fight,
And loyal in their truths.

K. Hen. We know it, Dawbeney:
For them we order thus; Oxford in chief,
Assisted by bold Essex and the Earl
Of Suffolk, shall lead on the first battalia;

[10] *Dawbeney;*] This person (Giles Lord Dawbeney) was "a man," Bacon says, "of great sufficiency and valour, the more because he was gentle and moderate." Yet he always appears on the side of violent counsels, and more forward with his flattery than any of the courtiers in the King's confidence.

Be that your charge.

Oxf. I humbly thank your majesty.

K. Hen. The next division we assign to Dawbeney:
These must be men of action, for on those
The fortune of our fortunes must rely.
The last and main ourself commands in person;
As ready to restore the fight at all times
As to consummate an assurèd victory.

Daw. The king is still oraculous.

K. Hen. But, Surrey,
We have employment of more toil for thee:
For our intelligence comes swiftly to us,
That James of Scotland late hath entertain'd
Perkin the counterfeit with more than common
Grace and respect, nay, courts him with rare favours.
The Scot is young and forward; we must look for
A sudden storm to England from the north;
Which to withstand, Durham shall post to Norham,
To fortify the castle and secure
The frontiers against an invasion there.
Surrey shall follow soon, with such an army
As may relieve the bishop, and encounter
On all occasions the death-daring Scots.
You know your charges all; 'tis now a time
To execute, not talk: Heaven is our guard still.
War must breed peace; such is the fate of kings.
[*Exeunt.*

SCENE III. *Edinburgh. An apartment in the palace.*

Enter CRAWFORD *and* DALYELL.

Craw. 'Tis more than strange; my reason cannot answer
Such argument of fine imposture, couch'd

In witchcraft of persuasion, that it fashions
Impossibilities, as if appearance
Could cozen truth itself: this dukeling mushroom
Hath doubtless charm'd the king.

Dal. He courts the ladies,
As if his strength of language chain'd attention
By power of prerogative.

Craw. It madded
My very soul to hear our master's motion:
What surety both of amity and honour
Must of necessity ensue upon
A match betwixt some noble of our nation
And this brave prince, forsooth!

Dal. 'Twill prove too fatal;
Wise Huntley fears the threatening. Bless the lady
From such a ruin!

Craw. How the counsel privy
Of this young Phaëthon do screw their faces
Into a gravity their trades, good people,
Were never guilty of! the meanest of 'em
Dreams of at least an office in the state.

Dal. Sure, not the hangman's; 'tis bespoke already
For service to their rogueships—Silence!

Enter King JAMES *and* HUNTLEY.

K. Ja. Do not
Argue against our will; we have descended
Somewhat—as we may term it—too familiarly
From justice of our birthright, to examine
The force of your allegiance,—sir, we have,—
But find it short of duty.

Hunt. Break my heart,
Do, do, king! Have my services, my loyalty,—
Heaven knows untainted ever,—drawn upon me
Contempt now in mine age, when I but wanted

A minute of a peace not to be troubled,[11]
My last, my long one? Let me be a dotard,
A bedlam, a poor sot, or what you please
To have me, so you will not stain your blood,
Your own blood, royal sir, though mix'd with mine,
By marriage of this girl[12] to a straggler:
Take, take my head, sir; whilst my tongue can wag,
It cannot name him other.

K. Ja. Kings are counterfeits
In your repute, grave oracle, not presently
Set on their thrones with sceptres in their fists.
But use your own detraction; 'tis our pleasure
To give our cousin York for wife our kinswoman,
The Lady Katherine: instinct of sovereignty
Designs the honour, though her peevish father
Usurps our resolution.

Hunt. O, 'tis well,
Exceeding well! I never was ambitious
Of using congees to my daughter-queen—
A queen! perhaps a quean![13]—Forgive me, Dalyell,

[11] *when I but wanted*
A minute of a peace not to be troubled,] i.e. when I am on the verge of the grave, and should spend the short remainder of my life in tranquillity.

[12] *By marriage of this* girl] See vol. i. p. 18.—The circumstance is thus briefly noticed by Lord Bacon; "To put it out of doubt that he took him [Perkin] to be a great prince, and not a representation only, he [King James] gave consent that this duke should take to wife the Lady Katherine Gordon, daughter to the Earl of Huntley, being a near kinswoman to the king himself, and a young virgin of excellent beauty and virtue."

[13] *A queen! perhaps a* quean!] I cannot reconcile myself to this reading, though I have adopted it. The noble Huntley would scarcely use such language of his daughter, however lightly he might be disposed to treat the young pretender to royalty. The passage stands thus in the old copy;

"I never was ambitious
Of using congeys to my *Daughter Queene:*
A *Queene*, perhaps a *Queene?*"

If the last line be read

"A *queen*, perhaps! a *queen!*"

it may seem to express his affected surprise at her advancement. But let the reader decide. [The reading in the text is, I think, right. D.]

Thou honourable gentleman;—none here
Dare speak one word of comfort?

Dal. Cruel misery!

Craw. The lady, gracious prince, may be hath settled
Affection on some former choice.

Dal. Enforcement
Would prove but tyranny.

Hunt. I thank ye heartily.
Let any yeoman of our nation challenge
An interest in the girl, then the king
May add a jointure of ascent in titles,
Worthy a free consent; now he pulls down
What old desert hath builded.

K. Ja. Cease persuasions.
I violate no pawns of faiths, intrude not
On private loves: that I have play'd the orator
For kingly York to virtuous Kate, her grant
Can justify, referring her contents
To our provision. The Welsh Harry henceforth
Shall therefore know, and tremble to acknowledge,
That not the painted idol of his policy
Shall fright the lawful owner from a kingdom.
We are resolv'd.

Hunt. Some of thy subjects' hearts,
King James, will bleed for this.

K. Ja. Then shall their bloods
Be nobly spent. No more disputes; he is not
Our friend who contradicts us.

Hunt. Farewell, daughter!
My care by one is lessen'd, thank the king for't:
I and my griefs will dance now.

Enter WARBECK, *leading, and complimenting with*, Lady KATHERINE; Countess of CRAWFORD, JANE DOU-

GLAS, FRION, JOHN A-WATER, ASTLEY, HERON, *and* SKELTON.

Look, lords, look;
Here's hand in hand already!
K. Ja. Peace, old frenzy!—
How like a king he looks! Lords, but observe
The confidence of his aspect; dross cannot
Cleave to so pure a metal—royal youth!
Plantagenet undoubted!
Hunt. [*aside*] Ho, brave!—Youth,[14]
But no Plantagenet, by'r lady, yet,
By red rose or by white.
War. An union this way
Settles possession in a monarchy
Establish'd rightly, as is my inheritance:
Acknowledge me but sovereign of this kingdom,
Your heart, fair princess, and the hand of providence
Shall crown you queen of me and my best fortunes.
Kath. Where my obedience is, my lord, a duty
Love owes true service.
War. Shall I?—
K. Ja. Cousin, yes,
Enjoy her; from my hand accept your bride;
[*He joins their hands.*
And may they live at enmity with comfort
Who grieve at such an equal pledge of troths!—
You are the prince's wife now.
Kath. By your gift, sir.
War. Thus I take seizure of mine own.
Kath. I miss yet
A father's blessing. Let me find it;—humbly
Upon my knees I seek it.

[14] *Ho, brave!*—Youth,] The old copy has "*lady.*" The Earl evidently meant to repeat the King's last words: the mistake probably arose from the printer's eye having been caught by the word immediately below it.

Hunt. I am Huntley,
Old Alexander Gordon,[15] a plain subject,
Nor more nor less; and, lady, if you wish for
A blessing, you must bend your knees to heaven;
For heaven did give me you. Alas, alas,
What would you have me say? May all the happiness
My prayers ever su'd to fall upon you
Preserve you in your virtues!—Prithee, Dalyell,
Come with me; for I feel thy griefs as full
As mine; let's steal away, and cry together.

Dal. My hopes are in their ruins.

[*Exeunt Hunt. and Dal.*

K. Ja. Good, kind Huntley
Is overjoy'd: a fit solemnity
Shall perfect these delights.—Crawford, attend
Our order for the preparation.

[*Exeunt all but Frion, Her. Skelt. J. a-Wat. and Ast.*

Fri. Now, worthy gentlemen, have I not follow'd
My undertakings with success? Here's entrance
Into a certainty above a hope.

Her. Hopes are but hopes; I was ever confident, when I traded but in remnants, that my stars had reserved me to the title of a viscount at least: honour is honour, though cut out of any stuffs.[16]

Skelt. My brother Heron hath right wisely delivered

[15] Hunt. *I am Huntley,*
Old Alexander *Gordon,*] This appears to be a mistake. The father of Katherine, as is said above, was *George* Gordon. His father, indeed, was named *Alexander*, and so was his son and successor; but the latter did not obtain the title till many years after this period. [Here in the 4to "*Gordon*" is "Guerdon." D.]

[16] *honour is honour, though cut out of any stuffs.*] Ford has made the speakers express themselves characteristically. Heron, or Herne, as Lord Bacon calls him, was a mercer; Sketon, or rather Skelton, was a tailor; and Astley a scrivener: they were all men of broken fortunes; a circumstance to which the poet frequently alludes. [The 4to has "Sketon" passim; and so Gifford: but see Lord Bacon and Hall. D.]

his opinion; for he that threads his needle with the sharp eyes of industry shall in time go through-stitch[17] with the new suit of preferment.

Ast. Spoken to the purpose, my fine-witted brother Skelton; for as no indenture but has its counterpane, no *noverint* but his condition or defeasance; so no right but may have claim, no claim but may have possession, any act of parliament to the contrary notwithstanding.

Fri. You are all read in mysteries of state,
And quick of apprehension, deep in judgment,
Active in resolution; and 'tis pity
Such counsel should lie buried in obscurity.
But why, in such a time and cause of triumph,
Stands the judicious Mayor of Cork so silent?
Believe it, sir, as English Richard prospers,
You must not miss employment of high nature.

J. a-Wat. If men may be credited in their mortality, which I dare not peremptorily aver but they may or not be, presumptions by this marriage are then, in sooth, of fruitful expectation. Or else I must not justify other men's belief, more than other should rely on mine.

Fri. Pith of experience! those that have borne office
Weigh every word before it can drop from them.
But, noble counsellors, since now the present
Requires in point of honour,—pray, mistake not,—
Some service to our lord, 'tis fit the Scots
Should not engross all glory to themselves
At this so grand and eminent solemnity.

Skelt. The Scots! the motion is defied: I had rather, for my part, without trial of my country, suffer persecution under the pressing-iron of reproach; or

[17] *through-stitch*] Gifford printed "thorough-*stitch*,"—the more usual form of the word. D.

let my skin be punched[18] full of eyelet-holes with the bodkin of derision.

Ast. I will sooner lose both my ears on the pillory of forgery.

Her. Let me first live a bankrupt, and die in the lousy Hole[19] of hunger, without compounding for six-pence in the pound.

J. a-Wat. If men fail not in their expectations, there may be spirits also that digest[20] no rude affronts, Master Secretary Frion, or I am cozened; which is possible, I grant.

Fri. Resolv'd like men of knowledge: at this feast, then,
In honour of the bride, the Scots, I know,
Will in some show, some masque, or some device,
Prefer their duties: now it were uncomely
That we be found less forward for our prince
Than they are for their lady; and by how much
We outshine them in persons of account,
By so much more will our endeavours meet with
A livelier applause. Great emperors
Have for their recreations undertook
Such kind of pastimes: as for the conceit,
Refer it to my study; the performance
You all shall share a thanks in: 'twill be grateful.

Her. The motion is allowed: I have stole to a dancing-school when I was a prentice.

Ast. There have been Irish hubbubs,[21] when I have made one too.

18 *punched*] The 4to has "pincht." D.
19 *Hole*] The name for one of the worst apartments in the Counter prison. D.
20 *digest*] Here the 4to has "disgest." D.
21 *Irish hubbubs,*] Tumultuous merry-meetings at wakes and fairs. The speakers, it should be observed, are all from Ireland. Astley, as has been said, was a pettifogger; his presence at these hubbubs, therefore, is natural enough.

Skelt. For fashioning of shapes and cutting a cross-caper, turn me off to my trade again.

J. a-Wat. Surely there is, if I be not deceived, a kind of gravity in merriment; as there is, or perhaps ought to be, respect of persons in the quality of carriage, which is as it is construed, either so or so.

Fri. Still you come home to me; upon occasion
I find you relish courtship with discretion;
And such are fit for statesmen of your merits.
Pray ye wait the prince, and in his ear acquaint him
With this design; I'll follow and direct ye.

[*Exeunt all but Frion.*

O, the toil
Of humouring this abject scum of mankind,
Muddy-brain'd peasants! princes feel a misery
Beyond impartial sufferance, whose extremes
Must yield to such abettors:—yet our tide[22]
Runs smoothly, without adverse winds: run on!
Flow to a full sea! time alone debates
Quarrels forewritten in the book of fates. [*Exit.*

ACT III.

SCENE I. *Westminster. The palace.*

Enter King HENRY, *with his gorget on, his sword, plume of feathers, and leading-staff (truncheon), followed by* URSWICK.

K. Hen. How runs the time of day?

Urs. Past ten, my lord.

K. Hen. A bloody hour will it prove to some,
Whose disobedience, like the sons o' th' earth,

[22] yet *our tide,* &c.] i.e. *hitherto, thus far,* &c. as in p. 162.

Throw[s] a defiance 'gainst the face of heaven.
Oxford, with Essex and stout De la Pole,
Have quieted the Londoners, I hope,
And set them safe from fear.

Urs. They are all silent.

K. Hen. From their own battlements they may behold
Saint George's-fields o'erspread with armèd men;
Amongst whom our own royal standard threatens
Confusion to opposers: we must learn
To practise war again in time of peace,
Or lay our crown before our subjects' feet;
Ha, Urswick, must we not?

Urs. The powers who seated
King Henry on his lawful throne will ever
Rise up in his defence.

K. Hen. Rage shall not fright
The bosom of our confidence: in Kent
Our Cornish rebels, cozen'd of their hopes,
Met brave resistance by that country's earl,
George Abergeny, Cobham, Poynings, Guilford,
And other loyal hearts; now, if Blackheath
Must be reserv'd the fatal tomb to swallow
Such stiff-neck'd abjects as with weary marches
Have travell'd from their homes, their wives, and children,
To pay, instead of subsidies, their lives,
We may continue sovereign. Yet, Urswick,
We'll not abate one penny what in parliament
Hath freely been contributed; we must not;
Money gives soul to action. Our competitor,
The Flemish counterfeit, with James of Scotland,
Will prove what courage need and want can nourish,
Without the food of fit supplies:—but, Urswick,
I have a charm in secret that shall loose

The witchcraft wherewith young King James is bound,
And free it at my pleasure without bloodshed.

Urs. Your majesty's a wise king, sent from heaven,
Protector of the just.

K. Hen. Let dinner cheerfully
Be serv'd in; this day of the week is ours,
Our day of providence; for Saturday
Yet never fail'd[1] in all my undertakings
To yield me rest at night. [*A flourish.*]—What means this warning?
Good fate, speak peace to Henry!

Enter DAWBENEY, Oxford, *and* Attendants.

Daw. Live the king,
Triumphant in the ruin of his enemies!

Oxf. The head of strong rebellion is cut off,
The body hew'd in pieces.

K. Hen. Dawbeney, Oxford,
Minions to noblest fortunes, how yet stands
The comfort of your wishes?

Daw. Briefly thus:
The Cornish under Audley, disappointed
Of flatter'd expectation, from the Kentish—
Your majesty's right-trusty liegemen—flew,
Feather'd by rage and hearten'd by presumption,
To take the field even at your palace-gates,
And face you in your chamber-royal: arrogance
Improv'd their ignorance; for they, supposing,
Misled by rumour, that the day of battle
Should fall on Monday, rather brav'd your forces

1 *for* Saturday
Yet never fail'd, &c.] The King's predilection for *Saturday* is noticed by Lord Bacon. Henry had taken great pains to induce the insurgents to believe that he intended to put-off the action till the succeeding Monday: they fell into the snare, and were accordingly unprepared for the attack, which took place on Saturday the 22d of June.

Than doubted any onset; yet this morning,
When in the dawning I, by your direction,
Strove to get Deptford-Strand-bridge,[2] there I found
Such a resistance as might show what strength
Could make: here arrows hail'd in showers upon us
A full yard long at least; but we prevail'd.
My Lord of Oxford, with his fellow peers
Environing the hill, fell fiercely on them
On the one side, I on the other, till, great sir,—
Pardon the oversight,—eager of doing
Some memorable act, I was engag'd
Almost a prisoner, but was freed as soon
As sensible of danger: now the fight
Began in heat, which quench'd in the blood of
Two thousand rebels, and as many more
Reserv'd to try your mercy, have return'd
A victory with safety.

K. Hen. Have we lost
An equal number with them?

Oxf. In the total
Scarcely four hundred. Audley, Flammock, Joseph,
The ringleaders[3] of this commotion,
Railèd in ropes,[4] fit ornaments for traitors,

[2] *Deptford-Strand-bridge,*] The 4to has "Dertford *Strand bridge.*" D.

[3] *Audley, Flammock, Joseph,*
The ringleaders, &c.] Lord Audley had been for some time in communication with the leaders of the Cornish men, but did not join them till they reached Wells in Somersetshire. He was, the historian says, "of an ancient family, but unquiet and popular, and aspiring to ruin." He was immediately, and "with great gladness and cries of joy, accepted as their general; they being now proud that they were led by a nobleman." Thomas Flammock, a common name in Cornwall, was a lawyer, who by various artifices had obtained great sway among them; and Michael Joseph, a blacksmith or farrier, of Bodmin, "a notable talking fellow, and no less desirous to be talked of." It should be added, that Ford is indebted to Lord Bacon for most of the incidents in Dawbeney's narrative.

[4] Railèd *in ropes,*] The 4to is imperfect [where? D.], and reads "*Raled* in ropes." As the *R* is very indistinct, I should have been inclined, perhaps, to make "*Haled*" out of it, had I not found the

Wait your determinations.

K. Hen. We must pay
Our thanks where they are only due: O, lords,
Here is no victory, nor shall our people
Conceive that we can triumph in their falls.
Alas, poor souls! let such as are escap'd
Steal to the country back without pursuit:
There's not a drop of blood spilt but hath drawn
As much of mine; their swords could have wrought wonders
On their king's part, who faintly were unsheath'd
Against their prince, but wounded their own breasts.
Lords, we are debtors to your care; our payment
Shall be both sure and fitting your deserts.

Daw. Sir, will you please to see those rebels, heads
Of this wild monster-multitude?

K. Hen. Dear friend,
My faithful Dawbeney, no; on them our justice
Must frown in terror; I will not vouchsafe
An eye of pity to them. Let false Audley
Be drawn upon an hurdle from the Newgate
To Tower-hill in his own coat of arms
Painted on paper, with the arms revers'd,
Defac'd and torn; there let him lose his head.
The lawyer and the blacksmith shall be hang'd,
Quarter'd; their quarters into Cornwall sent
Examples to the rest, whom we are pleas'd
To pardon and dismiss from further quest.—
My Lord of Oxford, see it done.

Oxf. I shall, sir.

K. Hen. Urswick!

---

expression in Bacon; "they were brought to London all *railed in ropes*, like a team of horses in a cart."—Flammock and Joseph were hanged at Tyburn. "The Lord Audley was *led* from Newgate to Tower-hill, *in a paper coat painted with his own arms*, the arms reversed, the coat torn, and at Tower-hill beheaded."

Urs. My lord?
K. Hen. To Dinham, our high-treasurer,
Say, we command commissions be new granted
For the collection of our subsidies
Through all the west, and that [right] speedily.—
Lords, we acknowledge our engagements due
For your most constant services.
Daw. Your soldiers
Have manfully and faithfully acquitted
Their several duties.
K. Hen. For it we will throw
A largess free amongst them, which shall hearten
And cherish-up their loyalties. More yet
Remains of like employment; not a man
Can be dismiss'd, till enemies abroad,
More dangerous than these at home, have felt
The puissance of our arms. O, happy kings
Whose thrones are raisèd in their subjects' hearts!
[*Exeunt.*

SCENE II. *Edinburgh. The palace.*

Enter HUNTLEY *and* DALYELL.

Hunt. Now, sir, a modest word with you, sad gentleman:
Is not this fine, I trow, to see the gambols,
To hear the jigs, observe the frisks, be enchanted
With the rare discord of bells, pipes, and tabors,
Hotch-potch of Scotch and Irish twingle-twangles,
Like to so many quiristers of Bedlam
Trolling a catch! The feasts, the manly stomachs,
The healths in usquebaugh and bonny-clabber,[5]

[5] *The healths in* bonny-clabber,] A common name, in our old writers, for curds-and-whey, or sour buttermilk. It appears to have been a favourite drink both with the Scotch and Irish. See *Jonson*, vol. v. p. 330.

The ale in dishes never fetch'd from China,
The hundred-thousand knacks not to be spoken of,—
And all this for King Oberon and Queen Mab,—
Should put a soul into ye. Look ye, good man,
How youthful I am grown: but, by your leave,
This new queen-bride must henceforth be no more
My daughter; no, by'r lady, 'tis unfit:
And yet you see how I do bear this change,
Methinks courageously: then shake-off care
In such a time of jollity.

Dal. Alas, sir,
How can you cast a mist upon your griefs?
Which, howsoe'er you shadow, but present
To any[6] judging eye the perfect substance,
Of which mine are but counterfeits.

Hunt. Foh, Dalyell!
Thou interrupt'st the part I bear in music
To this rare bridal-feast; let us be merry,
Whilst flattering calms secure us against storms:
Tempests, when they begin to roar, put out
The light of peace, and cloud the sun's bright eye
In darkness of despair; yet we are safe.

Dal. I wish you could as easily forget
The justice of your sorrows as my hopes
Can yield to destiny.

Hunt. Pish! then I see
Thou dost not know the flexible condition
Of my apt[7] nature: I can laugh, laugh heartily,
When the gout cramps my joints; let but the stone
Stop in my bladder, I am straight a-singing;
The quartan-fever, shrinking every limb,

[6] *any*] Gifford bracketed this word, as if omitted in the old edition. But both the 4to in the King's Library, British Museum, and a copy in my possession have the word. D.

[7] *apt*] So the two 4tos just mentioned.—Gifford printed "[tough]." D.

Sets me a-capering straight; do but[8] betray me,
And bind me a friend ever: what! I trust
The losing of a daughter, though I doted
On every hair that grew to trim her head,
Admits not any pain like one of these.
Come, thou'rt deceiv'd in me: give me a blow,
A sound blow on the face, I'll thank thee for't;
I love my wrongs: still thou'rt deceiv'd in me.

Dal. Deceiv'd! O, noble Huntley, my few years
Have learnt experience of too ripe an age
To forfeit fit credulity: forgive
My rudeness, I am bold.

Hunt. Forgive me first
A madness of ambition; by example
Teach me humility, for patience scorns
Lectures, which schoolmen use to read to boys
Uncapable of injuries: though old,
I could grow tough in fury, and disclaim
Allegiance to my king; could fall at odds
With all my fellow-peers that durst not stand
Defendants 'gainst the rape done on mine honour:
But kings are earthly gods, there is no meddling
With their anointed bodies; for their actions
They only are accountable to heaven.
Yet in the puzzle of my troubled brain
One antidote's reserv'd against the poison
Of my distractions; 'tis in thee t' apply it.

Dal. Name it; O, name it quickly, sir!

Hunt. A pardon
For my most foolish slighting thy deserts;
I have cull'd out this time to beg it: prithee,

[8] *but*] Bracketed by Gifford, though found in the two 4tos just mentioned.—It is possible that Gifford may have used a 4to of *the same edition* with the variations here noticed: see note, vol. i. p. 34. D.

Be gentle; had I been so, thou hadst own'd
A happy bride, but now a castaway,
And never child of mine more.

Dal. Say not so, sir;
It is not fault in her.

Hunt. The world would prate
How she was handsome; young I know she was,
Tender, and sweet in her obedience;
But lost now: what a bankrupt am I made
Of a full stock of blessings! Must I hope
A mercy from thy heart?

Dal. A love, a service,
A friendship to posterity.

Hunt. Good angels
Reward thy charity! I have no more
But prayers left me now.

Dal. I'll lend you mirth, sir,
If you will be in consort.

Hunt. Thank ye truly:
I must; yes, yes, I must;—here's yet some ease,
A partner in affliction: look not angry.

Dal. Good, noble sir! [*Flourish.*

Hunt. O, hark! we may be quiet,
The King and all the others come; a meeting
Of gaudy sights: this day 's the last of revels;
To-morrow sounds of war; then new exchange;
Fiddles must turn to swords.—Unhappy marriage!

A flourish. Enter King JAMES, WARBECK *leading* KATHERINE, CRAWFORD *and his* Countess; JANE DOUGLAS, *and other* Ladies. HUNTLEY *and* DALYELL *fall among them.*

K. Ja. Cousin of York, you and your princely bride
Have liberally enjoy'd such soft delights

As a new-married couple could forethink;
Nor has our bounty shorten'd expectation:
But after all those pleasures of repose,
Of amorous safety, we must rouse the ease
Of dalliance with achievements of more glory
Than sloth and sleep can furnish: yet, for farewell,
Gladly we entertain a truce with time,
To grace the joint endeavours of our servants.

War. My royal cousin, in your princely favour
Th' extent of bounty hath been so unlimited,
As only an acknowledgment in words
Would breed suspicion in our state and quality.
When we shall, in the fulness of our fate,—
Whose minister, Necessity, will perfect,[9]—
Sit on our own throne; then our arms, laid open
To gratitude, in sacred memory
Of these large benefits, shall twine them close,
Even to our thoughts and heart, without distinction.
Then James and Richard, being in effect
One person, shall unite and rule one people,
Divisible in titles only.

K. Ja. Seat ye.—
Are the presenters ready?

Craw. All are entering.

Hunt. Dainty sport toward, Dalyell! sit; come, sit,
Sit and be quiet; here are kingly bug's-words![10]

[9] The sentence seems incomplete, for want of a relative; the meaning, however, is clear enough: in plain words, Necessity, the agent of Destiny, will bring her design to perfection; i.e. give me the kingdom.

[10] *bug's-words!*] [Altered to "bug-*words*" by Gifford, who, in his Introd., sneers at Weber for retaining the other form: but see my note on *Philaster*, Beaumont and Fletcher's *Works*, vol. i. p. 297. D.] Generally speaking, terrific, alarming words; from the Celtic *bwg*, a fiend, a frightful hobgoblin: here, however, they sarcastically allude to the pompous high-sounding language of the imaginary monarch. A similar expression occurs in the *Tamer tamed* [by Fletcher]; "Indeed, these are *bug-words!*"

Enter at one door Four Scotch Antics, *accordingly habited;*[11] *at another*, WARBECK'S *followers, disguised as* Four Wild Irish *in trowses*,[11] *long-haired, and accordingly habited. Music. A dance by the Masquers.*

K. Ja. To all a general thanks!

War. In the next room
Take your own shapes[12] again; you shall receive
Particular acknowledgment. [*Exeunt the Masquers.*

K. Ja. Enough
Of merriments.—Crawford, how far's our army
Upon the march?

Craw. At Hedon-hall, great king;
Twelve thousand, well prepar'd.

K. Ja. Crawford, to-night
Post thither. We in person, with the prince,
By four o'clock to-morrow after dinner
Will be wi' ye; speed away!

Craw. I fly, my lord. [*Exit.*

K. Ja. Our business grows to head now: where's your secretary,
That he attends ye not to serve?

War. With Marchmont,
Your herald.

K. Ja. Good: the proclamation's ready;
By that it will appear how th' English stand
Affected to your title.—Huntley, comfort
Your daughter in her husband's absence; fight
With prayers at home for us, who for your honours
Must toil in fight abroad.

Hunt. Prayers are the weapons

11 *Four Scotch Antics*, accordingly *habited;*] i.e. *characteristically*. The *trowses*, or *trosses*, of the "wild Irish," mentioned in the next line, were drawers closely fitted to the shape, and which, together with the long shaggy hair of these people, are often made the subject of mirth by our old dramatists.

12 *Take your* own shapes] i.e. resume your ordinary dress.

Which men so near their graves as I do use;
I've little else to do.

K. Ja. To rest, young beauties!—
We must be early stirring; quickly part:
A kingdom's rescue craves both speed and art.—
Cousins,[13] good-night. [*A flourish.*

War. Rest to our cousin-king.

Kath. Your blessing, sir.

Hunt. Fair blessings on your highness! sure, you need 'em.

[*Exeunt all but War. Kath. and Jane.*

War. Jane, set the lights down, and from us return
To those in the next room this little purse;
Say we'll deserve their loves.

Jane. It shall be done, sir. [*Exit.*

War. Now, dearest, ere sweet sleep shall seal those eyes,
Love's precious tapers, give me leave to use
A parting ceremony; for to-morrow
It would be sacrilege t' intrude upon
The temple of thy peace: swift as the morning
Must I break from the down of thy embraces,
To put on steel, and trace the paths which lead
Through various hazards to a careful throne.

Kath. My lord, I'd fain go wi' ye; there's small fortune
In staying here behind.

War. The churlish brow
Of war, fair dearest, is a sight of horror
For ladies' entertainment: if thou hear'st
A truth of my sad ending by the hand
Of some unnatural subject, thou withal
Shalt hear how I died worthy of my right,

[13] *Cousins,*] Is right, if the king addresses Katherine as well as Warbeck: but qy. "Cousin"? D.

By falling like a king; and in the close,
Which my last breath shall sound, thy name, thou fairest,
Shall sing a requiem to my soul, unwilling
Only of greater glory, 'cause divided
From such a heaven on earth as life with thee.
But these are chimes for funerals: my business
Attends on fortune of a sprightlier triumph;
For love and majesty are reconcil'd,
And vow to crown thee empress of the west.

Kath. You have a noble language, sir; your right
In me is without question, and however
Events of time may shorten my deserts
In others' pity, yet it shall not stagger
Or constancy or duty in a wife.
You must be king of me; and my poor heart
Is all I can call mine.

War. But we will live,
Live, beauteous virtue, by the lively test
Of our own blood, to let the counterfeit
Be known the world's contempt.

Kath. Pray, do not use
That word; it carries fate in't. The first suit
I ever made, I trust your love will grant.

War. Without denial, dearest.

Kath. That hereafter,
If you return with safety, no adventure
May sever us in tasting any fortune:
I ne'er can stay behind again.

War. You're lady
Of your desires, and shall command your will;
Yet 'tis too hard a promise.

Kath. What our destinies
Have rul'd-out in their books we must not search,
But kneel to.

War. Then to fear when hope is fruitless,
Were to be desperately miserable;
Which poverty our greatness dares not dream of,
And much more scorns to stoop to: some few minutes
Remain yet; let's be thrifty in our hopes. [*Exeunt.*

SCENE III. *The palace at Westminster.*

Enter King HENRY, HIALAS, *and* URSWICK.

K. Hen. Your name is Pedro Hialas,[13] a Spaniard?
Hial. Sir, a Castilian born.
K. Hen. King Ferdinand,
With wise Queen Isabel his royal consort,
Write ye a man of worthy trust and candour.
Princes are dear to heaven who meet with subjects
Sincere in their employments; such I find
Your commendation, sir. Let me deliver
How joyful I repute the amity
With your most fortunate master, who almost
Comes near a miracle in his success
Against the Moors, who had devour'd his country,
Entire now to his sceptre. We, for our part,
Will imitate his providence, in hope
Of partage in the use on't: we repute
The privacy of his advisement to us
By you, intended an ambassador
To Scotland, for a peace between our kingdoms,
A policy of love, which well becomes

[13] *Your name is Pedro Hialas,* &c.] "Amongst these troubles," Lord Bacon says, "came into England from Spain Peter *Hialas*, some call him *Elias* (surely he was the *forerunner* of the good hap that we enjoy at this day; for his ambassage set the truce between England and Scotland; the truce drew on the peace; the peace the marriage; and the marriage the union of the kingdoms); a man of great wisdom, and, as those times were, not unlearned."

His wisdom and our care.

Hial. Your majesty
Doth understand him rightly.

K. Hen. Else
Your knowledge can instruct me; wherein, sir,
To fall on ceremony would seem useless,
Which shall not need; for I will be as studious
Of your concealment in our conference
As any council shall advise.

Hial. Then, sir,
My chief request is, that on notice given
At my dispatch in Scotland, you will send
Some learnèd man of power and experience
To join entreaty with me.

K. Hen. I shall do it,
Being that way well provided by a servant
Which may attend ye ever.

Hial. If King James,
By any indirection, should perceive
My coming near your court, I doubt the issue
Of my employment.

K. Hen. Be not your own herald:
I learn sometimes without a teacher.

Hial. Good days
Guard all your princely thoughts!

K. Hen. Urswick, no further
Than the next open gallery attend him.—
A hearty love go with you!

Hial. Your vow'd beadsman.[14]
[*Exeunt Urs. and Hial.*

K. Hen. King Ferdinand is not so much a fox,
But that a cunning huntsman may in time

[14] *Your vow'd* beadsman.] One bound to *pray* for you; from *bede*, the old English word for *prayer*. At this time, however, the expression was sufficiently familiar, and meant little more than the common language of civility—your vowed or devoted *servant*.

Fall on the scent: in honourable actions
Safe imitation best deserves a praise.

Re-enter URSWICK.

What, the Castilian's pass'd away?
Urs. He is,
And undiscover'd; the two hundred marks
Your majesty convey'd, he gently purs'd
With a right modest gravity.
K. Hen. What was't
He mutter'd in the earnest of his wisdom?
He spoke not to be heard; 'twas about—
Urs. Warbeck:
How if King Henry were but sure of subjects,
Such a wild runagate might soon be cag'd,
No great ado withstanding.
K. Hen. Nay, nay; something
About my son Prince Arthur's match.
Urs. Right, right, sir:
He humm'd it out, how that King Ferdinand
Swore that the marriage 'twixt the Lady Katherine
His daughter and the Prince of Wales your son
Should never be consummated as long
As any Earl of Warwick liv'd in England,
Except by new creation.
K. Hen. I remember
'Twas so, indeed: the king his master swore it?
Urs. Directly, as he said.
K. Hen. An Earl of Warwick!—
Provide a messenger for letters instantly
To Bishop Fox. Our news from Scotland creeps;
It comes so[15] slow, we must have airy spirits;
Our time requires dispatch.—[*Aside*] The Earl of Warwick!

[15] *so*] Gifford printed "too." D.

Let him be son to Clarence,[16] younger brother
To Edward! Edward's daughter is, I think,
Mother to our Prince Arthur.—Get a messenger.
[*Exeunt.*

SCENE IV. *Before the castle of Norham.*

Enter King JAMES, WARBECK, CRAWFORD, DALYELL, HERON, ASTLEY, JOHN A-WATER, SKELTON, *and Soldiers.*

K. Ja. We trifle time against these castle-walls;
The English prelate will not yield: once more
Give him a summons. [*A parley is sounded.*

Enter on the walls the Bishop of Durham *armed, a truncheon in his hand, with Soldiers.*

War. See, the jolly clerk
Appears, trimm'd like a ruffian!
K. Ja. Bishop, yet
Set ope the ports, and to your lawful sovereign,
Richard of York, surrender up this castle,
And he will take thee to his grace; else Tweed
Shall overflow his banks with English blood,
And wash the sand that cements those hard stones
From their foundation.
Dur. Warlike King of Scotland,
Vouchsafe a few words from a man enforc'd
To lay his book aside, and clap on arms[17]
Unsuitable to my age or my profession.
Courageous prince, consider on what grounds
You rend the face of peace, and break a league

[16] *Let him be son to Clarence,* &c.] These are ominous musings of the King, who eagerly caught at the words of Ferdinand, as given above, and sought "to export the odium of this innocent prince's execution out of the land, and lay it upon his new ally." [The substance, not the exact words, of Bacon's *Hist.* D.]

[17] *and* clap *on arms*] So the old copy: it is not improbable, however, that the poet's word was "*clasp.*" [No, no. D.]

With a confederate king that courts your amity;
For whom too? for a vagabond, a straggler,
Not noted in the world by birth or name,
An obscure peasant, by the rage of hell
Loos'd from his chains to set great kings at strife.
What nobleman, what common man of note,
What ordinary subject hath come in,
Since first you footed on our territories,
To only feign a welcome? Children laugh at
Your proclamations, and the wiser pity
So great a potentate's abuse by one
Who juggles merely with the fawns and youth
Of an instructed compliment: such spoils,
Such slaughters as the rapine of your soldiers
Already have committed, is enough
To show your zeal in a conceited justice.
Yet, great king, wake not yet my master's vengeance;
But shake that viper off which gnaws your entrails.
I and my fellow-subjects are resolv'd,
If you persist, to stand your utmost fury,
Till our last blood drop from us.

War. O, sir, lend
No ear to this traducer[18] of my honour!—
What shall I call thee, thou gray-bearded scandal,
That kick'st against the sovereignty to which
Thou ow'st allegiance?—Treason is bold-fac'd
And eloquent in mischief: sacred king,
Be deaf to his known malice.

Dur. Rather yield
Unto those holy motions which inspire
The sacred heart of an anointed body.
It is the surest[19] policy in princes

[18] *to this* traducer, &c.] The 4to, by an evident oversight, reads "to this *seducer*," &c. There is another misprint in the same line, "*Me*" for "*No*"

[19] *surest*] So perhaps Ford wrote: but qy. "surer"? D.

To govern well their own than seek encroachment
Upon another's right.
Craw. The king is serious,
Deep in his meditation[s].
Dal. Lift them up
To heaven, his better genius!
War. Can you study
While such a devil raves? O, sir!
K. Ja. Well, bishop,
You'll not be drawn to mercy?
Dur. Construe me
In like case by a subject of your own:
My resolution's fix'd: King James, be counsell'd,
A greater fate waits on thee.
[*Exeunt Durham and Soldiers from the walls.*
K. Ja. Forage through
The country; spare no prey of life or goods.
War. O, sir, then give me leave to yield to nature;
I am most miserable: had I been
Born what this clergyman would by defame
Baffle belief with, I had never sought
The truth of mine inheritance with rapes
Of women or of infants murder'd, virgins
Deflower'd, old men butcher'd, dwellings fir'd,
My land depopulated, and my people
Afflicted with a kingdom's devastation:
Show more remorse, great king, or I shall never
Endure to see such havoc with dry eyes;
Spare, spare, my dear, dear England!
K. Ja. You fool your piety,
Ridiculously careful of an interest
Another man possesseth. Where's your faction?
Shrewdly the bishop guess'd of your adherents,
When not a petty burgess of some town,
No, not a villager, hath yet appear'd

In your assistance: that should make ye whine,
And not your country's sufferance, as you term it.
Dal. The king is angry.
Craw. And the passionate duke
Effeminately dolent.[20]
War. The experience
In former trials, sir, both of mine own
Or other princes cast out of their thrones,
Have[21] so acquainted me how misery
Is destitute of friends or of relief,
That I can easily submit to taste
Lowest reproof without contempt or words.
K. Ja. An humble-minded man!

Enter FRION.

Now, what intelligence
Speaks Master Secretary Frion?
Fri. Henry
Of England hath in open field o'erthrown
The armies who oppos'd him in the right
Of this young prince.
K. Ja. His subsidies, you mean:—
More, if you have it?
Fri. Howard Earl of Surrey,
Back'd by twelve earls and barons of the north,
An hundred knights and gentlemen of name,
And twenty thousand soldiers, is at hand
To raise your siege. Brooke, with a goodly navy,
Is admiral at sea; and Dawbeney follows
With an unbroken army for a second.

[20] *And the* passionate *duke*
Effeminately dolent.] Thus Bacon; "It is said that Perkin, acting the part of a prince handsomely, when he saw the Scotch fell to waste the country, came to the King in a *passionate* [plaintive, tearful] manner, making great *lamentation*," &c. "Whereunto the King answered, half in sport," much as we have it above.

[21] *Have*] Gifford printed "Hath." See note, vol. i. p. 85. D.

War. 'Tis false! they come to side with us.
K. Ja. Retreat;
We shall not find them stones and walls to cope with.—
Yet, Duke of York, for such thou sayst thou art,
I'll try thy fortune to the height: to Surrey,
By Marchmont, I will send a brave defiance
For single combat; once a king will venture
His person to an earl,[22] with condition
Of spilling lesser blood: Surrey is bold,
And James resolv'd.
War. O, rather, gracious sir,
Create me to this glory, since my cause
Doth interest this fair quarrel; valu'd least,
I am his equal.
K. Ja. I will be the man.—
March softly off: where victory can reap
A harvest crown'd with triumph, toil is cheap.
[*Exeunt.*

ACT IV.

SCENE I. *The English camp near Ayton, on the Borders.*

Enter Surrey, Durham, *Soldiers, with drums and colours.*

Sur. Are all our braving enemies shrunk back,
Hid in the fogs of their distemper'd climate,
Not daring to behold our colours wave
In spite of this infected air? Can they
Look on the strength of Cundrestine defac'd?

[22] *His person to an* earl,] Here, and in p. 178 ["The *earl* shall deliver," &c.], *earl* is used as a dissyllable. It is necessary to notice this, as Ford occasionally varies in the measure of this and similar words in the course of the same speech.

The glory of Hedon-hall devasted? that
Of Edington cast down? the pile of Fulden
O'erthrown? and this, the strongest of their forts,
Old Ayton-castle,[1] yielded and demolish'd?
And yet not peep abroad? The Scots are bold,
Hardy in battle; but it seems the cause
They undertake, considerèd, appears
Unjointed in the frame on't.

Dur. Noble Surrey,
Our royal master's wisdom is at all times
His fortune's harbinger; for when he draws
His sword to threaten war, his providence
Settles on peace, the crowning of an empire.

[*A trumpet within.*

Sur. Rank all in order: 'tis a herald's sound;
Some message from King James: keep a fix'd station.

Enter MARCHMONT *and another in heralds' coats.*

March. From Scotland's awful majesty we come
Unto the English general.

Sur. To me?
Say on.

March. Thus, then; the waste and prodigal
Effusion of so much guiltless blood
As in two potent armies of necessity
Must glut the earth's dry womb, his sweet compassion
Hath studied to prevent; for which to thee,
Great Earl of Surrey, in a single fight

[1] *and this, the strongest of their forts,*
Old Ayton-castle,] The castle of Aton, Bacon says, was then esteemed one of the strongest places between Berwick and Edinburgh. With the capture of this place the struggle terminated; little to the honour, and less to the advantage, of either side. The noble historian says nothing of the main business of this scene, which must, I believe, be placed entirely to the account of the poet; though it is in some measure justified by the chivalrous and romantic character of James IV.

He offers his own royal person; fairly
Proposing these conditions only, that
If victory conclude our master's right,
The earl shall deliver for his ransom
The town of Berwick to him, with the fishgarths;
If Surrey shall prevail, the king will pay
A thousand pounds down present for his freedom,
And silence further arms: so speaks King James.

Sur. So speaks King James! so like a king he speaks.
Heralds, the English general returns
A sensible devotion from his heart,
His very soul, to this unfellow'd grace:
For let the king know, gentle heralds, truly,
How his descent from his great throne, to honour
A stranger subject with so high a title
As his compeer in arms, hath conquer'd more
Than any sword could do; for which—my loyalty
Respected—I will serve his virtues ever
In all humility: but Berwick, say,
Is none of mine to part with; in affairs
Of princes subjects cannot traffic rights
Inherent to the crown. My life is mine,
That I dare freely hazard; and—with pardon
To some unbrib'd vainglory—if his majesty
Shall taste a change of fate, his liberty
Shall meet no articles. If I fall, falling
So bravely, I refer me to his pleasure
Without condition; and for this dear favour,
Say, if not countermanded, I will cease
Hostility, unless provok'd.

March. This answer
We shall relate[2] unpartially.

[2] *relate*] Gifford printed "repeat." D.

Dur. With favour,
Pray have a little patience.—[*Aside to Surrey*] Sir, you find
By these gay flourishes how wearied travail
Inclines to willing rest; here's but a prologue,
However confidently utter'd, meant
For some ensuing acts of peace: consider
The time of year, unseasonableness of weather,
Charge, barrenness of profit; and occasion
Presents itself for honourable treaty,
Which we may make good use of. I will back,
As sent from you, in point of noble gratitude
Unto King James, with these his heralds: you
Shall shortly hear from me, my lord, for order
Of breathing or proceeding; and King Henry,
Doubt not, will thank the service.

Sur. [*aside to Dur.*] To your wisdom,
Lord Bishop, I refer it.

Dur. [*aside to Sur.*] Be it so, then.

Sur. Heralds, accept this chain and these few crowns.

March. Our duty, noble general.

Dur. In part
Of retribution for such princely love,
My lord the general is pleas'd to show
The king your master his sincerest zeal,
By further treaty, by no common man:
I will myself return with you.

Sur. Y' oblige
My faithfullest affections t'ye,[3] Lord Bishop.

March. All happiness attend your lordship!

[*Exit with Her.*

Sur. Come, friends

[3] *Y'oblige . . . t'ye,*] I may notice that so the 4to reads.—Gifford printed "You *oblige*" and "to you." D.

And fellow-soldiers; we, I doubt, shall meet
No enemies but woods and hills to fight with;
Then 'twere as good to feed and sleep at home:
We may be free from danger, not secure. [*Exeunt.*

SCENE II. *The Scottish camp.*

Enter WARBECK *and* FRION.

War. Frion, O, Frion, all my hopes of glory
Are at a stand! the Scottish king grows dull,
Frosty, and wayward, since this Spanish agent
Hath mix'd discourses with him; they are private,
I am not call'd to council now:—confusion
On all his crafty shrugs! I feel the fabric
Of my designs are tottering.[4]
Fri. Henry's policies
Stir with too many engines.
War. Let his mines,
Shap'd in the bowels of the earth, blow up
Works rais'd for my defence, yet can they never
Toss into air the freedom of my birth,
Or disavow my blood Plantagenet's:
I am my father's son still. But, O, Frion,
When I bring into count with my disasters
My wife's compartnership, my Kate's, my life's,
Then, then my frailty feels an earthquake. Mischief
Damn Henry's plots! I will be England's king,
Or let my aunt of Burgundy report
My fall in the attempt deserv'd our ancestors!
Fri. You grow too wild in passion: if you will
Appear a prince indeed, confine your will

[4] *the fabric
Of my designs are tottering.*] See note, vol. i. p. 85.

To moderation.

War. What a saucy rudeness
Prompts this distrust! If? If I will appear!
Appear a prince! death throttle such deceits
Even in their birth of utterance! cursèd cozenage
Of trust! Ye make me mad: 'twere best, it seems,
That I should turn impostor to myself,
Be mine own counterfeit, belie the truth
Of my dear mother's womb, the sacred bed
Of a prince murder'd and a living baffled!

Fri. Nay, if you have no ears to hear, I have
No breath to spend in vain.

War. Sir, sir, take heed!
Gold and the promise of promotion rarely
Fail in temptation.

Fri. Why to me this?

War. Nothing.
Speak what you will; we are not sunk so low
But your advice may piece again the heart
Which many cares have broken: you were wont
In all extremities to talk of comfort;
Have ye none left now? I'll not interrupt ye.
Good, bear with my distractions! If King James
Deny us dwelling here, next whither must I?
I prithee, be not angry.

Fri. Sir, I told ye
Of letters come from Ireland; how the Cornish
Stomach their last defeat, and humbly sue
That with such forces as you could partake
You would in person land in Cornwall, where
Thousands will entertain your title gladly.

War. Let me embrace thee, hug thee; thou'st reviv'd
My comforts; if my cousin-king will fail,
Our cause will never.

Enter JOHN A-WATER, HERON, ASTLEY, SKELTON.

Welcome, my tried friends!
You keep your brains awake in our defence.—
Frion, advise with them of these affairs,
In which be wondrous secret; I will listen
What else concerns us here: be quick and wary. [*Exit.*

Ast. Ah, sweet young prince!—Secretary, my fellow-counsellors and I have consulted, and jump all in one opinion directly; an if these Scotch garboils do not fadge to our minds, we will pell-mell run amongst the Cornish choughs presently and in a trice.

Skelt. 'Tis but going to sea and leaping ashore, cut ten or twelve thousand unnecessary throats, fire seven or eight towns, take half a dozen cities, get into the market-place, crown him Richard the Fourth, and the business is finished.

J. a-Wat. I grant ye, quoth I, so far forth as men may do, no more than men may do; for it is good to consider when consideration may be to the purpose, otherwise — still you shall pardon me—little said is soon amended.

Fri. Then you conclude the Cornish action surest?

Her. We do so, and doubt not but to thrive abundantly. Ho, my masters, had we known of the commotion when we set sail out of Ireland, the land had been ours ere this time.

Skelt. Pish, pish! 'tis but forbearing being an earl or a duke a month or two longer. I say, and say it again, if the work go not on apace, let me never see new fashion more. I warrant ye, I warrant ye; we will have it so, and so it shall be.

Ast. This is but a cold phlegmatic country, not stirring enough for men of spirit. Give me the heart of England for my money!

Skelt. A man may batten there in a week only, with hot loaves and butter,[5] and a lusty cup of muscadine and sugar at breakfast, though he make never a meal all the month after.

J. a-Wat. Surely, when I bore office I found by experience that to be much troublesome was to be much wise and busy: I have observed how filching and bragging has been the best service in these last wars; and therefore conclude peremptorily on the design in England. If things and things may fall out, as who can tell what or how—but the end will show it.

Fri. Resolv'd like men of judgment! Here to linger
More time is but to lose it: cheer the prince,
And haste him on to this; on this depends
Fame in success, or glory in our ends. [*Exeunt.*

SCENE III. *Another part of the same.*

Enter King JAMES, Durham, *and* HIALAS.

Hial. France, Spain, and Germany combine a league
Of amity with England: nothing wants
For settling peace through Christendom, but love
Between the British monarchs, James and Henry.

Dur. The English merchants, sir, have been receiv'd
With general procession into Antwerp;
The emperor confirms the combination.

Hial. The King of Spain resolves a marriage
For Katherine his daughter with Prince Arthur.

Dur. France courts this holy contract.

[5] *with* hot loaves *and butter.*] Our ancestors must have found something peculiarly amusing in a tailor's breakfast to justify the comic writers in these eternal references to it. It is more than once noticed by Jonson; and see Massinger, vol. iii. p. 447.

Hial. What can hinder
A quietness in England?—
Dur. But your suffrage
To such a silly creature, mighty sir,
As is but in effect an apparition,
A shadow, a mere trifle?
Hial. To this union
The good of both the church and commonwealth
Invite ye.
Dur. To this unity, a mystery
Of providence points out a greater blessing
For both these nations than our human reason
Can search into. King Henry hath a daughter,
The Princess Margaret; I need not urge,
What honour, what felicity can follow
On such affinity 'twixt two Christian kings
Inleagu'd by ties of blood; but sure I am,
If you, sir, ratify the peace propos'd,
I dare both motion and effect this marriage
For weal of both the kingdoms.
K. Ja. Dar'st thou, Lord Bishop?
Dur. Put it to trial, royal James, by sending
Some noble personage to the English court
By way of embassy.
Hial. Part of the business
Shall suit my mediation.
K. Ja. Well; what heaven
Hath pointed out to be, must be: you two
Are ministers, I hope, of blessèd fate.
But herein only I will stand acquitted,
No blood of innocents shall buy my peace:
For Warbeck, as you nick him, came to me,
Commended by the states of Christendom,
A prince, though in distress; his fair demeanour,
Lovely behaviour, unappallèd spirit,

Spoke him not base in blood, however clouded.
The brute beasts have both[6] rocks and caves to fly to,
And men the altars of the church; to us
He came for refuge: kings come near in nature
Unto the gods in being touch'd with pity.[7]
Yet, noble friends, his mixture with our blood,
Even with our own, shall no way interrupt
A general peace; only I will dismiss him
From my protection, throughout my dominions,
In safety; but not ever to return.

Hial. You are a just king.

Dur. Wise, and herein happy.

K. Ja. Nor will we dally in affairs of weight:
Huntley, Lord Bishop, shall with you to England
Ambassador from us: we will throw down
Our weapons; peace on all sides! Now repair
Unto our council; we will soon be with you.

Hial. Delay shall question no dispatch; heaven crown it! [*Exeunt Dur. and Hial.*

K. Ja. A league with Ferdinand! a marriage
With English Margaret! a free release
From restitution for the late affronts!
Cessation from hostility! and all
For Warbeck, not deliver'd, but dismiss'd!
We could not wish it better.—Dalyell!

Enter DALYELL.

Dal. Here, sir.

K. Ja. Are Huntley and his daughter sent for?

Dal. Sent for,
And come, my lord.

K. Ja. Say to the English prince,

[6] *both*] Gifford printed "their." D.

[7] *kings . . . . . with pity.*] The 4to marks this with inverted commas, which Gifford very improperly retained: see note, p. 130. D.

We want his company.
Dal. He is at hand, sir.

Enter WARBECK, KATHERINE, JANE, FRION, HERON, SKELTON, JOHN A-WATER, ASTLEY.

K. Ja. Cousin, our bounty, favours, gentleness,
Our benefits, the hazard of our person,
Our people's lives, our land, hath evidenc'd
How much we have engag'd on your behalf:
How trivial and how dangerous our hopes
Appear, how fruitless our attempts in war,
How windy, rather smoky, your assurance
Of party shows, we might in vain repeat:
But now obedience to the mother church,
A father's care upon his country's weal,
The dignity of state, direct our wisdom
To seal an oath of peace through Christendom;
To which we're sworn already: it is you
Must only seek new fortunes in the world,
And find an harbour elsewere. As I promis'd
On your arrival, you have met no usage
Deserves repentance in your being here;
But yet I must live master of mine own:
However, what is necessary for you
At your departure, I am well content
You be accommodated with, provided
Delay prove not my enemy.
War. It shall not,
Most glorious prince. The fame of my designs
Soars higher than report of ease and sloth
Can aim at: I acknowledge all your favours
Boundless and singular; am only wretched
In words as well as means to thank the grace
That flow'd so liberally. Two empires firmly
You're lord of,—Scotland and Duke Richard's heart:

My claim to mine inheritance shall sooner
Fail than my life to serve you, best of kings;
And, witness Edward's blood in me! I am
More loth to part with such a great example
Of virtue than all other mere respects.
But, sir, my last suit is, you will not force
From me what you have given,—this chaste lady,
Resolv'd on all extremes.

Kath. I am your wife;
No human power can or shall divorce
My faith from duty.

War. Such another treasure
The earth is bankrupt of.

K. Ja. I gave her, cousin,
And must avow the gift; will add withal
A furniture becoming her high birth
And unsuspected constancy; provide
For your attendance: we will part good friends.
[*Exit with Dalyell.*

War. The Tudor hath been cunning in his plots;
His Fox of Durham would not fail at last.
But what? our cause and courage are our own:
Be men, my friends, and let our cousin-king
See how we follow fate as willingly
As malice follows us. Ye're all resolv'd
For the west parts of England?

All. Cornwall, Cornwall!

Fri. Th' inhabitants expect you daily.

War. Cheerfully
Draw all our ships out of the harbour, friends;
Our time of stay doth seem too long, we must
Prevent intelligence; about it suddenly.

All. A prince, a prince, a prince!
[*Exeunt Heron, Skelton, Astley, and John a-Water.*

War. Dearest, admit not into thy pure thoughts
The least of scruples, which may charge their softness
With burden of distrust. Should I prove wanting
To noblest[8] courage now, here were the trial:
But I am perfect, sweet; I fear no change,
More than thy being partner in my sufferance.

Kath. My fortunes, sir, have arm'd me to encounter
What chance soe'er they meet with.—Jane, 'tis fit
Thou stay behind, for whither wilt thou wander?

Jane. Never till death will I forsake my mistress,
Nor then in wishing to die with ye gladly.

Kath. Alas, good soul!

Fri. Sir, to your aunt of Burgundy
I will relate your present undertakings:
From her expect on all occasions welcome.
You cannot find me idle in your services.

War. Go, Frion, go: wise men know how to soothe
Adversity, not serve it: thou hast waited
Too long on expectation; never yet
Was any nation read of so besotted
In reason as t' adore the setting sun.
Fly to the archduke's court; say to the duchess,
Her nephew, with fair Katherine his wife,
Are on their expectation to begin
The raising of an empire: if they fail,
Yet the report will never. Farewell, Frion!

[*Exit Frion.*

This man, Kate, has been true, though now of late
I fear too much familiar with the Fox.[9]

[8] *noblest*] Gifford printed "noble." D.

[9] *the Fox.*] i.e. the Bishop of Durham, lord privy-seal, whom Bacon calls "a wise man, and one that could see through the present to the future." He stood deservedly high in Henry's confidence and favour. With respect to Frion, Warbeck was right. The defection of James showed the secretary but too clearly that the fortunes of his master were on the ebb; he therefore withdrew from him previously to the Cornish expedition, and returned no more.

Re-enter DALYELL *with* HUNTLEY.

Hunt. I come to take my leave: you need not
doubt
My interest in this sometime child of mine;
She's all yours now, good sir.—O, poor lost creature,
Heaven guard thee with much patience! if thou canst
Forget thy title to old Huntley's family,
As much of peace will settle in thy mind
As thou canst wish to taste but in thy grave.
Accept my tears yet, prithee; they are tokens
Of charity as true as of affection.

Kath. This is the cruell'st farewell!

Hunt. Love, young gentleman,
This model of my griefs; she calls you husband;
Then be not jealous of a parting kiss,—
It is a father's, not a lover's offering;
Take it, my last [*Kisses her*].—I am too much a child.
Exchange of passion is to little use,
So I should grow too foolish: goodness guide thee!
[*Exit.*

Kath. Most miserable daughter!—Have you aught
To add, sir, to our sorrows?

Dal. I resolve,
Fair lady, with your leave, to wait on all
Your fortunes in my person, if your lord
Vouchsafe me entertainment.

War. We will be bosom-friends, most noble Dalyell;[10]
For I accept this tender of your love

[10] *most noble Dalyell;*] Noble indeed! No drama that I am acquainted with offers four such admirable characters as Huntley and his daughter, the Lady Jane, and Dalyell. Of the Lady Jane Douglas, who follows Katherine with such affectionate duty, I have nothing with certainty to say. It is not improbable that she was one of the numerous daughters of George fourth Earl of Angus, among whom I find a *Joan* or Joanna.

Beyond ability of thanks to speak it.—
Clear thy drown'd eyes, my fairest: time and industry,
Will show us better days, or end the worst. [*Exeunt.*

SCENE IV. *The palace at Westminster.*

Enter Oxford *and* DAWBENEY.

Oxf. No news from Scotland yet, my lord?
Daw. Not any
But what King Henry knows himself: I thought
Our armies should have march'd that way; his mind,
It seems, is alter'd.
Oxf. Victory attends
His standard everywhere.
Daw. Wise princes, Oxford,
Fight not alone with forces. Providence
Directs and tutors strength; else elephants
And barbèd horses might as well prevail
As the most subtle stratagems of war.
Oxf. The Scottish king show'd more than common bravery
In proffer of a combat hand to hand
With Surrey.
Daw. And but show'd it: northern bloods
Are gallant being fir'd; but the cold climate,
Without good store of fuel, quickly freezeth
The glowing flames.
Oxf. Surrey, upon my life,
Would not have shrunk an hair's-breadth.
Daw. May he forfeit
The honour of an English name and nature,
Who would not have embrac'd it with a greediness
As violent as hunger runs to food!

'Twas an addition any worthy spirit
Would covet, next to immortality,
Above all joys of life: we all miss'd shares
In that great opportunity.

Enter King HENRY, *in close conversation with* URSWICK.

Oxf. The king!
See, he comes smiling.
Daw. O, the game runs smooth
On his side, then, believe it: cards well shuffled
And dealt with cunning bring some gamester thrift,
But others must rise losers.
K. Hen. The train takes?
Urs. Most prosperously.
K. Hen. I knew it should[11] not miss.
He fondly angles who will hurl his bait
Into the water 'cause the fish at first
Plays round about the line and dares not bite.—
Lords, we may reign your king yet: Dawbeney, Oxford,
Urswick, must Perkin wear the crown?
Daw. A slave!
Oxf. A vagabond!
Urs. A glow-worm!
K. Hen. Now, if Frion,
His practis'd politician, wear a brain
Of proof, King Perkin will in progress ride
Through all his large dominions; let us meet him,
And tender homage: ha, sirs! liegemen ought
To pay their fealty.
Daw. Would the rascal were,
With all his rabble, within twenty miles
Of London!

[11] *should*] Gifford printed "could." D.

K. Hen. Farther off is near enough
To lodge him in his home: I'll wager odds,
Surrey and all his men are either idle
Or hasting back; they have not work, I doubt,
To keep them busy.

Daw. 'Tis a strange conceit, sir.

K. Hen. Such voluntary favours as our people
In duty aid us with, we never scatter'd
On cobweb parasites, or lavish'd out
In riot or a needless hospitality:
No undeserving favourite doth boast
His issues from our treasury; our charge
Flows through all Europe, proving us but steward
Of every contribution which provides
Against the creeping canker of disturbance.
Is it not rare, then, in this toil of state
Wherein we are embark'd, with breach of sleep,
Cares, and the noise of trouble, that our mercy
Returns nor thanks nor comfort? Still the West
Murmur and threaten innovation,
Whisper our government tyrannical,
Deny us what is ours, nay, spurn their lives,
Of which they are but owners by our gift:
It must not be.

Oxf. It must not, should not.

Enter a Messenger *with a packet.*

K. Hen. So then—
To whom?

Mess. This packet to your sacred majesty.

K. Hen. Sirrah, attend without. [*Exit Mess.*

Oxf. News from the North, upon my life.

Daw. Wise Henry
Divines aforehand of events; with him
Attempts and execution are one act.

K. Hen. Urswick, thine ear: Frion is caught; the man
Of cunning is outreach'd; we must be safe.
Should reverend Morton, our archbishop, move
To a translation higher yet,[12] I tell thee
My Durham owns a brain deserves that see;
He's nimble in his industry, and mounting—
Thou hear'st me?

Urs. And conceive your highness fitly.

K. Hen. Dawbeney and Oxford, since our army stands
Entire, it were a weakness to admit
The rust of laziness to eat amongst them:
Set forward toward Salisbury; the plains
Are most commodious for their exercise.
Ourself will take a muster of them there;
And or disband them with reward, or else
Dispose as best concerns us.

Daw. Salisbury!
Sir, all is peace at Salisbury.

K. Hen. Dear friend,
The charge must be our own; we would a little
Partake the pleasure with our subjects' ease.—
Shall I entreat your loves?

Oxf. Command our lives.

K. Hen. Ye're men know how to do, not to fore-think.
My bishop is a jewel tried and perfect;
A jewel, lords. The post who brought these letters
Must speed another to the Mayor of Exeter;

[12] *To a translation* higher *yet,*] i.e. *to heaven.* Moreton was at this time Archbishop of Canterbury. He died about three years after this period, at the great age of ninety. The King seems to have changed his opinion with respect to Fox, who was removed on the archbishop's death, not to Canterbury, but to Winchester, in which see he died. Moreton and Fox were fast friends; they rank high among our prelates, and were, in fact, both very eminent men.

Urswick, dismiss him not.
Urs. He waits your pleasure.
K. Hen. Perkin a king? a king!
Urs. My gracious lord,—
K. Hen. Thoughts busied in the sphere of royalty
Fix not on creeping worms without their stings,
Mere excrements of earth. The use of time
Is thriving safety, and a wise prevention
Of ills expected. We're resolv'd for Salisbury.
[*Exeunt.*

SCENE V. *The coast of Cornwall.*

A general shout within. Enter WARBECK, DALYELL, KATHERINE, *and* JANE.

War. After so many storms as wind and seas
Have threaten'd to our weather-beaten ships,
At last, sweet fairest, we are safe arriv'd
On our dear mother earth, ingrateful only
To heaven and us in yielding sustenance
To sly usurpers of our throne and right.
These general acclamations are an omen
Of happy process to their welcome lord:
They flock in troops, and from all parts with wings
Of duty fly to lay their hearts before us.—
Unequall'd pattern of a matchless wife,
How fares my dearest yet?
Kath. Confirm'd in health,
By which I may the better undergo
The roughest face of change; but I shall learn
Patience to hope, since silence courts affliction,
For comforts, to this truly noble gentleman,—
Rare unexampled pattern of a friend!—
And my belovèd Jane, the willing follower
Of all misfortunes.

Dal. Lady, I return
But barren crops of early protestations,
Frost-bitten in the spring of fruitless hopes.

Jane. I wait but as the shadow to the body;
For, madam, without you let me be nothing.

War. None talk of sadness; we are on the way
Which leads to victory: keep cowards thoughts
With desperate sullenness! The lion faints not
Lock'd in a grate, but loose disdains all force
Which bars his prey,—and we are lion-hearted,—
Or else no king of beasts. [*Another general shout within.*]—Hark, how they shout,
Triumphant in our cause! bold confidence
Marches on bravely, cannot quake at danger.

Enter SKELTON.

Skelt. Save King Richard the Fourth! save thee, king of hearts! The Cornish blades are men of mettle; have proclaimed, through Bodmin[13] and the whole county, my sweet prince Monarch of England: four thousand tall yeomen, with bow and sword, already vow to live and die at the foot of King Richard.

Enter ASTLEY.

Ast. The mayor, our fellow-counsellor, is servant for an emperor. Exeter is appointed for the rendezvous, and nothing wants to victory but courage and resolution. *Sigillatum et datum decimo Septembris, anno regni regis primo, et cætera; confirmatum est.* All's cock-sure.

War. To Exeter! to Exeter, march on!
Commend us to our people: we in person
Will lend them double spirits; tell them so.

Skelt. and Ast. King Richard, King Richard!
[*Exeunt Skelt. and Ast.*

[13] *Bodmin*] The 4to has "Bodnam;" and so Gifford. D.

War. A thousand blessings guard our lawful arms!
A thousand horrors pierce our enemies' souls!
Pale fear unedge their weapons' sharpest points!
And when they draw their arrows to the head,
Numbness shall strike their sinews! Such advantage
Hath Majesty in its pursuit of justice,
That on the proppers-up of Truth's old throne
It both enlightens counsel and gives heart
To execution; whiles the throats of traitors
Lie bare before our mercy. O, divinity
Of royal birth! how it strikes dumb the tongues
Whose prodigality of breath is brib'd
By trains to greatness! Princes are but men
Distinguish'd in the fineness of their frailty,
Yet not so gross in beauty of the mind;
For there's a fire more sacred purifies
The dross of mixture. Herein stand the odds,
Subjects are men on earth, kings men and gods.
[*Exeunt.*

ACT V.

SCENE I. *Saint Michael's Mount,*[1] *Cornwall.*

Enter KATHERINE *and* JANE *in riding-suits, with one Servant.*

Kath. It is decreed; and we must yield to fate,
Whose angry justice, though it threaten ruin,
Contempt, and poverty, is all but trial
Of a weak woman's constancy in suffering.
Here, in a stranger's and an enemy's land,

[1] *Saint Michael's Mount,*] It appears that when Perkin marched on his ill-fated expedition Lady Katherine was left at this place, from which she was now preparing to withdraw, on some rumours of her husband's want of success.

Forsaken and unfurnish'd of all hopes
But such as wait on misery, I range,
To meet affliction wheresoe'er I tread.
My train and pomp of servants is reduc'd
To one kind gentlewoman and this groom.—
Sweet Jane, now whither must we?

Jane. To your ships,
Dear lady, and turn home.

Kath. Home! I have none.
Fly thou to Scotland; thou hast friends will weep
For joy to bid thee welcome; but, O, Jane,
My Jane! my friends are desperate of comfort,
As I must be of them: the common charity,
Good people's alms and prayers of the gentle,
Is the revenue must support my state.
As for my native country, since it once
Saw me a princess in the height of greatness
My birth allow'd me, here I make a vow
Scotland shall never see me being fall'n
Or lessen'd in my fortunes. Never, Jane,
Never to Scotland more will I return.
Could I be England's queen,—a glory, Jane,
I never fawn'd on,—yet the king who gave me
Hath sent me with my husband from his presence,
Deliver'd us suspected to his nation,
Render'd us spectacles to time and pity;
And is it fit I should return to such
As only listen after our descent
From happiness enjoy'd to misery
Expected, though uncertain? Never, never!
Alas, why dost thou weep? and that poor creature
Wipe his wet cheeks too? let me feel alone
Extremities, who know to give them harbour;
Nor thou nor he has cause: you may live safely.

Jane. There is no safety whiles your dangers, madam,

Are every way apparent.
Serv. Pardon, lady,
I cannot choose but show my honest heart;
You were ever my good lady.
Kath. O, dear souls,
Your shares in grief are too-too much!

Enter DALYELL.

Dal. I bring,
Fair princess, news of further sadness yet
Than your sweet youth hath been acquainted with.
Kath. Not more, my lord, than I can welcome: speak it;
The worst, the worst I look for.
Dal. All the Cornish
At Exeter were by the citizens
Repuls'd, encounter'd by the Earl of Devonshire
And other worthy gentlemen of the country.
Your husband march'd to Taunton, and was there
Affronted by King Henry's chamberlain;[2]
The king himself in person with his army
Advancing nearer, to renew the fight
On all occasions: but the night before
The battles were to join, your husband privately,
Accompanied with some few horse, departed
From out the camp, and posted none knows whither.
Kath. Fled without battle given?

[2] Affronted *by King Henry's chamberlain;*] i.e. *met directly in front* by Dawbeney. It is sufficiently clear, from the exulting language of this wily monarch in the scene with Urswick, p. 191, that he had made himself sure of the overthrow of Warbeck, whom he had by this time environed with his agents: hence the disgraceful flight of the usurper, the recourse to the sanctuary of Bewley, and subsequent surrender. Bacon shrewdly observes on this occasion, that "the king was . . . grown to be such a partner with Fortune, as nobody could tell what actions the one, and what the other, owned. For it was believed generally," he adds, "that Perkin was betrayed, and that" the king "had him all the time of his flight in a line;" a fact to which he does not seem disposed to give credit.

Dal. Fled, but follow'd
By Dawbeney; all his parties left to taste
King Henry's mercy,[3]—for to that they yielded,—
Victorious without bloodshed.

Kath. O, my sorrows!
If both our lives had prov'd the sacrifice
To Henry's tyranny, we had fall'n like princes,
And robb'd him of the glory of his pride.

Dal. Impute it not to faintness or to weakness
Of noble courage, lady, but [to] foresight;
For by some secret friend he had intelligence
Of being bought and sold by his base followers.
Worse yet remains untold.

Kath. No, no, it cannot.

Dal. I fear you are betray'd: the Earl of Oxford
Runs hot in your pursuit.[4]

---

[3] *all his parties left to taste*
King Henry's mercy.] The construction is—"all his parties (partisans) *were* [*being*?] left to taste King Henry's mercy."

[4] *the Earl of Oxford*
Runs hot in your pursuit.] "There were also sent," Lord Bacon says, "with all speed some horse to St. Michael's Mount in Cornwall, where the Lady Katherine Gordon was left by her husband, whom in all fortunes she entirely loved, adding the virtues of a wife to the virtues of her sex." The reader, in whose breast the extraordinary merits of this high-born lady can scarcely fail to have created some degree of interest, will not be displeased, perhaps, with the brief recital of her subsequent fortunes, as given by Sir R. Gordon, whom Douglas calls the historian of the family. After quoting the preceding passage from Bacon, Sir Robert adds; "shoe wes brought from St. Michael's Mount in Cornuall, and delyvered to King Henrie the Seaventh, who intertayned her honorablie, and for her better mantenance, according to her birth and vertue, did assigne vnto her good lands and rents for all the dayes of her lyff. After the death of her husband Richard, shoe mareid Sir Mathie Cradock (a man of great power at that tyme in Clamorganshyre in Wales), of the which mariage is descended this William Earle of Pembroke, by his grandmother, and had some lands by inheritance from the Cradockes. Lady Katheren Gordon died in Wales, and was buried in a chappell at one of the Earle of Pembrok his dwelling-places in that cuntrey. The Englesh histories doe much commend her for her beauty, comliness, and chastetie." It would be a pity to omit the pretty passage with which Bacon winds-up her eventful story; "the name of the White Rose, which had been given to her husband's false title, was continued in common speech to her true beauty."

Kath. He shall not need;
We'll run as hot in resolution gladly
To make the earl our jailor.

Jane. Madam, madam,
They come, they come!

Enter OXFORD *with his Followers.*

Dal. Keep back! or he who dares
Rudely to violate the law of honour
Runs on my sword.

Kath. Most noble sir, forbear.—
What reason draws you hither, gentlemen?
Whom seek ye?

Oxf. All stand off!—With favour, lady,
From Henry, England's king, I would present
Unto the beauteous princess, Katherine Gordon,
The tender of a gracious entertainment.

Kath. We are that princess, whom your master-king
Pursues with reaching arms to draw into
His power: let him use his tyranny,
We shall not be his subject.[5]

Oxf. My commission
Extends no further, excellentest lady,
Than to a service; 'tis King Henry's pleasure
That you, and all that have relation t'ye,
Be guarded as becomes your birth and greatness;
For, rest assur'd, sweet princess, that not aught
Of what you do call yours shall find disturbance,
Or any welcome other than what suits
Your high condition.

Kath. By what title, sir,
May I acknowledge you?

Oxf. Your servant, lady,
Descended from the line of Oxford's Earls,

[5] *subject.*] The 4to has "Subjects;" and so Gifford. D.

Inherits what his ancestors before him
Were owners of.
Kath. Your king is herein royal,
That by a peer so ancient in desert
As well as blood commands us to his presence.
Oxf. Invites ye, princess, not commands.
Kath. Pray use
Your own phrase as you list: to your protection
Both I and mine submit.
Oxf. There's in your number
A nobleman whom fame hath bravely spoken.
To him the king my master bade me say
How willingly he courts his friendship; far
From an enforcement, more than what in terms
Of courtesy so great a prince may hope for.
Dal. My name is Dalyell.
Oxf. 'Tis a name hath won
Both thanks and wonder from report, my lord:
The court of England emulates your merit,
And covets to embrace ye.
Dal. I must wait on
The princess in her fortunes.
Oxf. Will you please,
Great lady, to set forward?
Kath. Being driven
By fate, it were in vain to strive with heaven. [*Exeunt.*

SCENE II. *Salisbury.*

Enter King HENRY, Surrey, URSWICK, *and a guard of Soldiers.*

K. Hen. The counterfeit, King Perkin, is escap'd:—
Escap'd![6] so let him; he is hedg'd too fast
Within the circuit of our English pale

[6] *Escap'd!*] The 4to has "Escape;" and so Gifford. D.

To steal out of our ports, or leap the walls
Which guard our land; the seas are rough and wider
Than his weak arms can tug with. Surrey, henceforth
Your king may reign in quiet; turmoils past,
Like some unquiet dream, have rather busied
Our fancy than affrighted rest of state.
But, Surrey, why,[7] in articling a peace
With James of Scotland, was not restitution
Of losses which our subjects did sustain
By the Scotch inroads question'd?

Sur. Both demanded
And urg'd, my lord; to which the king replied,
In modest merriment, but smiling earnest,
How that our master Henry was much abler
To bear the detriments than he repay them.

K. Hen. The young man, I believe, spake honest truth;
He studies to be wise betimes.—Has, Urswick,
Sir Rice ap Thomas, and Lord Brook our steward,
Return'd the Western gentlemen full thanks
From us for their tried loyalties?

Urs. They have;
Which, as if health and life[8] had reign'd amongst 'em,
With open hearts they joyfully receiv'd.

K. Hen. Young Buckingham is a fair-natur'd prince,
Lovely in hopes, and worthy of his father;

[7] *But, Surrey, why,* &c.] Henry seems to have taken an odd time to question Surrey on this point. Perhaps the poet here, as in a former scene, intended to characterise the eager cupidity of the king, always alive to his pecuniary interests. The passage stands thus in Bacon; "The Bishop (Fox) also . . . demanded restitution of the spoils taken by the Scotish, or damages for the same. But the Scotish commissioners answered, that that was but as water spilt upon the ground, which could not be gotten up again; and that the king's people *were better able to bear the loss than their master to repair it.*"

[8] *health and life*] Altered by Gifford to "life and health:" but the reading of the old copy is a not indefensible sort of hysteron-proteron. D.

Attended by an hundred knights and squires
Of special name he tender'd humble service,
Which we must ne'er forget: and Devonshire's wounds,
Though slight, shall find sound cure in our respect.

Enter DAWBENEY *with a Guard, leading in* WARBECK, HERON, JOHN A-WATER, ASTLEY, *and* SKELTON, *chained.*

Daw. Life to the king, and safety fix his throne!
I here present you, royal sir, a shadow
Of majesty, but in effect a substance
Of pity; a young man, in nothing grown
To ripeness but th' ambition of your mercy,—
Perkin, the Christian world's strange wonder.

K. Hen. Dawbeney,
We observe no wonder: I behold, 'tis true,
An ornament of nature, fine and polish'd,
A handsome youth indeed, but not admire him.
How came he to thy hands?

Daw. From sanctuary
At Bewley, near Southampton; register'd,
With these few followers, for persons privileg'd.

K. Hen. I must not thank you, sir; you were to blame
T' infringe the liberty of houses sacred:
Dare we be irreligious?

Daw. Gracious lord,
They voluntarily resign'd themselves
Without compulsion.

K. Hen. So? 'twas very well;
'Twas very, very well.—Turn now thine eyes,
Young man, upon thyself and thy past actions;
What revels in combustion through our kingdom
A frenzy of aspiring youth hath danc'd,
Till, wanting breath, thy feet of pride have slipt

To break thy neck!
War. But not my heart; my heart
Will mount till every drop of blood be frozen
By death's perpetual winter: if the sun
Of majesty be darken'd, let the sun
Of life be hid from me in an eclipse
Lasting and universal. Sir, remember
There was a shooting-in of light when Richmond,
Not aiming at a crown, retir'd, and gladly,
For comfort to the Duke of Bretaine's court.
Richard, who sway'd the sceptre, was reputed
A tyrant then; yet then a dawning glimmer'd
To some few wandering remnants, promising day
When first they ventur'd on a frightful shore
At Milford Haven;—
Daw. Whither speeds his boldness?
Check his rude tongue, great sir.
K. Hen. O, let him range:
The player's on the stage still, 'tis his part;
He does but act.—What follow'd?
War. Bosworth Field;
Where, at an instant, to the world's amazement,
A morn to Richmond, and a night to Richard,
Appear'd at once: the tale is soon applied;
Fate, which crown'd these attempts when least assur'd,
Might have befriended others like resolv'd.
K. Hen. A pretty gallant! Thus, your aunt of Burgundy,
Your duchess-aunt, inform'd her nephew; so,
The lesson prompted and well conn'd, was moulded
Into familiar dialogue, oft rehears'd,
Till, learnt by heart, 'tis now receiv'd for truth.
War. Truth, in her pure simplicity, wants art
To put a feignèd blush on: scorn wears only
Such fashion as commends to gazers' eyes

Sad ulcerated novelty, far beneath
The sphere of majesty: in such a court
Wisdom and gravity are proper robes,
By which the sovereign is best distinguish'd
From zanies to his greatness.

K. Hen. Sirrah, shift
Your antic pageantry, and now appear
In your own nature, or you'll taste the danger
Of fooling out of season.

War. I expect
No less than what severity calls justice,
And politicians safety; let such beg
As feed on alms: but if there can be mercy
In a protested enemy, then may it
Descend to these poor creatures, whose engagements,
To th' bettering of their fortunes, have incurr'd
A loss of all; to them if any charity
Flow from some noble orator, in death
I owe the fee of thankfulness.

K. Hen. So brave!
What a bold knave is this!—Which of these rebels
Has been the Mayor of Cork?

Daw. This wise formality.—
Kneel to the king, ye rascals! [*They kneel.*

K. Hen. Canst thou hope
A pardon, where thy guilt is so apparent?

J. a-Wat. Under your good favours, as men are men, they may err; for I confess, respectively, in taking great parts, the one side prevailing, the other side must go down: herein the point is clear, if the proverb hold, that hanging goes by destiny, that it is to little purpose to say, this thing or that shall be thus or thus; for, as the Fates will have it, so it must be; and who can help it?

Daw. O, blockhead! thou a privy-counsellor?
Beg life, and cry aloud, "Heaven save King Henry!"

J. a-Wat. Every man knows what is best, as it happens; for my own part, I believe it is true, if I be not deceived, that kings must be kings and subjects subjects; but which is which, you shall pardon me for that: whether we speak or hold our peace, all are mortal; no man knows his end.

K. Hen. We trifle time with follies.

Her. John a-W. Ast. Skelt. Mercy, mercy!

K. Hen. Urswick, command the dukeling and these fellows [*They rise.*
To Digby, the Lieutenant of the Tower:
With safety let them be convey'd to London.
It is our pleasure no uncivil outrage,
Taunts or abuse be suffer'd to their persons;
They shall meet fairer law than they deserve.
Time may restore their wits, whom vain ambition
Hath many years distracted.

War. Noble thoughts
Meet freedom in captivity: the Tower,—
Our childhood's dreadful nursery!

K. Hen. No more!

Urs. Come, come, you shall have leisure to bethink ye.

[*Exit Urs. with Perk. and his Followers, guarded.*

K. Hen. Was ever so much impudence in forgery?
The custom, sure, of being styl'd a king
Hath fasten'd in his thought that he is such;
But we shall teach the lad another language:
'Tis good we have him fast.

Daw. The hangman's physic
Will purge this saucy humour.

K. Hen. Very likely;

Yet we could temper mercy with extremity,
Being not too far provok'd.

Enter OXFORD, KATHERINE *in her richest attire*, DALYELL, JANE, *and Attendants.*

Oxf. Great sir, be pleas'd,
With your accustom'd grace to entertain
The Princess Katherine Gordon.

K. Hen. Oxford, herein
We must beshrew thy knowledge of our nature.
A lady of her birth and virtues could not
Have found us so unfurnish'd of good manners
As not, on notice given, to have met her
Half way in point of love.—Excuse, fair cousin,
The oversight: O, fie! you may not kneel;
'Tis most unfitting: first, vouchsafe this welcome,
A welcome to your own; for you shall find us
But guardian to your fortune[s] and your honours.

Kath. My fortunes and mine honours are weak champions,
As both are now befriended, sir: however,
Both bow before your clemency.

K. Hen. Our arms
Shall circle them from malice—A sweet lady!
Beauty incomparable!—here lives majesty
At league with love.

Kath. O, sir, I have a husband.

K. Hen. We'll prove your father, husband, friend, and servant,
Prove what you wish to grant us.—Lords, be careful
A patent presently be drawn for issuing
A thousand pounds from our exchequer yearly
During our cousin's life.—Our queen shall be
Your chief companion, our own court your home,
Our subjects all your servants.

Kath. But my husband?

K. Hen. By all descriptions, you are noble Dalyell,
Whose generous truth hath fam'd a rare observance.
We thank ye; 'tis a goodness gives addition
To every title boasted from your ancestry,
In all most worthy.

Dal. Worthier than your praises,
Right princely sir, I need not glory in.

K. Hen. Embrace him, lords.—Whoever calls you mistress
Is lifted in our charge.—A goodlier beauty
Mine eyes yet ne'er encounter'd.

Kath. Cruel misery
Of fate! what rests to hope for?

K. Hen. Forward, lords,
To London.—Fair, ere long I shall present ye
With a glad object, peace, and Huntley's blessing.
[*Exeunt.*

SCENE III. *London. The Tower-hill.*

Enter Constable *and* Officers, WARBECK, URSWICK, *and* LAMBERT SIMNEL *as a falconer, followed by the rabble.*

Const. Make room there! keep off, I require ye; and none come within twelve foot of his majesty's new stocks, upon pain of displeasure.—Bring forward the malefactors.—Friend, you must to this gear, no remedy.—Open the hole, and in with his[9] legs, just in the middle hole; there, that hole. [*Warbeck is put in the stocks.*]—Keep off, or I'll commit you all: shall not a man in authority be obeyed?—So, so, there; 'tis as it should be: put on the padlock, and give me the key.—Off, I say, keep off!

[9] *his*] Gifford printed "the." D.

Urs. Yet, Warbeck, clear thy conscience: thou
hast tasted
King Henry's mercy liberally; the law
Has forfeited thy life; an equal jury
Have doom'd thee to the gallows; twice most wickedly,
Most desperately, hast thou escap'd the Tower,
Inveigling to thy party with thy witchcraft
Young Edward Earl of Warwick, son to Clarence,
Whose head must pay the price of that attempt;
Poor gentleman, unhappy in his fate,
And ruin'd by thy cunning! so a mongrel
May pluck the true stag down. Yet, yet, confess
Thy parentage; for yet the king has mercy.

Sim. You would be Dick the Fourth; very likely!
Your pedigree is publish'd;[10] you are known
For Osbeck's son of Tournay, a loose runagate,
A landloper; your father was a Jew,
Turn'd Christian merely to repair his miseries:
Where's now your kingship?

War. Baited to my death?
Intolerable cruelty! I laugh at
The Duke of Richmond's practice on my fortunes:
Possession of a crown ne'er wanted heralds.

Sim. You will not know who I am?

Urs. Lambert Simnel,
Your predecessor in a dangerous uproar;

[10] *Your pedigree is publish'd,* &c.] From Bacon; "Thus therefore it came to pass. There was a townsman of Tournay . . . whose name was John Osbeck, a converted Jew, married to Katherine de Faro, whose business drew him to live for a time with his wife at London, in King Edward the IVth's days. During which time he had a son by her; and being known in court, the king . . . did him the honour as to be godfather to his child, and named him *Peter.* But afterwards proving a dainty and effeminate youth, he was commonly called by the diminutive of his name, *Peter-kin* or Perkin." The term landloper, applied to him by Simnel, is also from the historian; "He (Perkin) had been from his childhood such a *wanderer,* or, as the king called it, such a *landloper,* as it was extreme hard to hunt out his nest."

But, on submission, not alone receiv'd
To grace, but by the king vouchsaf'd his service.

Simn. I would be Earl of Warwick, toil'd and ruffled
Against my master, leap'd to catch the moon,
Vaunted my name Plantagenet, as you do;
An earl, forsooth! whenas in truth I was,
As you are, a mere rascal: yet his majesty,
A prince compos'd of sweetness,—Heaven protect him!—
Forgave me all my villanies, repriev'd
The sentence of a shameful end, admitted
My surety of obedience to his service,
And I am now his falconer; live plenteously,
Eat from the king's purse, and enjoy the sweetness
Of liberty and favour; sleep securely:
And is not this, now, better than to buffet
The hangman's clutches, or to brave the cordage
Of a tough halter which will break your neck?
So, then, the gallant totters!—prithee, Perkin,
Let my example lead thee; be no longer
A counterfeit; confess, and hope for pardon.

War. For pardon! hold, my heart-strings, whiles contempt
Of injuries, in scorn, may bid defiance
To this base man's foul language!—Thou poor vermin,
How dar'st thou creep so near me? thou an earl!
Why, thou enjoy'st as much of happiness
As all the swing of slight ambition flew at.
A dunghill was thy cradle. So a puddle,
By virtue of the sunbeams, breathes a vapour
T' infect the purer air, which drops again
Into the muddy womb that first exhal'd it.
Bread and a slavish ease, with some assurance

From the base beadle's whip, crown'd all thy hopes:
But, sirrah, ran there in thy veins one drop
Of such a royal blood as flows in mine,
Thou wouldst not change condition, to be second
In England's state, without the crown itself.
Coarse creatures are incapable of excellence:
But let the world, as all to whom I am
This day a spectacle, to time deliver,
And by tradition fix posterity
Without another chronicle than truth,
How constantly my resolution suffer'd
A martyrdom of majesty.

Simn. He's past
Recovery; a Bedlam cannot cure him.

Urs. Away, inform the king of his behaviour.

Simn. Perkin, beware the rope! the hangman's coming. [*Exit.*

Urs. If yet thou hast no pity of thy body,
Pity thy soul!

Enter KATHERINE, JANE, DALYELL, *and* Oxford.

Jane. Dear lady!—

Oxf. Whither will ye,
Without respect of shame?

Kath. Forbear me, sir,
And trouble not the current of my duty.—
O, my lov'd lord! can any scorn be yours
In which I have no interest?—Some kind hand
Lend me assistance, that I may partake
Th' infliction of this penance.—My life's dearest,
Forgive me; I have stay'd too long from tendering
Attendance on reproach; yet bid me welcome.

War. Great miracle of constancy! my miseries
Were never bankrupt of their confidence
In worst afflictions, till this; now I feel them.

Report and thy deserts, thou best of creatures,
Might to eternity have stood a pattern
For every virtuous wife without this conquest.
Thou hast outdone belief; yet may their ruin
In after-marriages be never pitied,
To whom thy story shall appear a fable!
Why wouldst thou prove so much unkind to greatness
To glorify thy vows by such a servitude?
I cannot weep; but trust me, dear, my heart
Is liberal of passion.—Harry Richmond,
A woman's faith hath robb'd thy fame of triumph!

Oxf. Sirrah, leave-off your juggling, and tie up
The devil that ranges in your tongue.

Urs. Thus witches,
Possess'd, even [to] their deaths deluded,[11] say
They have been wolves and dogs, and sail'd in egg-shells
Over the sea, and rid on fiery dragons,
Pass'd in the air more than a thousand miles,
All in a night:—the enemy of mankind
Is powerful, but false, and falsehood confident.[12]

Oxf. Remember, lady, who you are; come from
That impudent impostor.

Kath. You abuse us:
For when the holy churchman join'd our hands,
Our vows were real then; the ceremony
Was not in apparition, but in act.—
Be what these people term thee, I am certain

11 *Thus witches,*
Possess'd, even [to] *their deaths deluded,* &c.] The old copy is imperfect here; it reads,

"Possess'd, *even* their deaths deluded," &c.

Perhaps it may be set right by a change still more slight than that of the text, by reading "*e'en in*" for "*even.*" Of the fact itself the age of our poet afforded unfortunately too many instances.

12 *and falsehood confident.*] Gifford unnecessarily printed "*and falsehood*'s *confident.*" D.

Thou art my husband, no divorce in heaven
Has been su'd-out between us; 'tis injustice
For any earthly power to divide us:
Or we will live or let us die together.
There is a cruel mercy.

War. Spite of tyranny
We reign in our affections, blessèd woman!
Read in my destiny the wreck of honour;
Point out, in my contempt of death, to memory
Some miserable happiness; since herein,
Even when I fell, I stood enthron'd a monarch
Of one chaste wife's troth pure and uncorrupted.
Fair angel of perfection, immortality
Shall raise thy name up to an adoration,
Court every rich opinion of true merit,
And saint it in the Calendar of Virtue,
When I am turn'd into the self-same dust
Of which I was first form'd.

Oxf. The lord ambassador,
Huntley, your father, madam, should he look on
Your strange subjection in a gaze so public,
Would blush on your behalf, and wish his country
Unleft for entertainment to such sorrow.

Kath. Why art thou angry, Oxford? I must be
More peremptory in my duty.—Sir,
Impute it not unto immodesty
That I presume to press you to a legacy
Before we part for ever.

War. Let it be, then,
My heart, the rich remains of all my fortunes.

Kath. Confirm it with a kiss, pray.

War. O, with that
I wish to breathe my last! upon thy lips,
Those equal twins of comeliness, I seal
The testament of honourable vows: [*Kisses her.*

Whoever be that man that shall unkiss
This sacred print next, may he prove more thrifty
In this world's just applause, not more desertful!

Kath. By this sweet pledge of both our souls, I swear
To die a faithful widow to thy bed;
Not to be forc'd or won: O, never, never![13]

Enter SURREY, DAWBENEY, HUNTLEY, *and* CRAWFORD.

Daw. Free the condemnèd person; quickly free him!
What has he yet confess'd?

[*Warbeck is taken out of the stocks.*

Urs. Nothing to purpose;
But still he will be king.

Sur. Prepare your journey
To a new kingdom, then, unhappy madman,[14]
Wilfully foolish!—See, my lord ambassador,
Your lady daughter will not leave the counterfeit
In this disgrace of fate.

Hunt. I never pointed
Thy marriage, girl; but yet, being married,
Enjoy thy duty to a husband freely.
The griefs are mine. I glory in thy constancy;
And must not say I wish that I had miss'd
Some partage in these trials of a patience.

Kath. You will forgive me, noble sir?

Hunt. Yes, yes;
In every duty of a wife and daughter

[13] The better genius of Ford, which had so admirably served him hitherto, appears to have *left his side* at this moment; he would not else have permitted Katherine to injure herself by a speech for which there was not the slightest occasion. She should have had nothing in common with the *Player Queen* [in *Hamlet*. D.], no, not even an oath.

[14] *unhappy* madman,
Wilfully foolish!] The 4to, by an unlucky transposition, reads "*madam.*"

I dare not disavow thee. To your husband,—
For such you are, sir,—I impart a farewell
Of manly pity; what your life has pass'd through,
The dangers of your end will make apparent;
And I can add, for comfort to your sufferance,
No cordial, but the wonder of your frailty,
Which keeps so firm a station. We are parted.

War. We are. A crown of peace renew thy age,
Most honourable Huntley!—Worthy Crawford!
We may embrace; I never thought thee injury.

Craw. Nor was I ever guilty of neglect
Which might procure such thought. I take my leave,
sir.

War. To you, Lord Dalyell,—what? accept a sigh,
'Tis hearty and in earnest.

Dal. I want utterance;
My silence is my farewell.

Kath. O, O!

Jane. Sweet madam,
What do you mean?—My lord, your hand. [*To Dal.*

Dal. Dear lady,
Be pleas'd that I may wait ye to your lodging.[15]
[*Exeunt Dal. and Jane, supporting Kath.*

Enter Sheriff *and* Officers *with* SKELTON, ASTLEY, HERON, *and* JOHN A-WATER, *with halters about their necks.*

Oxf. Look ye; behold your followers, appointed
To wait on ye in death!

War. Why, peers of England,
We'll lead 'em on courageously: I read
A triumph over tyranny upon
Their several foreheads.—Faint not in the moment
Of victory! our ends, and Warwick's head,

[15] *lodging.*] Gifford printed "lodgings." D.

Innocent Warwick's head,—for we are prologue
But to his tragedy,—conclude the wonder
Of Henry's fears;[16] and then the glorious race
Of fourteen kings, Plantagenets, determines
In this last issue male; Heaven be obey'd!
Impoverish time of its amazement, friends,
And we will prove as trusty in our payments
As prodigal to nature in our debts.
Death? pish! 'tis but a sound; a name of air;
A minute's storm, or not so much: to tumble
From bed to bed, be massacred alive
By some physicians, for a month or two,
In hope of freedom from a fever's torments,
Might stagger manhood; here the pain is past
Ere sensibly 'tis felt. Be men of spirit!
Spurn coward passion! so illustrious mention
Shall blaze our names, and style us Kings o'er Death.

Daw. Away, impostor beyond precedent!

[*Exeunt Sheriff and Officers with the Prisoners.*

No chronicle records his fellow.

Hunt. I have
Not thoughts left: 'tis sufficient in such cases
Just laws ought to proceed.

Enter King HENRY, Durham, *and* HIALAS.

K. Hen. We are resolv'd.
Your business, noble lords, shall find success
Such as your king impórtunes.

Hunt. You are gracious.

K. Hen. Perkin, we are inform'd, is arm'd to die;

[16] *our ends, and* Warwick's *head,—conclude the wonder Of Henry's fears;*] This poor prince, as Lord Bacon calls him, was undoubtedly sacrificed to the barbarous policy of the king. He was brought to trial almost immediately after Warbeck's death, condemned, and executed for conspiring with the former to raise sedition! He made no defence, and probably quitted without much regret a life that had never known one happy day.

In that we'll honour him. Our lords shall follow
To see the execution; and from hence
We gather this fit use,[17]—that public states,
As our particular bodies, taste most good
In health when purgèd of corrupted blood. [*Exeunt.*

[17] *We gather this fit* use,] The poet seems to apply this word in the puritanical sense (then sufficiently familiar) of doctrinal or practical deduction. See *Massinger*, vol. iii. p. 293, and *Jonson*, vol. vi. p. 55.

I cannot dismiss this "chronicle history," as Ford calls it, without observing that it has been much underrated. That the materials are borrowed from Lord Bacon is sufficiently clear; but the poet has arranged them with skill, and conducted his plot with considerable dexterity to the fatal catastrophe. Perkin is admirably drawn; and it would be unjust to the author to overlook the striking consistency with which he has marked his character. Whatever might be his own opinion of this person's pretensions, he has never suffered him to betray his identity with the Duke of York in a single thought or expression. Perkin has no soliloquies, no side-speeches, to compromise his public assertions; and it is pleasing to see with what ingenuity Ford has preserved him from the contamination of real history, and contrived to sustain his dignity to the last with all imaginable decorum, and thus rendered him a fit subject for the tragic Muse.

Of Huntley, the noble Huntley, and Dalyell, I have already spoken: the author seems, in truth, to have lavished most of his care on the Scotch characters, and with a success altogether proportioned to his exertions. Of his English personages much cannot be said, except, indeed, that he has given a most faithful portraiture of the cold, calculating, stern, shrewd, and avaricious Henry.

It is observable that the style of this piece, though occasionally deficient in animation, is more equable, clear, and dignified than that of any other of his works. It is such as the historic drama ought to appear in, and may justly excite some regret that the author had not more frequently taken his plots from our domestic struggles. Another thing, too, may be noticed. In most of his tragedies the trivial and comic personages are poorly drawn: if they attempt to be witty, they usually fall into low buffoonry; and if they aim at a scene of mirth, are sure to create sadness or disgust. The low characters of this play do neither. They are uniformly sustained; their language, though technical, is not repulsive; and the style of that "wise piece of formality," the Mayor of Cork, who does not venture on one positive expression from first to last, is not only supported with undeviating skill, but rendered really amusing.

EPILOGUE.

HERE has appear'd, though in a several fashion,
The threats of majesty, the strength of passion,
Hopes of an empire, change of fortunes ; all
What can to theatres of greatness fall,
Proving their weak foundations. Who will please,
Amongst such several sights, to censure these
No births abortive, nor[18] a bastard brood,—
Shame to a parentage or fosterhood,—
May warrant by their loves all just excuses,
And often find a welcome to the Muses.

[18] *nor*] Gifford printed "not." D.

THE

FANCIES CHASTE AND NOBLE.

The title-page of this comedy, of which there is but one edition, stands thus in the 4to; "The Fancies, Chast and Noble: Presented by the Queenes Maiesties Servants, At the Phœnix in Drury-lane. Fide Honor. London, Printed by E. P. for Henry Seile, and are to be sold at his shop, at the Tygers Head in Fleetstreet, over-against Saint Dunstans Church, 1638." It was probably licensed for the stage in 1637, as Ford brought out a new piece (*The Lady's Trial*) this year.

TO

THE RIGHT NOBLE LORD, THE LORD

RANDAL MACDONNELL,

EARL OF ANTRIM IN THE KINGDOM OF IRELAND, LORD VISCOUNT DUNLUCE.[1]

MY LORD,

PRINCES and worthy personages of your own eminence have entertained poems of this nature with a serious welcome. The desert of their authors might transcend mine, not their study of service. A practice of courtship to greatness hath not hitherto, in me, aimed at any thrift; yet I have ever honoured virtue, as the richest ornament to the noblest titles. Endeavour of being known to your lordship by such means I conceive no ambition, the extent being

[1] "This nobleman was the son of Sir Randal Macdonnell, who in his youth joined in Tyrone's rebellion, but subsequently became a loyal subject of King James, and contributed greatly to the civilisation of Ireland, for which service he was created successively Viscount Dunluce, and Earl of Antrim. He died 18th December 1636. The peer who succeeded him, and to whom the present play is dedicated, was born in 1609. He attended King Charles I. in his expedition against Scotland in 1639; was accused of joining the rebels in Ireland in 1642, but cleared; but subsequently joined them for the benefit of his royal master. He was twice imprisoned by Major-General Monro in Carrickfergus, but escaped both times. In 1643 he was created Marquis of Antrim. Though he made his peace with Cromwell, he assisted Charles II. in his escape after the battle of Worcester. He died in the year 1673, aged 64."

bounded by humility: so neither can the argument appear ungracious, nor the writer in that without allowance. You enjoy, my lord, the general suffrage for your freedom of merits: may you likewise please, by this particular presentment, amongst the number of such as faithfully honour those merits to admit[2] into your noble construction

JOHN FORD.

[2] *amongst the number of such as faithfully honour those merits to admit*, &c.] The 4to has "Amongst the number of such as *I* faithfully honour, those merits," &c.; which to me is unintelligible. There can be little doubt that the pronoun was inserted through mistake, or misapprehension of the poet's meaning; most probably the latter.—There is something pleasing in this short Dedication. It displays a spirit of independence very honourable to the poet, and yet is sufficiently respectful to his patron.

DRAMATIS PERSONÆ.

OCTAVIO, marquis of Sienna.
TROYLO-SAVELLI, his nephew.
LIVIO, brother to Castamela.
ROMANELLO, brother to Flavia.
JULIO DE VARANA, lord of Camerino.
CAMILLO, } attendants on Julio.
VESPUCCI, }
FABRICIO, a merchant, Flavia's first husband.
NITIDO, a page, }
SECCO, a barber, } attendants on the Marquis.
SPADONE, }

CASTAMELA, sister to Livio.
CLARELLA, }
SILVIA, } the Fancies.
FLORIA, }
FLAVIA, wife to Julio.
MOROSA, guardianess to the Fancies.

SCENE—*Sienna.*

PROLOGUE.

THE Fancies! that's our play: in it is shown
Nothing but what our author knows his own
Without a learnèd theft; no servant here
To some fair mistress borrows for his ear
His lock,[3] his belt, his sword, the fancied grace
Of any pretty ribbon; nor, in place
Of charitable friendship, is brought in
A thriving gamester, that doth chance to win
A lusty sum, while the good hand doth ply him,
And Fancies this or that to him sits by him.
His free invention runs but in conceit
Of mere imaginations; there's the height
Of what he writes; which if traduc'd by some,
'Tis well, he says, he's far enough from home.
For you, for him, for us, then this remains,
Fancy your own opinions[4] for our pains.

[3] *borrows for his ear*
His lock,] This allusion is to the ribbon, or love-lock, worn as an ornament in the ear. [A *love-lock* was a long lock of hair, often tied and plaited with ribbon, worn on the left side, and hanging down by the shoulder. D.]

[4] *Fancy your own opinions*] The old copy reads "Fancy your *even* opinions." Ford appears to have been on the Continent when this piece was first given to the stage.

THE

FANCIES CHASTE AND NOBLE.

ACT I.

SCENE I. *An apartment in the palace.*

Enter TROYLO-SAVELLI *and* LIVIO.

Troy. Do, do; be wilful-desperate; 'tis manly.
Build on your reputation! such a fortune
May furnish-out your tables, trim your liveries,
Enrich your heirs with purchase of a patrimony
Which shall hold-out beyond the waste of riot;
Stick honours on your heraldry, with titles
As swelling and as numerous as may likely
Grow to a pretty volume,—here's eternity!
All this can reputation, marry, can it;
Indeed, what not?
Liv. Such language from a gentleman
So noble in his quality as you are,
Deserves, in my weak judgment, rather pity
Than a contempt.
Troy. Couldst thou consider, Livio,
The fashion of the times, their study, practice,
Nay, their ambitions, thou wouldst soon distinguish
Betwixt the abject lowness of a poverty

And the applauded triumph[1] of abundance,
Though compass'd by the meanest service. Wherein
Shall you betray your guilt to common censure,
Waving the private charge of your opinion,
By rising up to greatness, or at least
To plenty, which now buys it?

Liv. Troylo-Savelli
Plays merrily on my wants.

Troy. Troylo-Savelli
Speaks to the friend he loves, to his own Livio.
Look, prithee, through the Great Duke's court in Florence,
Number his favourites, and then examine
By what steps some chief officers in state
Have reach'd the height they stand in.

Liv. By their merits.

Troy. Right, by their merits: well he merited
Th' intendments o'er the galleys at Ligorne,[2]—
Made grand collector of the customs there,—
Who led the prince unto his wife's chaste bed,
And stood himself by in his night-gown, fearing
The jest might be discover'd: was't not handsome?
The lady knows not yet on't.

Liv. Most impossible.

Troy. He merited well to wear a robe of chamlet
Who train'd his brother's daughter, scarce a girl,
Into the arms of Mont-Argentorato;[3]
Whiles the young lord of Telamon, her husband,
Was packeted to France to study courtship,[4]

[1] *triumph*] Gifford printed "triumphs." D.

[2] *Ligorne,*] Altered here by Gifford to "Leghorn:" but see vol. i. p. 141, where he retains the earlier form of the name. D.

[3] *Mont-Argentorato;*] The 4to has "*Mont-Angentorato.*" D.

[4] *to study* courtship,] i.e. the language and manners of a court. Thus Massinger;

"What she wanted
In *courtship* was, I hope, supplied in civil
And modest entertainment." *Great Duke of Florence.*

Under, forsooth, a colour of employment,—
Employment! yea, of honour.

Liv. You're well read
In mysteries of state.

Troy. Here in Sienna,
Bold Julio de Varana, lord of Camerine,
Held it no blemish to his blood and greatness
From a plain merchant with a thousand ducats
To buy his wife, nay, justify the purchase;
Procur'd it by a dispensation
From Rome, allow'd and warranted: 'twas thought
By his physicians that she was a creature
Agreed best with the cure of the disease
His present new infirmity then labour'd in.
Yet these are things in prospect of the world,
Advanc'd, employ'd, and eminent.

Liv. At best
'Tis but a goodly panderism.

Troy. Shrewd business!
Thou child in thrift, thou fool of honesty,
Is't a disparagement for gentlemen,
For friends of lower rank, to do the offices
Of necessary kindness without fee
For one another, courtesies of course,
Mirths of society; when petty mushrooms,
Transplanted from their dunghills, spread on mountains,
And pass for cedars by their servile flatteries
On great men's vices? Pander! thou'rt deceiv'd;
The word includes preferment; 'tis a title
Of dignity: I could add somewhat more else.

Liv. Add anything of reason.

Troy. Castamela,
Thy beauteous sister, like a precious tissue
Not shap'd into a garment fit for wearing,

Wants the adornments of the workman's cunning
To set the richness of the piece at view,
Though in herself all wonder. Come, I'll tell thee:
A way there may be—know, I love thee, Livio—
To fix this jewel in a ring of gold,
Yet lodge it in a cabinet of ivory,
White, pure, unspotted ivory: put case,
Livio himself shall keep the key on't?

Liv. O, sir,
Create me what you please of yours; do this,
You are another nature.

Troy. Be, then, pliable
To my first rules of your advancement.—See!
Octavio, my good uncle, the great Marquis
Of our Sienna, comes, as we could wish,
In private.

Enter OCTAVIO.[5]

Noble sir!

Oct. My bosom's secretary,
My dearest, best-lov'd nephew!

Troy. We've been thirsty
In our pursuit.[6]—Sir, here's a gentleman
Desertful of your knowledge, and as covetous
Of entertainment from it: you shall honour
Your judgment to intrust him to your favours;
His merits will commend it.

Oct. Gladly welcome;
Your own worth is a herald to proclaim it.
For taste of your preferment, we admit you
The chief provisor of our horse.

[5] Enter *Octavio.*] The 4to adds "and Nitido" (his page); which Gifford omitted, as inconsistent with the preceding "In private." D.

[6] *We've been* thirsty
In our pursuit.] i. e. sharp, eager, active.

Liv. Your bounty
Styles me your ever servant.
Troy. [*aside to Oct.*] He's our own;
Surely, nay, most persuadedly.—My thanks, sir,
Owes to this just engagement.[7]
Oct. Slack no time
To enter on your fortunes.—Thou art careful,
My Troylo, in the study of a duty.
His name is?—
Troy. Livio.[8]
Liv. Livio, my good lord.
Oct. Again, you're welcome to us.—[*Aside to Troy.*]
Be as speedy,
Dear nephew, as thou'rt constant.—Men of parts,
Fit parts and sound, are rarely to be met with;
But being met with, therefore to be cherish'd
With love and with supportance. While I stand,
Livio can no way fall:—yet once more, welcome!
[*Exit.*

Troy. An honourable liberality,
Timely dispos'd without delay or question,
Commands a gratitude. Is not this better
Than waiting three or four months at livery,
With cap and knee unto this chair of state
And to that painted arras, for a nod[9]
From goodman-usher or the formal secretary;

7 *My thanks, sir,*
Owes to this just engagement.] Our old writers sometimes used *thanks* (like *means*, &c.) with a verb singular. The sense is—"My thanks are due, or owing, to this just engagement."

8 *Livio.*] This word forms the conclusion of the preceding speech in the 4to. D.

9 *And to* that *painted arras, for a* nod] The 4to reads "And to *their* painted arras for a *need*," which I do not understand. Troylo is evidently congratulating Livio on his entering at once into the good graces of his lord, without stooping (as was too frequently the case) to the meanness of flattering the proud and formal domestics of his patron's establishment, the steward, gentleman-usher, &c. If the reader prefers *need* to *nod*, I see no great objection. "*Cup* and

Especially the juggler with the purse,
That pays some shares in all? A younger brother,
Sometimes an elder, not well trimm'd i' th' headpiece,
May spend what his friend left, in expectation
Of being turn'd out of service—for attendance![10]
Or marry a waiting-woman, and be damn'd for't
To open laughter, and, what's worse, old beggary!—
What thinks my Livio of this rise at first?
Is't not miraculous?

Liv. It seems the bargain
Was driven before between ye.

Troy. 'Twas, and nothing
Could void it but the peevish resolution
Of your dissent from goodness, as you call it;
A thin, a threadbare honesty, a virtue
Without a living to't.

Liv. I must resolve
To turn my sister whore? speak a home-word
For my old bachelor lord?—so! is't not so?
A trifle in respect of[11] present means;
Here's all.

Troy. Be yet more confident; the slavery
Of such an abject office shall not tempt
The freedom of thy[12] spirit: stand ingenious
To thine own fate,[13] and we will practise wisely
Without the charge of scandal.

Liv. May it prove so! [*Exeunt.*

---

knee" [the reading of the 4to, which Gifford retained], I doubt not, should be "*cap* and knee," as we have it in *The Sun's Darling*. It was not usual to present the *cup* kneeling to any but princes.

10 *Of being turn'd out of service—for attendance!*] i.e. as the sole reward of his pains.

11 *of*] Gifford printed "to." D.

12 *thy*] The 4to has "my." D.

13 *stand ingenious*
To thine own fate,] i.e. labour to forward the plans of fortune by thy own dexterity, &c.

SCENE II. *The street.*

Enter SECCO *with a casting-bottle,*[14] *sprinkling his hat and face, and a little looking-glass at his girdle, setting his countenance.*

Sec. Admirable! incomparably admirable! to be the minion, the darling, the delight of love; 'tis a very tickling to the marrow, a kissing i' the blood, a bosoming the ecstasy, the rapture of virginity, soul and paradise of perfection,—ah, pity of generation, Secco, there are no more such men!

Enter SPADONE.

Spa. Oyes! if any man, woman, or beast, have found, stolen, or taken up a fine, very fine male barber, of the age of above or under eighteen, more or less—

Sec. Spadone, hold; what's the noise?

Spa. Umph! pay the crier: I have been almost lost myself in seeking you: here's a letter from—

Sec. Whom, whom, my dear Spadone? whom?

Spa. Soft and fair! an you be so brief, I'll return it whence it came, or look out a new owner.—Oyes!

Sec. Low, low! what dost mean? is't from the glory of beauty, Morosa, the fairest fair? Be gentle to me; here's a ducat: speak low, prithee.

Spa. Give me one, and take t'other: 'tis from the party. [*Receives the ducat from Secco, and gives him the letter.*] Golden news, believe it.

Sec. Honest Spadone!—Divine Morosa! [*Reads.*

Spa. [*aside*]. Fairest fair, quoth'a? so is an old rotten coddled mongrel, parcel-bawd, parcel-midwife;

[14] *with a casting-bottle,* &c.] A small phial for perfumes, sweet waters, &c., which in Ford's time were in more general use than at present. For the fashion of wearing mirrors at the girdle and in the hat, see *Massinger*, vol. iv. p. 8, and *Jonson*, vol. ii. p. 263.

all the marks are quite out of her mouth; not the stump of a tooth left in her head to mumble the curd of a posset.—Signor, 'tis as I told ye; all's right.

Sec. Right, just as thou toldest me; all's right.

Spa. To a very hair, *Signor mio.*

Sec. For which, Sirrah Spadone, I will make thee a man; a man, dost hear? I say, a man.

Spa. Thou'rt a prick-eared foist,[15] a cittern-headed gewgaw, a knack, a snipper-snapper. Twit me with the decrement of my pendants! though I am made a gelding, and, like a tame buck, have lost my dowsets,—more a monster than a cuckold with his horns seen,—yet I scorn to be jeered by any checker-approved barbarian[16] of ye all. Make me a man! I defy thee.

Sec. How now, fellow, how now! roaring ripe indeed!

Spa. Indeed! thou'rt worse: a dry shaver, a copper-basined suds-monger.

Sec. Nay, nay; by my mistress' fair eyes, I meant no such thing.

Spa. Eyes in thy belly! The reverend madam shall know how I have been used. I will blow my nose in thy casting-bottle, break the teeth of thy combs, poison thy camphire-balls, slice out thy towels

15 *Thou'rt a prick-eared* foist, &c.] This stuff is hardly worth explaining; but it may be noticed *en passant,* that *foist* is one of the thousand cant terms for a *rogue* of any kind; that *cittern-headed* means *ugly,* in allusion to the grotesque and monstrous figures with which these and similar musical instruments were *ornamented;* that *knack* is a slight inconsiderate *toy;* and *snipper-snapper* whatever of vituperative the reader pleases. [In what follows the 4to has "decrements;" and so Gifford. D.]

16 *by any* checker-approved *barbarian*] i.e. by any favourite of taverns and their frequenters. Or, as Secco is not tainted with the vice of drunkenness, may we venture to suppose that a barber's shop, like a tavern, was occasionally denoted by the sign of the *chequers?* Ford seems tickled with his facetious pun on *barber;* for he uses it again in a subsequent passage, where Spadone calls Secco, who is about to shave him, "a precious *barbarian.*"

with thine own razor, betallow thy tweezes, and urine in thy basin:—make me a man!

Sec. Hold, take another ducat. As I love new clothes,—

Spa. Or cast old ones.

Sec. Yes, or cast old ones,—I intended no injury.

Spa. [*taking the ducat*] Good, we are pieced again: reputation, signor, is precious.

Sec. I know it is.

Spa. Old sores would not be rubbed.

Sec. For me, never.

Spa. The lady guardianess, the mother of the Fancies, is resolved to draw with ye in the wholesome [yoke] of matrimony suddenly.

Sec. She writes as much: and, Spadone, when we are married,—

Spa. You will to bed, no doubt.

Sec. We will revel in such variety of delights,—

Spa. Do miracles, and get babies.

Sec. Live so sumptuously,—

Spa. In feather and old furs.

Sec. Feed so deliciously,—

Spa. On pap and bull-beef.

Sec. Enjoy the sweetness of our years,—

Spa. Eighteen and threescore with advantage.

Sec. Tumble and wallow in abundance,—

Spa. The pure crystal puddle of pleasures.

Sec. That all the world should[17] wonder.

Spa. A pox on them that envy ye!

Sec. How do the beauties, my dainty knave? live, wish, think, and dream, sirrah, ha!

Spa. Fumble one with another on the gambos of imagination between their legs; eat they do and sleep, game, laugh, and lie down, as beauties ought to do; there's all.

[17] *should*] Gifford printed "shall." D.

Sec. Commend me to my choicest, and tell her the minute of her appointment shall be waited on; say to her she shall find me a man at all points.

Spa. Why, there's another quarrel,—"man" once more, in spite of my nose!

Enter NITIDO.

Nit. Away, Secco, away! my lord calls; he has a loose hair started from his fellows; a clip of your art is commanded.

Sec. I fly, Nitido.—Spadone, remember me. [*Exit.*

Nit. Trudging between an old moil[17] and a young calf, my nimble intelligencer? What, thou fattenest apace on capon still?

Spa. Yes, crimp; 'tis a gallant life to be an old lord's pimp-whiskin:[18] but beware of the porter's lodge,[19] for carrying tales out of the school.

Nit. What a terrible sight to a libbed breech is a sow-gelder!

17 *moil*] i. e. mule.—Altered by Gifford to "mule." D.

18 *pimp-whiskin*:] *Whiskin* (a diminutive of *whiske*, a hand-broom) was used by our old dramatists as a contemptuous term for a low menial of either sex. By the usual progress of such language, the poor harmless word came at length to denote a ready implement of corruption, and to be coupled with the most odious and repulsive epithets. This is the simple history of the expression; which, it should be noted, is commonly applied, as here, to a *domestic* or *dependent*. Thus Brome, in *The Novella*;

"This is ['Tis] the proud brache's *whiske*."

Again;

"I collect[ed] as much by your young *whiskin* that brought me hither." *City Wit.*

Again [in *The Demoiselle*];

"Stay, stay [dele second "stay"]! here she comes, and the *pimp whiskin* with her."

In all these instances, and in several others which I at first thought of giving from Shirley, the person spoken of is a *servant*, and is supposed by the speaker to be a *pander*.

19 *beware of the* porter's lodge, &c.] i. e. of the place where punishment was usually inflicted on refractory servants. See *Jonson*, vol. vii. p. 434.

Spa. Not so terrible as a cross-tree that never grows to a wag-halter page.

Nit. Good! witty rascal, thou'rt a satire, I protest, but that the nymphs[20] need not fear the evidence of thy mortality:—go, put on a clean bib, and spin amongst the nuns, sing 'em a bawdy song: all the children thou gettest shall be christened in wassail-bowls,[21] and turned into a college of men-midwives. Farewell, nightmare!

Spa. Very, very well: if I die in thy debt for this, crack-rope, let me be buried in a coal-sack. I'll fit ye, ape's-face! look for't.

Nit. [*sings*] *And still the urchin would, but could not do.*

Spa. Mark the end on't, and laugh at last.

[*Exeunt.*

SCENE III. *A room in the house of* LIVIO.

Enter ROMANELLO *and* CASTAMELA.

Rom. Tell me you cannot love me.

Cast. You impórtune
Too strict a resolution: as a gentleman
Of commendable parts and fair deserts
In every sweet condition that becomes
A hopeful expectation, I do honour
Th' example of your youth; but, sir, our fortunes,
Concluded on both sides in narrow bands,

[20] but *that the nymphs*] i.e. except that, &c. This would have called for no notice, had I not ventured to alter the pointing of the former editions, which deprived the passage of all meaning. Ford plays on the similarity of the words *satyr* and *satire.* [Formerly *satire* was frequently used as equivalent to *satirist:* see vol. i. p. 71. D.]

[21] *shall be christened in* wassail-bowls,] i.e. in ale or wine instead of water. Nitido is still jesting with the incapacity of Spadone.

Move you to construe gently my forbearance
In argument of fit consideration.

Rom. Why, Castamela, I have shap'd thy virtues,
Even from our childish years, into a dowry
Of richer estimation than thy portion
Doubled an hundred times can equal: now
I clearly find thy current of affection
Labours to fall into the gulf of riot,[22]
Not the free ocean of a soft content.
You'd marry pomp and plenty: 'tis the idol,
I must confess, that creatures of the time
Bend their devotions to; but I have fashion'd
Thoughts much more excellent of you.

Cast. Enjoy
Your own prosperity; I am resolv'd
Never by any charge with me to force
A poverty upon ye, want of love.
'Tis rarely cherish'd with the love of want.[23]
I'll not be your undoing.

Rom. Sure, some dotage
Of living stately, richly, lend[s] a cunning
To eloquence. How is this piece of goodness
Chang'd to ambition! O, you are most miserable
In your desires! the female curse has caught ye.

Cast. Fie, fie! how ill this suits!

22 *Labours to fall into the* gulf *of riot,*] The old copy has "*guilt,*" which the whole context shows to be a misprint.

23 *want of love.*
'Tis rarely cherish'd with the love of want.] I have adopted the pointing of the old copy, simply because I could not satisfy myself with any new arrangement. It is not easy to guess at the speaker's meaning; she appears to consider *poverty* and *want of love* as synonymous, with a reference, perhaps, to the insinuation of the old proverb, that the latter is a necessary consequence of the former. In the next line she seems to say: It (love) is rarely cherished by those who, like Romanello, embrace a voluntary poverty. But this is all conjecture. The reader must decide whether the play on words has led the poet into this perplexed expression, or whether any part of it has been corrupted at the press.

Rom. A devil of pride
Ranges in airy thoughts to catch a star,
Whiles ye grasp mole-hills.

Cast. Worse and worse, I vow.

Rom. But that some remnant of an honest sense
Ebbs a full tide of blood to shame, all women
Would prostitute all honour to the luxury
Of ease and titles.

Cast. Romanello, know
You have forgot the nobleness of truth,
And fix'd on scandal now.

Rom. A dog, a parrot,
A monkey, a caroch, a guarded[24] lackey,
A waiting-woman with her lips seal'd up,
Are pretty toys to please my Mistress Wanton!
So is a fiddle too; 'twill make it dance,
Or else be sick and whine.

Cast. This is uncivil:
I am not, sir, your charge.

Rom. My grief you are;
For all my services are lost and ruin'd.

Cast. So is my chief opinion of your worthiness,
When such distractions tempt ye: you would prove
A cruel lord, who dare, being yet a servant,
As you profess, to bait my best respects
Of duty to your welfare; 'tis a madness
I have not oft observ'd. Possess your freedom,
You have no right in me: let this suffice;
I wish your joys much comfort.

Enter LIVIO *richly habited.*

Liv. Sister, look ye,
How, by a new creation of my tailor's,

[24] *guarded*] See note, vol. i. p. 18. D.

I've shook-off old mortality; the rags
Of home-spun gentry—prithee, sister, mark it—
Are cast by, and I now appear in fashion
Unto men, and receiv'd. Observe me, sister;
The consequence concerns you.

Cast. True, good brother;
For my well-doing must consist in yours.

Liv. Here's Romanello, a fine-temper'd gallant,
Of decent carriage, of indifferent means,
Considering that his sister, new hoist up
From a lost merchant's warehouse to the titles[24]
Of a great lord's bed, may supply his wants;—
Not sunk in his acquaintance, for a scholar
Able enough, and one who may subsist
Without the help of friends, provided always
He fly not upon wedlock without certainty
Of an advancement; else a bachelor
May thrive by observation on a little.
A single life's no burthen;[25] but to draw
In yokes is chargeable, and will require
A double maintenance: why, I can live
Without a wife, and purchase.

Rom. Is't a mystery
You've lately found out, Livio, or a cunning
Conceal'd till now for wonder?

Liv. Pish! believe it,
Endeavours and an active brain are better
Than patrimonies left by parents. Prove it.
One thrives by cheating; shallow fools and unthrifts
Are game knaves only fly at: then a fellow
Presumes on his hair, and that his back can toil
For fodder from the city;—lies: another,

[24] *titles*] Qy. "title"? D.
[25] *A single life's no burthen;*] For "*A*" the 4to reads "*As* single life's," &c.

Reputed valiant, lives by the sword,[26] and takes up
Quarrels, or braves them, as the novice likes,
To gild his reputation ;—most improbable.
A world of desperate undertakings possibly
Procures some hungry meals, some tavern-surfeits,
Some frippery to hide nakedness, perhaps
The scambling half a ducat[27] now and then
To roar and noise it with the tattling hostess
For a week's lodging; these are pretty shifts,
Souls bankrupt of their royalty submit to.
Give me a man whose practice and experience
Conceives not barely the philosopher's stone,
But indeed has it; one whose wit's his Indies:
The poor is most ridiculous.

Rom. You're pleasant
In new discoveries of fortune: use them
With moderation, Livio.

Cast. Such wild language
Was wont to be a stranger to your custom:
However, brother, you are pleas'd to vent it,
I hope, for recreation.

Liv. Name and honour,
What are they? a mere sound without supportance,

[26] *another,*
Reputed valiant, lives by the sword, &c.] Thus Fletcher;
"Your high offers
Taught by the masters of dependencies,
That by compounding differences 'tween others
Supply their own necessities, with me
Will never carry it." [*The Elder Brother*, act v. sc. 1.]

These "masters of dependencies," as they called themselves, were a set of low bullies and bravoes, who undertook to instruct such country novices as aspired to the reputation of valour in the fashionable mode of getting-up a quarrel, and, if need were, submitted to be beaten by them. They are noticed with ridicule and contempt by most of our old dramatists.

[27] *The* scambling *half a ducat,* &c.] "*Scambling*" appears to be used in this place for obtaining by impudent importunity, by false pretences, &c.; in a word, much in the sense of *skelder*, as we have it in Jonson, Decker, and others.

A begging: chastity, youth, beauty, handsomeness,
Discourse, behaviour which might charm attention
And curse the gazer's eyes into amazement,
Are nature's common bounties; so are diamonds
Uncut, so flowers unworn, so silkworms' webs
Unwrought, gold unrefin'd: then all those glories
Are of esteem when us'd and set at price:
There's no dark sense in this.

Rom. I understand not
The drift on't, nor how meant, nor yet to whom.

Cast. Pray, brother, be more plain.

Liv. First, Romanello,
This for your satisfaction: if you waste
More hours in courtship to this maid, my sister,
Weighing her competency with your own,
You go about to build without foundation;
So that care will prove void.

Rom. A sure acquittance,
If I must be discharg'd.

Liv. Next, Castamela,
To thee, my own lov'd sister, let me say,
I have not been so bountiful in showing
To fame the treasure which this age hath open'd
As thy true value merits.

Cast. You are merry.

Liv. My jealousy of thy fresh-blooming years
Prompted a fear of husbanding too charily
Thy growth to such perfection as no flattery
Of art can perish now.

Cast. Here's talk in riddles![28]

[38] *Here's talk in riddles!*] Here is, indeed; and, what is worse, no Œdipus at hand to solve them. It would be mere presumption to alter the text; but if the reader, in the following line,

"Prompted a *fear* of husbanding *too* charily,"

be pleased to suppose "*care*" and "*so*" in the place of "*fear*" and "*too*," he will catch, I believe, some glimpse of the poet's meaning.

Brother, the exposition?
Liv. I'll no longer
Chamber thy freedom: we have been already
Thrifty enough in our low fortunes; henceforth
Command thy liberty, with that thy pleasures.
Rom. Is't come to this?
Cast. You're wondrous full of courtesy.
Liv. Ladies of birth and quality are suitors
For being known t'ye; I have promis'd, sister,
They shall partake your company.
Cast. What ladies?
Where, when, how, who?
Liv. A day, a week, a month,
Sported amongst such beauties is a gain
On time; they're young, wise, noble, fair, and chaste.
Cast. Chaste?
Liv. Castamela, chaste; I would not hazard
My hopes, my joys of thee on dangerous trial.
Yet if, as it may chance, a neat-cloth'd merriment
Pass without blush in tattling,—so[29] the words
Fall not too broad, 'tis but a pastime smil'd at
Amongst yourselves in counsel;[30] but beware
Of being overheard.
Cast. This is pretty!
Rom. [*aside*] I doubt I know not what, yet must be silent.

Enter TROYLO, FLORIA, CLARELLA, SILVIA, *and* NITIDO.

Liv. They come as soon as spoke of.—Sweetest fair ones,
My sister cannot but conceive this honour

[29] *so*] The 4to has "to." D.

[30] *Amongst yourselves* in counsel;] i.e. in secret, in *private:* the expression is common to all our old writers.

Particular in your respects.—Dear sir,
You grace us in your favours.

Troy. Virtuous lady!

Flo. We are your servants.

Clar. Your sure friends.

Sil. Society
May fix us in a league.

Cast. All fitly welcome.
I find not reason, gentle ladies, whereon
To cast this debt of mine; but my acknowledgment
Shall study to pay thankfulness.

Troy. Sweet beauty,
Your brother hath indeed been too much churl
In this concealment from us all, who love him,
Of such desir'd a presence.

Sil. Please to enrich us
With your wish'd amity.

Flo. Our coach attends;
We cannot be denied.

Clar. Command it, Nitido.

Nit. Ladies, I shall.—[*Aside*] Now for a lusty harvest!
'Twill prove a cheap year, should these barns be fill'd once. [*Exit.*

Cast. Brother, one word in private.

Liv. Phew! anon
I shall instruct at large.[31]—We are prepar'd,
And easily entreated;—'tis good manners
Not to be troublesome.

Troy. Thou'rt perfect, Livio.

Cast. Whither?—[*Aside*] But he's my brother.

Troy. Fair, your arm;

[31] *instruct at large.*] Gifford printed "*instruct* you *at large;*" an addition hardly necessary for the sense, and violating the metre. D.

I am your usher, lady.
Cast. As you please, sir.
Liv. I wait you to your coach.—[*To Rom.*] Some two hours hence
I shall return again. [*Exeunt all but Rom.*
Rom. Troylo-Savelli,
Next heir unto the marquis! and the page too,
The marquis's own page! Livio transform'd
Into a sudden bravery,[32] and alter'd
In nature, or I dream! Amongst the ladies,
I not remember I have seen one face.
There's cunning in these changes: I am resolute,
Or to pursue the trick on't, or lose labour. [*Exit.*

ACT II.

SCENE I. *An apartment in* JULIO'S *house.*

Enter FLAVIA, *supported by* CAMILLO *and* VESPUCCI.

Flav. Not yet return'd?
Cam. Madam?
Flav. The lord our husband
We mean. Unkind! four hours are almost past,—
But twelve short minutes wanting by the glass,—
Since we broke company; was never, gentlemen,
Poor princess us'd so!
Ves. With your gracious favour,
Peers, great in rank and place, ought of necessity
To attend on state-employments.
Cam. For such duties

[32] *Into a sudden* bravery,] i.e. gallantry of attire, finery of dress, —*freshly* [*fresh*] *suited*, as the margin says [as the stage-direction in the 4to has it when Livio enters at p. 239. D.].

Are all their toil and labour; but their pleasures
Flow in the beauties they enjoy, which conquers
All sense of other travail.

Flav. Trimly spoken.
When we were common, mortal, and a subject,
As other creatures of Heaven's making are,—
The more the pity,—bless us, how we waited
For the huge play-day, when the pageants flutter'd
About the city![1] for we then were certain
The madam-courtiers would vouchsafe to visit us,
And call us by our names, and eat our viands;
Nay, give us leave to sit at th' upper end
Of our own tables, telling us how welcome
They'd make us when we came to court: full little
Dreamt I at that time of the wind that blew me
Up to the weathercock of th' honours now
Are thrust upon me; but we'll bear the burthen,
Were't twice as much as 'tis. The next great feast
We'll grace the city-wives, poor souls, and see
How they'll behave themselves before our presence:
You two shall wait on us.

Ves. With best observance,
And glory in our service.

Cam. We are creatures
Made proud in your commands.

Flav. Believe't you are so;

[1] *For the huge play-day, when the pageants flutter'd About the city!*] The huge play-day (for Ford's *Sienna* is only another name for London) was probably the Lord-Mayor's day, when the company to which he belonged exhibited, in honour of his installation, those rude but splendid pageantries and processions which, however they may now excite a smile, were then viewed with equal wonder and delight, and not altogether, perhaps, without profit, which is more than can be said of the tattered remnants of them that are annually dragged abroad to shame us. They were not, however, confined to one festival, but "fluttered about the city" on every joyous occasion. There is truth as well as humour in Flavia's pleasant description of the condescension of the "madam-courtiers" on these huge play-days. The satire is not yet quite obsolete.

And you shall find us readier in your pleasures
Than you in your obedience. Fie! methinks
I have an excellent humour to be pettish,
A little toysome:—'tis a pretty sign
Of breeding, is't not, sirs? I could, indeed, la,
Long for some strange good things now.

Cam. Such news, madam,
Would overjoy my lord your husband.

Ves. Cause
Bonfires and bell-ringings.

Flav. I must be with child, then,
An't be but for the public jollity;
Or lose my longings, which were mighty pity.

Cam. Sweet fates forbid it!

Enter FABRICIO.

Fab. Noblest lady,—

Ves. Rudeness!
Keep off, or I shall—Saucy groom, learn manners;
Go swab amongst your goblins.

Flav. Let him stay;
The fellow I have seen, and now remember
His name, Fabricio.

Fab. Your poor creature, lady;
Out of your gentleness, please you to consider
The brief of this petition, which contains
All hope of my last fortunes.[2]

Flav. Give it from him.

Cam. Here, madam. [*Takes the paper from Fab., and delivers it to Flav., who walks aside with it.*]—Mark, Vespucci, how the wittol

[2] *All hope of my* last fortunes.] Meaning probably (for the language is constrained) "my final hope, my last resource." The object of this request appears to be more money to enable him to expatriate himself.

Stares on his sometime wife; sure, he imagines
To be a cuckold by consent is purchase
Of approbation in a state.

Ves. Good reason:
The gain repriev'd him from a bankrupt's statute,
And fil'd him in the charter of his freedom.
"She had seen the fellow"! did'st observe?

Cam. Most punctually;
Could call him by his name too! why, 'tis possible
She has not yet forgot he was her husband.

Ves. That were [most] strange: O, 'tis a precious trinket!
Was ever puppet so slipt up?

Cam. The tale
Of Venus' cat, man, chang'd into a woman,
Was emblem but to this. She turns.

Ves. He stands
Just like Actæon in the painted cloth.[3]

Cam. No more.

Flav. Friend, we have read and weigh'd the sum
Of what your scrivener—which, in effect,
Is meant your counsel learnèd—has drawn for ye:
'Tis a fair hand, in sooth, but the contents
Somewhat unseasonable; for, let us tell ye,
You've been a spender, a vain spender; wasted
Your stock of credit and of wares unthriftily:
You are a faulty man; and should we urge
Our lord as often for supplies as shame
Or wants drive you to ask, it might be constru'd
An impudence, which we defy; an impudence,
Base in base women, but in noble sinful.

[3] *He stands*
Just like Actæon *in the painted cloth.*] i.e. in the act of gazing at Diana in a posture of mingled awe and surprise. There is some humour in the expression.

Are ye not asham'd yet of yourself?

Fab. Great lady,
Of my misfortunes I'm asham'd.

Cam. [*aside to Ves.*] So, so!
This jeer twangs roundly, does it not, Vespucci?

Ves. [*aside to Cam.*] Why, here's a lady worshipful!

Flav. Pray, gentlemen,
Retire a while: this fellow shall resolve
Some doubts that stick about me.

Cam.
Ves. } As you please. [*Exeunt.*

Flav. To thee, Fabricio,—O, the change is cruel,—
Since I find some small leisure, I must justify
Thou art unworthy of the name of man.
Those holy vows which we, by bonds of faith,
Recorded in the register of truth,
Were kept by me unbroken; no assaults
Of gifts, of courtship, from the great and wanton,
No threats nor sense of poverty, to which
Thy riots had betray'd me, could betray
My warrantable thoughts to impure folly.
Why wouldst thou force me miserable?

Fab. The scorn
Of rumour is reward enough to brand
My lewder actions: 'twas, I thought, impossible
A beauty fresh as was your youth could brook
The last of my decays.

Flav. Did I complain?
My sleeps between thine arms were even as sound,
My dreams as harmless, my contents as free,
As when the best of plenty crown'd our bride-bed.
Amongst some of a mean but quiet fortune,
Distrust of what they call their own, or jealousy
Of those whom in their bosoms they possess
Without control, begets a self-unworthiness;

For which [through] fear, or, what is worse,[4] desire
Of paltry gain, they practise art, and labour
To pander their own wives; those wives, whose innocence,
Stranger to language, spoke obedience only;
And such a wife was Flavia to Fabricio.

Fab. My loss is irrecoverable.

Flav. Call not
Thy wickedness thy loss: without my knowledge
Thou sold'st me, and in open court protested'st
A pre-contráct unto another falsely,
To justify a separation. Wherein
Could I offend, to be believ'd thy strumpet,
In best sense an adultress? so conceiv'd
In all opinions, that I am shook off
Even from mine own blood, which, although I boast
Not noble, yet 'twas not mean: for Romanello,
Mine only brother, shuns me, and abhors
To own me for his sister.

Fab. 'Tis confest
I am the shame of mankind.

Flav. I live happy
In this great lord's love now; but could his cunning
Have train'd me to dishonour, we had never
Been sunder'd by th' temptation of his purchase.
In troth, Fabricio, I am little proud of
My unsought honours, and so far from triumph,
That I am not more fool to such as honour me
Than to myself, who hate this antic carriage.[5]

Fab. You are an angel rather to be worshipp'd
Than grossly to be talk'd with.

[4] *worse,*] The 4to has "worst." D.

[5] *this* antic *carriage.*] This childish and ridiculous affectation of levity, which she assumed, partly to humour the count, but chiefly, as she afterwards says, to defeat the "lascivious villanies" of her attendants, Camillo and Vespucci.

Flav. [*gives him money*] Keep those ducats;
I shall provide you better:—'twere a bravery,
Could you forget the place wherein you've render'd
Your name for ever hateful.

Fab. I will do't,
Do't, excellentest goodness, and conclude
My days in silent sadness.[6]

Flav. You may prosper
In Spain, in France, or elsewhere, as in Italy.
Besides, you are a scholar bred, however
You interrupted study with commérce.
I'll think of your supplies: meantime, pray, storm not
At my behaviour t'ye; I have forgot
Acquaintance with mine own—keep your first distance.— [*He draws back.*
Camillo! who is near? Vespucci!

Enter JULIO, *with* CAMILLO *and* VESPUCCI.

Jul. What!
Our lady's cast familiar?

Flav. O, my stomach
Wambles at sight of—sick, sick,—I am sick—
I faint at heart—[*To Jul.*] Kiss me; nay, prithee, quickly,
Or I shall swoon. You've stay'd a sweet while from me.
And this companion[7] too—beshrew him!

Jul. Dearest,
Thou art my health, my blessing.—Turn the bankrupt
Out of my doors!—Sirrah, I'll have thee whipt,
If thou com'st here again.

[6] *My days in silent* sadness.] The old copy has "*goodness*," evidently repeated, by mistake, from the word immediately above it. "*Sadness*" is not given as the author's expression, but as conveying what might, perhaps, have been his meaning.

[7] *companion*] A term of contempt,—"fellow." D.

Cam. Hence, hence, you vermin!
[*Exit Fab.*

Jul. How is't, my best of joys?

Flav. Prettily mended,
Now we have our own lord here: I shall never
Endure to spare you long out of my sight.—
See, what the thing presented. [*Gives him the paper.*

Jul. A petition,
Belike, for some new charity?

Flav. We must not
Be troubled with his needs; a wanting creature
Is monstrous, is as ominous—fie upon't!
Dispatch the silly mushroom once for all,
And send him with some pittance out o' th' country,
Where we may hear no more of him.

Jul. Thy will
Shall stand a law, my Flavia.

Flav. You have been
In private with our fellow-peers now: shall not we
Know how the business stands? Sure, in some country
Ladies are privy-counsellors, I warrant ye;
Are they not, think ye? there the land is doubtless
Most politicly govern'd; all the women
Wear swords and breeches, I have heard most certainly:
Such sights were excellent.[8]

Jul. Thou'rt a matchless pleasure;
No life is sweet without thee: in my heart
Reign empress, and be styl'd thy Julio's sovereign,
My only precious dear.

Flav. We'll prove no less t'ye. [*Exeunt.*

[8] *Such sights were excellent.*] Flavia is pleased to be satirical on the influence supposed to be possessed by some of the ladies of Charles's court.

SCENE II. *A room in the palace.*

Enter TROYLO *and* LIVIO.

Troy. Sea-sick ashore still! thou couldst rarely scape
A calenture in a long voyage, Livio,
Who in a short one, and at home, art subject
To such faint stomach-qualms; no cordials comfort
The business of thy thoughts, for aught I see:
What ails thee, man? be merry, hang up jealousies.
Liv. Who, I? I jealous? no, no, here's no cause
In this place; 'tis a nunnery, a retirement
For meditation; all the difference extant
But puzzles only bare belief, not grounds it.
Rich services in plate, soft and fair lodgings,
Varieties of recreations, exercise
Of music in all changes, neat attendance,
Princely, nay, royal furniture of garments,
Satiety of gardens, orchards, waterworks,
Pictures so ravishing that ranging eyes
Might dwell upon a dotage of conceit
Without a single wish for livelier substance,—
The great world in a little world of fancy
Is here abstracted: no temptation proffer'd
But such as fools and mad folks can invite to;
And yet—
Troy. And yet your reason cannot answer
Th' objections of your fears, which argue danger.
Liv. Danger! dishonour, Troylo: were my sister
In safety from those charms, I must confess
I could live here for ever.
Troy. But you could not,
I can assure ye; for 'twere then scarce possible
A door might open t'ye, hardly a loophole.

Liv. My presence, then, is usher to her ruin,
And loss of her the fruit of my preferment?

Troy. Briefly partake a secret; but be sure
To lodge it in the inmost of thy bosom,
Where memory may not find it for discovery;
By our firm truth of friendship, I require thee.

Liv. By our firm truth of friendship, I subscribe
To just conditions.

Troy. Our great uncle-marquis,
Disabled from his cradle by an impotence
In nature first, that impotence since seconded
And render'd more infirm by a fatal breach
Receiv'd in fight against the Turkish galleys,
Is made uncapable of any faculty
Of active manhood, more than what affections
Proper unto his sex must else distinguish;
So that no helps of art can warrant life,
Should he transcend the bounds his weakness limits.

Liv. On; I attend with eagerness.

Troy. 'Tis strange
Such natural defects at no time check
A full and free sufficiency of spirit,
Which flows both in so clear and fix'd a strength,
That to confirm belief, it seems, where nature
Is in the body lame, she is supplied
In fine proportion of the mind: a word
Concludes all—to a man his enemy
He is a dangerous threatening; but to women,
However pleasurable, no way cunning
To show abilities of friendship, other
Than what his outward senses can delight in,
Or charge and bounty court with.

Liv. Good, good, Troylo.
O, that I had a lusty faith to credit it,
Though none of all this wonder should be possible!

Troy. As I love honour and an honest name,
I falter not, my Livio, in one syllable.
Liv. News admirable! 'tis, 'tis so—pish, I know
it—
Yet he has a kind heart of his own to girls,
Young, handsome girls; yes, yes, so he may;
'Tis granted:—he would now and then be piddling,
And play the wanton, like a fly that dallies
About a candle's flame; then scorch his wings,
Drop down, and creep away, ha?
Troy. Hardly that, too;
To look upon fresh beauties, to discourse
In an unblushing merriment of words,
To hear them play or sing, and see them dance;
To pass the time in pretty amorous questions,
Read a chaste verse of love, or prattle riddles,
Is th' height of his temptations.
Liv. Send him joy on't!
Troy. His choices are not of the courtly train
Nor city's practice; but the country's innocence;
Such as are gentle-born, not meanly; such
To whom both gaudiness and ape-like fashions
Are monstrous; such as cleanliness and decency
Prompt to a virtuous envy; such as study
A knowledge of no danger but themselves.
Liv. Well, I have liv'd in ignorance: the ancients,
Who chatted of the golden age, feign'd trifles.
Had they dreamt this, they would have truth'd it
heaven;[9]
I mean an earthly heaven, less it is not.
Troy. Yet is this bachelor-miracle not free
From the epidemical headache.

[9] *they would have* truth'd *it heaven;*] Our poet uses "*truth*," whether as a substantive (vol. i. p. 16), or, as in this place, a verb, in a way somewhat peculiar to himself. It here means, they would have affirmed, maintained, as a *truth*, that this society was heaven.

Liv. The yellows?

Troy. Huge jealous fits; admitting none to enter
But me, his page and barber, with an eunuch,
And an old guardianess. It is a favour
Not common, that the license of your visits
To your own sister, now and then, is wink'd at.

Liv. But why are you his instrument? his nephew!
'Tis ominous in nature.

Troy. Not in policy:
Being his heir, I may take truce a little
With mine own fortunes.

Liv. Knowing how things stand too.

Troy. At certain seasons, as the humour takes him,
A set of music are permitted peaceably
To cheer their solitariness, provided
They're strangers, not acquainted near the city;
But never the same twice, pardon him that;
Nor must their stay exceed an hour, or two
At farthest, as at this wise wedding; wherefore
His barber is the master to instruct
The lasses both in song and dance, by him
Train'd up in either quality.

Liv. A caution
Happily studied.

Troy. Farther to prevent
Suspicion, he has married his young barber
To the old matron, and withal is pleas'd
Report should mutter him a mighty man
For th' game, to take-off all suspicion
Of insufficiency; and this strict company
He calls his Bower of Fancies.

Liv. Yes, and properly,
Since all his recreations are in fancy.
I'm infinitely taken.—Sister! marry,

Would I had sisters in a plenty, Troylo,
So to bestow them all, and turn them Fancies!—
Fancies! why, 'tis a pretty name, methinks.

Troy. Something remains, which in conclusion shortly
Shall take thee fuller.— [*Music within.*
Hark, the wedding-jollity!
With a bride-cake, on my life, to grace the nuptials!
Perhaps the ladies will turn songsters.

Liv. Silence!

A SONG *within.*

After which enter in procession, with the bride-cake, SECCO *and* MOROSA, *with* CASTAMELA, FLORIA, CLARELLA, SILVIA, SPADONE, *and Musicians.*

Sec. Passing neat and exquisite, I protest, fair creatures. These honours to our solemnity are liberal and uncommon; my spouse and myself, with our posterity, shall prostitute our services to your bounties:—shall's not, duckling?

Mor. Yes, honeysuckle; and do as much for them one day, if things stand right as they should stand. Bill, pigeon, do; thou'st be my cat-a-mountain, and I thy sweet-brier, honey.—We'll lead you to kind examples, pretty ones, believe it; and you shall find us one in one, whiles hearts do last.

Sec. Ever mine own, and ever.

Spa. Well said, old touch-hole.

Liv. All happiness, all joy!

Troy. A plenteous issue,
A fruitful womb!—Thou hast a blessing, Secco.

Mor. Indeed he has, sir, if ye know all, as I conceive you know enough, if not the whole; for you have, I may say, tried me to the quick through and through, and most of my carriage, from time to time.

Spa. [*aside*] 'Twould wind-break a moil[10] or a ringed mare to vie burthens with her.

Mor. What's that you mumble, gelding, hey?[11]

Spa. Nothing, forsooth, but that you're a bouncing couple well met, and 'twere pity to part ye, though you hung together in a smoky chimney.

Mor. 'Twere e'en pity, indeed, Spadone; nay, thou'st a foolish loving nature of thine own, and wishest well to plain dealings, o' my conscience.

Spa. Thank your brideship—[*Aside*] your bawdship.

Flo. Our sister is not merry.

Clar. Sadness cannot
Become a bridal harmony.

Sil. At a wedding
Free spirits are requir'd.

Troy. You should dispense
With serious thoughts now, lady.

Mor. Well said, gentlefolks!

Liv. Fie, Castamela, fie!

All. A dance, a dance!

Troy. By any means, the day is not complete else.

Cast. Indeed, I'll be excus'd.

Troy. By no means, lady.

Sec. We all are suitors.

Cast. With your pardons, spare me
For this time; grant me license to look on.

Troy. Command your pleasures, lady.[12]—Every one hand
Your partner:—nay, Spadone must make one;
These merriments are free.

10 *moil*] See note, p. 236. D.

11 *hey?*] The 4to has "shey." D.

12 Troy. *Command your pleasures, lady,* &c.] The 4to gives this as a continuation of Castamela's speech. It evidently belongs to Troylo.

Spa. With all my heart; I'm sure I am not the heaviest in the company.—Strike up for the honour of the bride and bridegroom. [*Music.*

A DANCE.

Troy. So, so, here's art in motion. On all parts
Ye have bestirr'd ye nimbly.

Mor. I could dance now,
E'en till I dropt again; but want of practice
Denies the scope of breath or so: yet, sirrah,
My cat-a-mountain, do not I trip quickly,
And with a grace too, sirrah?

Sec. Light as a feather.

Spa. Sure, you are not without a stick of liquorice in your pocket, forsooth. You have, I believe, stout lungs of your own, you swim about so roundly without rubs; 'tis a tickling sight to be young still.

Enter NITIDO.

Nit. Madam Morosa!

Mor. Child?

Nit. [*takes her aside*] To you in secret.

Spa. That earwig scatters the troop now; I'll go near to fit him.[13]

Liv. My lord, upon my life,—

Troy. Then we must sever.

Mor. Ladies and gentlemen, your ears.
[*Whispers them.*

Spa. O, 'twas ever a wanton monkey! he will wriggle into a starting-hole so cleanly: an it had been on my wedding-day, I know what I know.

Sec. Sayest so, Spadone?

Spa. Nothing, nothing; I prate sometimes beside the purpose—whoreson, lecherous weasel!

[13] *him.*] The 4to has "'em." D.

Sec. Look, look, look, how officious the little knave is!—but—

Spa. Why, there's the business; buts on one's forehead are but scurvy buts.

Mor. Spadone, discharge the fiddlers instantly.

Spa. Yes, I know my postures—O monstrous, buts!

[*Exit with the Musicians.*

Mor. [*to Sec.*] Attend within, sweeting.—Your pardons, gentlemen.—To your recreations, dear virgins.—Page, have a care.

Nit. My duty, reverend madam.

Troy. Livio, away!—Sweet beauties—

Cast. Brother!

Liv. Suddenly
I shall return.—[*Aside*] Now for a round temptation.

[*Exeunt severally; Mor. stays Cast.*

Mor. One gentle word in private with your ladyship;
I shall not hold you long.

Cast. What means this huddle
Of flying several ways thus? who has frighted 'em?
They live not at devotion here or pension:
Pray, quit me of distrust.

Mor. May't please your goodness,
You'll find him even in every point as honourable
As flesh and blood can vouch him.

Cast. Ha! him! whom?
What him?

Mor. He will not press beyond his bounds;
He will but chat and toy, and feel your—

Cast. Guard me
A powerful Genius!—Feel—

Mor. Your hands to kiss them,
Your fair, pure, white hands: what strange business is it?

These melting twins of ivory, but softer
Than down of turtles, shall but feed the appetite—
Cast. A rape upon my ears!
Mor. The appetite
Of his poor ravish'd eye; should he swell higher
In his desires, and soar upon ambition
Of rising in humility by degrees,
Perhaps he might crave leave to clap—
Cast. Fond woman,
In thy grave sinful!
Mor. Clap or pat the dimples
Where Love's tomb stands erected on your cheeks.
Else, pardon those slight exercises, pretty one;
His lordship is as harmless a weak implement
As e'er young lady trembled under.
Cast. Lordship!—
Stead me, my modest anger!—'tis belike, then,
Religious matron, some great man's prison,
Where virgins' honours suffer martyrdom,
And you are their tormentor: let's lay down
Our ruin'd names to the insulter's mercy!
Let's sport and smile on scandal!—[*Aside*] Rare calamity,
What hast thou toil'd me in!—You nam'd his lordship;
Some gallant youth and fiery?
Mor. No, no, 'deed, la!
A very grave stale bachelor, my dainty one;
There's the conceit: he's none of your hot rovers,
Who ruffle at first dash, and so disfigure
Your dresses and your sets of blush at once;
He's wise in years, and of a temperate warmth,
Mighty in means and power, and withal liberal;
A wanton in his wishes, but else,—farther
He cannot—cause—he cannot—
Cast. Cannot! prithee

Be plainer; I begin to like thee strangely;
What cannot?

Mor. You urge timely and to purpose:
He cannot do,—the truth is truth,—do any thing—
As one should say—that's any thing; put case,—
I do but put the case, forsooth,—he find ye.

Cast. [*aside*] My stars, I thank ye for being ignorant
Of what this old-in-mischief can intend!—
And so we might be merry, bravely merry?

Mor. You hit it—what else!—[*Aside*] She is cunning.—Look ye,
Pray lend your hand, forsooth.

Cast. Why, prithee, take it.

Mor. You have a delicate moist palm—umph—can ye
Relish that tickle there?

Cast. And laugh, if need were.

Mor. And laugh! why, now you have it; what hurt, pray,
Perceive ye? there's all, all: go to, you want tutoring,
Are an apt scholar; I'll neglect no pains
For your instruction.

Cast. Do not.—But his lordship,
What may his lordship be?

Mor. No worse man[14]
Than Marquis of Sienna, the great master
Of this small family: your brother found him
A bounteous benefactor;[15] 'has advanc'd him
The gentleman o' th' horse: in a short time
He means to visit you himself in person,

[14] *man*] Qy. "a *man*"? D.

[15] *your* brother *found him*
A bounteous benefactor;] For "*brother*" the 4to reads "*master;*" an evident misprint, from the compositor's eye being caught by the word immediately above it.

As kind as loving an old man!
Cast. We'll meet him
With a full flame of welcome. Is't the marquis?
No worse?
Mor. No worse, I can assure your ladyship;
The only free maintainer of the Fancies.
Cast. Fancies! how mean ye that?
Mor. The pretty souls
Who are companions in the house; all daughters
To honest virtuous parents and right worshipful;
A kind of chaste collapsèd ladies.
Cast. Chaste too,
And yet collapsèd?
Mor. Only in their fortunes.
Cast. Sure, I must be a Fancy in the number.
Mor. A Fancy principal: I hope you'll fashion
Your entertainment, when the marquis courts you,
As that I may stand blameless.
Cast. Free suspicion.
My brother's raiser?
Mor. Merely.
Cast. My supporter?
Mor. Undoubtedly.
Cast. An old man and a lover?
Mor. True, there's the music, the content, the harmony.
Cast. And I myself a Fancy?
Mor. You are pregnant.[16]
Cast. The chance is thrown; I now am fortune's minion;
I will be bold and resolute.
Mor. Blessing on thee! [*Exeunt.*

[16] *You are pregnant.*] i.e. intelligent, shrewd, quick at guessing; in other words, you are fully possessed of the case.

ACT III.

SCENE I. *The street.*

Enter ROMANELLO.

Rom. Prosper me now, my fate! some better Genius
Than such a one as waits on troubled passions
Direct my courses to a noble issue!
My thoughts have wander'd in a labyrinth;
But if the clue I have laid hold on fail not,
I shall tread-out the toil of these dark paths,
In spite of politic reaches. I am punish'd
In mine own hopes by her unlucky fortunes
Whose fame is ruin'd; Flavia, my lost sister!
Lost to report by her unworthy husband,
Though heighten'd by a greatness, in whose mixtures
I hate to claim a part.

Enter NITIDO.

O, welcome, welcome,
Dear boy! thou keep'st time with my expectations
As justly as the promise of my bounties
Shall reckon with thy service.
Nit. I have fashion'd
The means of your admittance.
Rom. Precious Nitido!
Nit. More, have bethought me of a shape, a quaint one,
You may appear in safe and unsuspected.
Rom. Thou'rt an ingenious boy.
Nit. Beyond all this,
Have so contriv'd the feat, that at first sight

Troylo himself shall court your entertainment,
Nay, force you to vouchsafe it.

Rom. Thou'st outdone
All counsel and all cunning.

Nit. True, I have, sir,
Fadg'd nimbly in my practices; but surely
There are some certain clogs, some roguish staggers,
Some—what shall I call 'em?—in the business.

Rom. Nitido,
What, faint now! dear heart, bear up:—what staggers,
What clogs? let me remove 'em.

Nit. Am I honest
In this discovery?

Rom. Honest! pish, is that all?
[*Gives him a purse.*
By this rich purse, and by the twenty ducats
Which line it, I will answer for thy honesty
Against all Italy, and prove it perfect:
Besides, remember I am bound to secrecy;
Thou'lt not betray thyself?

Nit. All fears are clear'd, then;
But if—

Rom. If what? out with't.

Nit. If we're discover'd,
You'll answer I am honest still?

Rom. Dost doubt it?

Nit. Not much; I have your purse in pawn for it.
Now to the shape.[1] You know the wit in Florence
Who in the Great Duke's court buffoons his compliment
According to the change of meats in season
At every free lord's table—

[1] *Now to the shape.*] The quaint *dress* or *disguise* which he has just mentioned. For "*you* know," in this line, the old copy reads "*and* know." [It also reads "wits." D.]

Rom. Or free meetings
In taverns ; there he sits at th' upper end,
And eats and prates, he cares not how nor what :
The very quack of fashions,[2] the very he that
Wears a stiletto on his chin ?[3]

Nit. You have him.
Like such a thing must you appear, and study,
Amongst the ladies, in a formal foppery,
To vent some curiosity of language
Above their apprehensions—or your own,
Indeed beyond sense ; you're the more the person.
Now amorous, then scurvy, sometimes bawdy ;
The same man still, but evermore fantastical,
As being the suppositor to laughter :[4]
It hath sav'd charge in physic.

Rom. When occasion
Offers itself,—for, whêre it does or not,[5]
I will be bold to take it,—I may turn
To some one in the company, and, changing
My method, talk of state, and rail against
Th' employment of the time, mislike the carriage
Of places, and mislike that men of parts,[6]
Of merit, such as myself am, are not

[2] *The very* quack *of fashions,*] So I read : i.e. a loud and boastful pretender to eminence in them. The 4to has "The very *quaik,*" of which I can make nothing. I observe that Mr. Nares has placed a *quere* at this word ; but he does not attempt to explain it.

[3] *a stiletto on his chin ?*] One of the many fantastical fashions of wearing the beard : it was sharp and pointed, as its name implies. It frequently occurs in our old writers under the name of *spade* (lance) or *dagger* beard, and appears to have been chiefly affected by soldiers and bravoes.

[4] *the* suppositor *to laughter :*] The excitement, the provocative : a medical term.

[5] *for,* whêre *it does or not,*] So it should be printed [or rather, "whêr." D.] : it is the old abbreviation of "*whether.*"

[6] *and* mislike *that men of parts,* &c.] Here again we have a repetition, from that fruitful source of error, the wandering of the eye to a preceding or following line. It is idle to think of replacing the genuine word ; but if we read "*complain,*" we shall not be far, perhaps, from the poet's meaning.

Thrust into public action : 'twill set-off
A privilege I challenge from opinion
With a more lively current.

Nit. On my modesty,
You are some kin to him.
Signor Prugnuolo ![7] Signor Mushrumpo !
Leap but into his antic garb, and trust me
You'll fit it to a thought.

Rom. The time ?

Nit. As suddenly
As you can be transform'd :—for the event,
'Tis pregnant.

Rom. Yet, my pretty knave, thou hast not
Discover'd where fair Castamela lives ;
Nor how, nor amongst whom.

Nit. Pish ! yet[8] more queries ?
Till your own eyes inform, be silent ; else
Take back your earnest. What, turn woman ? fie !
Be idle and inquisitive ?

Rom. No more.
I shall be speedily provided : ask for
A note at mine own lodging.

Nit. I'll not fail ye. [*Exit Rom.*
Assuredly, I will not fail you, signor,
My fine inamorato : twenty ducats !
They're half his quarter's income : love, O, love,
What a pure madness art thou ! I shall fit him,
Fit, quit, and split him too.

Enter TROYLO.

Most bounteous sir !

Troy. Boy, thou art quick and trusty ;

[7] *Prugnuolo !*] Here the 4to has "Prugnioli," and towards the conclusion of the play (p. 320), "Prugniolo's." Gifford printed "Pragnioli." (In Italian *prugnuolo* means *a kind of mushroom*). D.

[8] *yet*] The 4to has "it." D.

Be withal close and silent, and thy pains
Shall meet a liberal addition.

Nit. Though, sir,
I'm but a child, yet you shall find me—

Troy. Man
In the contrivements; I will speak for thee.
Well, he does relish the disguise?

Nit. Most greedily,
Swallows it with a liquorish delight,
Will instantly be shap'd in't, instantly.
And, on my conscience, sir, the supposition,
Strengthen'd by imposition,[9] will transform him
Into the beast itself he does resemble.

Troy. Spend that, and look for more, boy.
[*Gives him money.*

Nit. Sir, it needs not:
I have already twenty ducats purs'd
In a gay case: 'las, sir, to you my service
Is but my duty.

Troy. Modesty in pages
Shows not a virtue, boy, when it exceeds
Good manners. Where must we meet?

Nit. Sir, at's lodging,
Or near about: he will make haste, believe it.

Troy. Wait th' opportunity, and give me notice;
I shall attend.

Nit. If I miss my part, hang me! [*Exeunt.*

SCENE II. *An apartment in* JULIO'S *house.*

Enter VESPUCCI *and* CAMILLO.

Ves. Come, thou art caught, Camillo.

Cam. Away, away,

[9] *imposition,*] The 4to has "supposition." D.

That were a jest indeed; I caught?
Ves. The lady
Does scatter glances, wheels her round and smiles;
Steals an occasion to ask how the minutes
Each hour have run in progress; then thou kissest
All thy four fingers; crouchest and sigh'st faintly,
"Dear beauty, if my watch keep fair decorum,
Three quarters have near pass'd the figure X;"
Or as the time of day goes—
Cam. So, Vespucci!
This will not do; I read it on thy forehead,
The grain of thy complexion is quite alter'd;
Once 'twas a comely brown, 'tis now of late
A perfect green and yellow; sure prognosticates
Of th' overflux o' th' gall and melancholy,
Symptoms of love and jealousy; poor soul!
Quoth she, *the* she, "Why hang thy locks like bell-ropes[10]
Out of the wheels?" thou, flinging down thy eyes
Low at her feet, repliedst, "Because, O, sovereign,
The great bell of my heart is crack'd, and never
Can ring in tune again till 't be new-cast by
One only skilful founderess!" Hereat
She turn'd aside, wink'd, thou stood'st still, and sta-red'st;
I did observe 't:—be plain, what hope?
Ves. She loves thee,
Dotes on thee; in my hearing told her lord
Camillo was the Pyramus and Thisbe
Of courtship and of compliment:—ah ha!
She nick'd it there!—I envy not thy fortunes;
For, to say truth, thou'rt handsome and deserv'st her,

10 *Why hang thy* locks like *bell-ropes*, &c.] The 4to has "looks;" to which Gifford (though he observed that "we might mend the expression, perhaps, by reading 'locks' for '*looks*'") most ridiculously adhered. D.

Were she as great again as she is.

Cam. I handsome?
Alas, alas, a creature of Heaven's making,
There's all! But, sirrah, prithee, let's be sociable:
I do confess, I think the goody-madam
May possibly be compass'd; I resolve, too,
To put in for a share, come what can come on't.

Ves. A pretty toy 'tis. Since thou'rt open-breasted,
Camillo, I presume she is [a] wanton,
And therefore mean to give the souse whenever
I find the game on wing.

Cam. Let us consider—
She's but a merchant's leavings.

Ves. Hatch'd i' th' country,
And fledg'd i' th' city.

Cam. 'Tis a common custom
'Mongst friends,—they are not friends else,—chiefly gallants,
To trade by turns in suchlike frail commodities:[11]
The one is but reversioner to t'other.

Ves. Why, 'tis the fashion, man.

Cam. Most free and proper;
One surgeon, one apothecary.

Ves. Thus, then;
When I am absent, use the gentlest memory
Of my endowments, my unblemish'd services
To ladies' favours; with what faith and secrecy
I live in her commands, whose special courtesies
Oblige me to particular engagements:
I'll do as much for thee.

[11] *in suchlike* frail commodities:] It seems almost a pity to take this out of its plain sense; but as the author has given it in italics, it is but justice to him to say that he means to be witty, and pun on the word *frail* (an osier basket, in which figs, raisins, &c. were packed), and often applied, as here, to the citizens' wives. Thus, in *Eastward Hoe;* "A plague on figs and such *frail commodities!* we shall make nothing of them."

Cam. With this addition,
Camillo, best of fairs, a man so bashful,
So simply harmless, and withal so constant,
Yet resolute in all true rights of honour;
That to deliver him in perfect character,
Were to detract from such a solid virtue
As reigns not in another soul; he is—

Ves. The thing a mistress ought to wish her servant.
Are we agreed?

Cam. Most readily. On t' other side,
Unto the lord her husband talk as coarsely
Of one another as we can.

Ves. I like it;
So shall we sift her love and his opinion.

Enter JULIO, FLAVIA, *and* FABRICIO.

Jul. Be thankful, fellow, to a noble mistress;
Two hundred ducats are no trifling sum
Nor common alms.

Flav. You must not loiter lazily,
And speak about the town,[12] my friend, in taverns,
In gaming-houses; nor sneak after dinner
To public shows, to interludes, in riot,
To some lewd painted baggage, trick'd-up gaudily
Like one of us:—O, fie upon 'em, giblets!
I have been told they ride in coaches, flaunt it
In braveries so rich that it's scarce possible
How[13] to distinguish one of these vile naughty packs
From true and arrant ladies: they'll inveigle
Your substance and your body,—think on that,—

[12] *And* speak *about the town*, &c.] So the 4to reads; but this cannot be right, as "gaming-houses" were not much noted in Ford's days for the resort of "idle praters." I suspect that the poet's word was "*lurk*." [Qy. "skulk"? D.]

[13] *How*] Omitted by Gifford: perhaps either "vile" or "naughty" should be thrown out. D.

I say, your body; look to't.—
Is't not sound counsel? [*Turns to Jul.*

Jul. It is more; 'tis heavenly.

Ves. [*aside to Cam.*] What hope, Camillo, now, if this tune hold?

Cam. [*aside to Ves.*] Hope fair enough, Vespucci, now as ever;
Why, any woman in her husband's presence
Can say no less.

Ves. [*aside to Cam.*] 'Tis true, and she hath leave here.

Fab. Madam, your care and charity at once
Have so new-moulded my resolves, that henceforth
Whene'er my mention falls into report,
It shall requite this bounty: I am travelling
To a new world.

Jul. I like your undertakings.

Flav. New world! where's that, I pray? Good, if you light on
A parrot or a monkey that has qualities
Of a new fashion, think on me.

Fab. Yes, lady,
I, I shall think on you; and my devotions,
Tender'd where they are due in single meekness,
With purer flames will mount, with free increase
Of plenty, honours, full contents, full blessings,
Truth and affection 'twixt your lord and you.
So, with my humblest, best leave, I turn from you;
Never, as now I am, t' appear before ye.
All joys dwell here, and lasting! [*Exit.*

Flav. Prithee, sweetest,
Hark in your ear,—beshrew 't, the brim of your hat
Struck in mine eye,—[*Aside*] Dissemble, honest tears,
The griefs my heart does labour in,—[it] smarts
Unmeasurably.

Jul. A chance, a chance; 'twill off,
Suddenly off: forbear; this handkercher
But makes it worse.

Cam. Wink, madam, with that eye;
The pain will quickly pass.

Ves. Immediately;
I know it by experience.

Flav. Yes, I find it.

Jul. Spare us a little, gentlemen. [*Exeunt Cam. and Ves.*]—Speak freely:
What wert thou saying, dearest?

Flav. Do you love me?
Answer in sober sadness: I'm your wife now;
I know my place and power.

Jul. What's this riddle?
Thou hast thyself replied to thine own question,
In being married to me; a sure argument
Of more than protestation.

Flav. Such it should be,
Were you as other husbands: it is granted,
A woman of my state may like good clothes,
Choice diet, many servants, change of merriments;
All these I do enjoy; and wherefore not?
Great ladies should command their own delights;
And yet, for all this, I am us'd but homely,—
But I am serv'd even well enough.

Jul. My Flavia,
I understand not what thou wouldst.

Flav. Pray pardon me;
I do confess I'm foolish, very foolish;
Trust me, indeed I am; for I could cry
Mine eyes out, being in the weeping humour.
You know I have a brother.

Jul. Romanello,
An unkind brother.

Flav. Right, right; since you bosom'd
My latter youth, he never would vouchsafe
As much as to come near me. O, it mads me,
Being but two, that we should live at distance,
As if I were a castaway;—and you,
For your part, take no care on't, nor attempt[14]
To draw him hither.

Jul. Say the man be peevish,
Must I petition him?

Flav. Yea, marry, must ye,
Or else you love not me. Not see my brother!
Yes, I will see him; so I will, will see him;—
You hear 't—O, my good lord, dear, gentle, prithee,—
You sha'n't be angry;—'las, I know, poor gentleman,
He bears a troubled mind: but let us meet
And talk a little; we perhaps may chide
At first, shed some few tears, and then be quiet;
There's all.

Jul. Write to him, and invite him hither,
Or go to him thyself. Come, no more sadness;
I'll do what thou canst wish.

Flav. And, in requital,
Believe I shall say something that may settle
A constancy of peace, for which thou'lt[15] thank me.
[*Exeunt.*

SCENE III. *An apartment in the palace.*

Enter SECCO *and* SPADONE.

Sec. The rarest fellow, Spadone! so full of gambols!—he talks so humorously; does he not?—so carelessly; O, rich! O' my hope of posterity, I could be in love with him.

Spa. His tongue trolls like a mill-clack; he touses

[14] *attempt*] The 4to has "attempted." D.
[15] *thou'lt*] Gifford printed "you'll." D.

the lady-sisters as a tumbling dog does young rabbits; hey here! dab there! your Madonna,—he has a catch at her too: there's a trick in the business,—I am a dunce else,—I say, a shrewd one.

Sec. Jump with me! I smell a trick too, if I could tell what.

Spa. Who brought him in? that would be known.

Sec. That did Signor Troylo; I saw the page part at the door. Some trick still; go to, wife; I must and I will have an eye to this gear.

Spa. A plain case; roguery, brokage and roguery, or call me bulchin. Fancies, quoth 'a? rather Frenzies. We shall all roar shortly, turn madcaps, lie open to what comes first: I may stand to't, that boy page is a naughty boy page;—let me feel your forehead: ha! O, hum,—yes,—there,—there again! I'm sorry for ye, a handsaw cannot cure ye: monstrous and apparent!

[*Feeling his forehead.*

Sec. What, what, what, what, what, Spadone?

Spa. What, what, what, what! nothing but velvet tips;[16] you are of the first head yet. Have a good heart, man: a cuckold, though he be a beast, wears invisible horns, else we might know a city-bull from a country-calf:—villanous boy, still!

Sec. My razor shall be my weapon, my razor.

Spa. Why, he's not come to the honour of a beard yet; he needs no shaving.

Sec. I will trim him and tram him.

Spa. Nay, she may do well enough for one.

Sec. One! ten, a hundred, a thousand, ten thousand; do beyond arithmetic! Spadone, I speak it with some passion, I am a notorious cuckold.

Spa. Gross and ridiculous!—look ye; point blank

[16] *nothing but* velvet tips;] Spadone alludes to the down or velvet upon the first sprouting horns of a young deer.

I dare not swear that this same mountebanking new-come foist is at least a procurer in the business, if not a pretender himself;—but I think what I think.

Sec. He, Troylo, Livio, the page, that hole-creeping page, all horn me, sirrah. I'll forgive thee from my heart; dost not thou drive a trade too in my bottom?

Spa. A likely matter! 'las, I'm metamorphosed, I: be patient, you'll mar all else.

[*Laughing within*] Ha, ha, ha, ha!

Sec. Now, now, now, now the game's rampant, rampant!

Spa. Leave your wild figaries, and learn to be a tame antic, or I'll observe no longer.

[*Within*] Ha, ha, ha, ha!

Enter TROYLO, CASTAMELA, FLORIA, CLARELLA, SILVIA, MOROSA, *and* ROMANELLO *disguised as* PRUGNUOLO.[17]

Sil. You are extremely busy, signor.

Flo. Courtly,
Without a fellow.

Clar. Have a stabbing wit.

Cast. But are you always, when you press on ladies
Of mild and easy nature, so much satire,[18]
So tart and keen as we do taste ye now?
It argues a lean brain.

Rom. Gip to your beauties!
You would be fair, forsooth, you would be monsters;
Fair women are such;—monsters to be seen
Are rare, and so are they.

Troy. Bear with him, ladies.

Mor. He is a foul-mouth'd man.

[17] *Prugnuolo*] See note, p. 267. D.

[18] *satire,*] i. e. satirist: see note, vol. i. p. 71, and note in p. 237 of this vol. D.

Sec. [*aside to Mor.*] Whore, bitch-fox, treddle![19]—
fa la la la!

Mor. How's that, my cat-a-mountain?

Spa. Hold her there, boy.

Clar. Were you e'er in love, fine signor?

Rom. Yes, for sport's sake,
But soon forgot it; he that rides a gallop
Is quickly weary. I esteem of love
As of a man in some huge place; it puzzles
Reason, distracts the freedom of the soul,
Renders a wise man fool, and a fool wise—
In's own conceit, not else; it yields effects
Of pleasure, travail; bitter, sweet; war, peace;
Thorns, roses; prayers, curses; longings, surfeits;
Despair, and then a rope. O, my trim lover!—
Yes, I have lov'd a score at once.

Spa. Out, stallion! as I am a man and no man, the baboon lies, I dare swear, abominably.

Sec. Inhumanly.—Keep your bow close, vixen.[20]
[*Pinches Mor.*

Mor. Beshrew your fingers, if you be in earnest!
You pinch too hard; go to; I'll pare your nails for't.

Spa. She means your horns; there's a bob for you!

Clar. Spruce signor, if a man may love so many,
Why may not a fair lady have like privilege
Of several servants?

Troy. Answer that; the reason
Holds the same weight.

Mor. Marry, and so it does,
Though he would spit his gall out.

[19] *treddle!*] That part of the loom on which the foot presses: vulgarly, a common creature, a street-walker.

[20] *Keep your* bow *close, vixen.*] This is taken from Ancient Pistol's injunction to his disconsolate spouse at parting [in Shakespeare's *Henry V.* act ii. sc. 3, where the 4tos (not the folio) have "buggle boe." D.]; and with her it might have been safely left.

Spa. Mark that, Secco.
Sil. D'ye pump for a reply?
Rom. The learnèd differ
In that point; grand and famous scholars often
Have argu'd *pro* and *con*, and left it doubtful;
Volumes have been writ on't. If, then, great clerks
Suspend their resolutions, 'tis a modesty
For me to silence mine.
Flo. Dull and phlegmatic!
Clar. Yet women, sure, in such a case are ever
More secret than men are.
Sil. Yea, and talk less.
Rom. That is a truth much fabled, never found.
You secret! when your dresses blab your vanities?
Carnation for your points?[21] there's a gross babbler;
Tawney? heigho! the pretty heart is wounded:
A knot of willow-ribbons? she's forsaken;
Another rides the cock-horse green and azure,
Wince and cry "wee-hee!" like a colt unbroken:
But desperate black puts 'em in mind of fish-days;
When Lent spurs on devotion, there's a famine:
Yet love and judgment may help all this pudder;
Where are they? not in females.
Flo. In all sorts
Of men, no doubt.
Sil. Else they were sots to choose.
Clar. To swear and flatter, sometimes lie, for profit.
Rom. Not so, forsooth: should love and judgment meet,
The old, the fool, the ugly and deform'd,
Could never be belovèd; for example,
Behold these two, this madam and this shaver.
Mor. I do defy thee; am I old or ugly?
Sec. Tricks, knacks, devices! now it trolls about.

[21] *points?*] See note, vol. i. p. 292. D.

Rom. Troll let it, stripling; thou hast yet firm footing,
And need'st not fear the cuckold's livery,
There's good philosophy for't: take this for comfort;
No hornèd beasts have teeth in either gums;
But thou art tooth'd on both sides, though she fail in't.

Mor. He is not jealous, sirrah.

Rom. That's his fortune;
Women, indeed, more jealous are than men,
But men have more cause.

Spa. There he rubb'd your forehead;
'Twas a tough blow.

Sec. It smarts.

Mor. Pox on him! let him
Put's finger[22] into any gums of mine,
He shall find I have teeth about me, sound ones.

Sec. You are a scurvy fellow, and I am made a cokes, an ass; and this same filthy crone's a flirt.
Whoop, do me no harm, good woman.[23] [*Exit.*

Spa. Now, now he's in! I must not leave him so. [*Exit.*

Troy. Morosa, what means this?

Mor. I know not, I;
He pinch'd me, call'd me names, most filthy names.—
[*To Rom.*] Will ye part hence, sir? I will set ye packing. [*Exit.*

Clar. You were, indeed, too broad, too violent.

Flo. Here's nothing meant but mirth.

Sil. The gentleman
Hath been a little pleasant.

[22] *finger*] Gifford printed "fingers." D.

[23] *Whoop, do me no harm, good man!* is the burthen of an old song; it is quoted by the clown in *Winter's Tale*, and is mentioned in several other places. Ritson says that the tune of the old ballad is still preserved in a collection of "Ayres for the Lute and Basse Violl, by W. Corbine, 1610."

Clar. Somewhat bitter
Against our sex.
Cast. For which I promise him
He ne'er proves choice of mine.
Rom. Not I your choice?
Troy. So she protested, signor.
Rom. Indeed!
Clar. Why, you are mov'd, sir.

Re-enter MOROSA.

Mor. Hence! there enters
A civiller companion for fair ladies
Than such a sloven.
Rom. Beauties,—
Troy. Time prevents us;
Love and sweet thoughts accompany this presence.
[*Exeunt Troy. and Rom.*

Enter OCTAVIO, SECCO *whispering him, and* LIVIO.[24]

Oct. [*to Sec.*] Enough: slip off, and on your life be secret. [*Exit Sec.*
A lovely day, young creatures! to you, Floria,
To you, Clarella, Silvia, to all, service!
But who is this fair stranger?
Liv. Castamela,
My sister, noble lord.
Oct. Let ignorance
Of what you were plead my neglect of manners,
And this soft touch excuse it. You've enrich'd
This little family, most excellent virgin,
With th' honour of your company.
Cast. I find them
Worthily graceful, sir.

[24] The 4to adds "and Nitido." D.

Liv. [*aside*] Are ye so taken?

Oct. Here are no public sights nor courtly visitants,
Which youth and active blood might stray in thought for;
The companies are few, the pleasures single,
And rarely to be brook'd, perhaps, by any
Not perfectly acquainted with this custom:
Are they not, lovely one?

Liv. Sir, I dare answer
My sister's resolution.[25] Free convérse
Amongst so many of her sex, so virtuous,
She ever hath preferr'd before the surquedry
Of protestation, or the vainer giddiness
Of popular attendants.

Cast. [*aside*] Well play'd, brother!

[*Music within.*

Oct. The meaning of this music?

Mor. Please your lordship,
It is the ladies' hour for exercise
In song and dance.

Oct. I dare not be the author
Of truanting the time then, neither will I.

Mor. Walk on, dear ladies.

Oct. 'Tis a task of pleasure.

Liv. Be now my sister, stand a trial bravely.

Mor. [*to Cast.*] Remember my instructions, or—

[*Exit, followed by Livio, Floria, Clarella, and Silvia.*

Oct. [*detaining Cast.*] With pardon,
You are not of the number, I presume, yet,
To be enjoin'd to hours. If you please,
We for a little while may sit as judges

[25] *My sister's* resolution.] i.e. her settled, her confirmed opinion. *Surquedry*, which occurs in the next line, is used by our old writers for *excess* of pride, presumption, &c.; from *sur* and *cuider*, French, over-conceit.

Of their proficience; pray, vouchsafe the favour.
Cast. I am, sir, in a place to be commanded,
As now the present urgeth.
Oct. No compulsion;
That were too hard a word; where you are sovereign,
Your yea and nay is law: I have a suit t'ye.
Cast. For what, sir?
Oct. For your love.
Cast. To whom? I am not
So weary of th' authority I hold
Over mine own contents in sleeps and wakings,
That I'd resign my liberty to any
Who should control it.
Oct. Neither I intend so:
Grant me an entertainment.
Cast. Of what nature?
Oct. T' acknowledge me your creature.
Cast. O, my lord,
You are too wise in years, too full of counsel,
For my green inexperience.
Oct. Love, dear maid,
Is but desire of beauty, and 'tis proper
For beauty to desire to be belov'd.
I am not free from passion, though the current
Of a more lively heat runs slowly through me;
My heart is gentle; and, believe, fresh girl,
Thou shalt not wish for any full addition,
Which may adorn thy rarities to boast 'em,
That bounty can withhold: this académy
Of silent pleasures is maintain'd, but only
To such a constant use.
Cast. You have, belike, then,
A patent for concealing virgins; otherwise,
Make plainer your intentions.
Oct. To be pleasant

In practice of some outward senses only;
No more.

Cast. No worse you dare not to imagine,
Where such an awful innocency as mine is
Outfaces every wickedness your dotage
Has lull'd you in. I scent your cruel mercies;
Your fact'ress hath been tampering for my misery,
Your old temptation, your she-devil:—bear with
A language which this place, and none but this, hath
Infected my tongue with. The time will come, too,
When he, unhappy man! whom your advancement
Hath ruin'd by being spaniel to your fortunes,
Will curse he train'd me hither,—Livio,—
I must not call him brother; this one act
Hath rent him off the ancestry he sprung from.

Oct. The proffer of a noble courtesy
Is check'd, it seems.

Cast. A courtesy!—a bondage:
You are a great man, vicious, much more vicious
Because you hold a seeming league with charity,
Of pestilent nature, keeping hospitality
For sensualists in your own sepulchre,
Even by your lifetime, yet are dead already.

Oct. How's this? come, be more mild.

Cast. You chide me soberly;
Then, sir, I tune my voice to other music.
You are an eminent statist; be a father
To such unfriended virgins as your bounty
Hath drawn into a scandal: you are powerful
In means; a bachelor, freed from the jealousies
Of wants; convert this privacy of maintenance
Into your own court; let this, as you call it,
Your académy, have a residence there;
And there survey your charity yourself:
That when you shall bestow on worthy husbands,

With fitting portions, such as you know worthy,
You may yield to the present age example,
And to posterity a glorious chronicle.
There were a work of piety: the other is
A scorn upon your tombstone; where the reader
Will but expound, that when you liv'd you pander'd
Your own purse and your fame. I am too bold, sir;
Some anger and some pity hath directed
A wandering trouble.

Oct. Be not known what passages
The time hath lent; for once I can bear with ye.

Cast. I'll countenance the hazard of suspicion,
And be your guest awhile.

Oct. Be; but hereafter—
I know not what.—Livio!

Re-enter LIVIO *and* MOROSA.

Liv. My lord?

Cast. Indeed, sir,
I cannot part w'ye yet.

Oct. Well, then, thou shalt not,
My precious Castamela.—Thou hast a sister,
A perfect sister, Livio.

Mor. [*aside*] All is nick'd[26] here,
Good soul, indeed!

Liv. I'd speak with you anon.

Cast. It may be so.

Oct. Come, fair one.

Liv. O, I'm cheated! [*Exeunt.*

[26] *nick'd*] The 4to has "inck'd,"—a manifest blunder; which, however, Gifford retained, writing as follows; "So the old copy. If the poet meant to endow this convenient character with any feeling of goodness, this may be an expression of regret at finding, as she supposed, Castamela giving way to the marquis: should this not be admitted, we might then read '*nick'd*,' a transposition of the letters of the former word. This must be allowed to be a very beautiful scene, and Castamela rises considerably in the reader's estimation. She does not fall in that which follows." D.

ACT IV.

SCENE I. *An apartment in the palace.*

Enter LIVIO *and* CASTAMELA.

Liv. Prithee, be serious.
Cast. Prithee, interrupt not
The paradise of my becharming thoughts,
Which mount my knowledge to the sphere I move in,
Above this useless tattle.
Liv. Tattle, sister!
D'ye know to whom you talk this?
Cast. To the Gentleman
Of my lord's horse, new-stept into the office!
'Tis a good place, sir, if you can be thankful.
Demean your carriage in it so, that negligence,
Or pride of your preferment, oversway not
The grace you hold in his esteem; such fortunes
Drop not down every day: observe the favour
That rais'd you to this fortune.
Liv. Thou mistak'st, sure,
What person thou hold'st speech with.
Cast. Strange and idle.
Liv. Is't possible? why, you are turn'd a mistress,
A mistress of the trim![1] Beshrew me, lady,
You keep a stately port; but it becomes you not.
Our father's daughter, if I err not rarely,
Delighted in a softer, humbler sweetness,
Not in a hey-de-gay of scurvy gallantry:
You do not brave it like a thing o' th' fashion,
You ape the humour faintly.
Cast. "Love, dear maid,

[1] *A mistress of the trim!*] Haughty, insolent, imperious.

Is but desire of beauty, and 'tis proper
For beauty to desire to be belov'd."

Liv. Fine sport!
You mind not me; will you yet hear me, madam?

Cast. "Thou shalt not wish for any full addition,
Which may adorn thy rarities to boast 'em,
That bounty can withhold." I know I shall not.

Liv. And so you clapt the bargain! the conceit on't
Tickles your contemplation! 'tis come out now:
A woman's tongue, I see, some time or other,
Will prove her traitor; this was all I sifted,
And here have found thee wretched.

Cast. We shall flourish;
Feed high henceforth, man, and no more be straiten'd
Within the limits of an empty patience;
Nor tire our feeble eyes with gazing only
On greatness, which enjoys the swing of pleasures;
But be ourselves the object of their envy,
To whom a service would have seem'd ambition.
It was thy cunning, Livio; I applaud it;
Fear nothing; I'll be thrifty in thy projects:
Want? misery? may all such want as think on't!
Our footing shall stand[2] firm.

Liv. You are much witty.
Why, Castamela, this to me? you counterfeit
Most palpably; I am too well acquainted
With thy condition, sister.[3] If the marquis
Hath utter'd one unchaste, one wanton syllable,
Provoking thy contempt, not all the flatteries
Of his assurance to our hopes of rising

[2] *stand*] Gifford printed "be." D.

[3] *I am too well acquainted*
With thy condition, *sister.*] i.e. natural disposition. We have had this in a former play (*The Broken Heart*); but as the word has an ambiguous appearance in this place, it seemed not improper to advert to it.

Can, or shall, slave our souls.
Cast. Indeed, not so, sir;
You are beside the point, most gentle signor!
I'll be no more your ward, no longer chamber'd
Nor mew'd-up to the lure of your devotion;
Trust me, I must not, will not, dare not; surely
I cannot, for my promise pass'd; and sufferance
Of former trials hath too strongly arm'd me:
You may take this for answer.
Liv. In such earnest!
Hath goodness left thee quite? Fool, thou art wandering
In dangerous fogs, which will corrupt the purity
Of every noble virtue dwelt within thee.
Come home again,—home, Castamela, sister,
Home to thine own simplicity; and rather
Than yield thy memory up to the witchcraft
Of an abusèd confidence, be courted
For Romanello.
Cast. Romanello!
Liv. Scorn'st thou
The name? thy thoughts, I find, then, are chang'd, rebels
To all that's honest,—that's to truth and honour.
Cast. So, sir, and in good time!
Liv. Thou art fall'n suddenly
Into a plurisy of faithless impudence;
A whorish itch infects thy blood, a leprosy
Of raging lust, and thou art mad to prostitute
The glory of thy virgin-dower basely
For common sale. This foulness must be purg'd,
Or thy disease will rankle to a pestilence,
Which can even taint the very air about thee:
But I shall study physic.
Cast. Learn good manners:

I take it, you are saucy.

Liv. Saucy! strumpet
In thy desires! 'tis in my power to cut off
The twist thy life is spun by.

Cast. Phew! you rave now:
But if you have not perish'd all your reason,[4]
Know I will use my freedom. You, forsooth,
For change of fresh apparel, and the pocketing
Of some well-looking ducats, were contented,
Passingly pleas'd—yes, marry were you, mark it—
T' expose me to the danger now you rail at!
Brought me, nay, forc'd me hither, without question
Of what might follow; here you find the issue:
And I distrust not but it was th' appointment
Of some succeeding fate that more concern'd me
Than widowèd virginity.

Liv. You're a gallant;
One of my old lord's Fancies. Peevish girl,[5]
Was't ever heard that youth could dote on sickness,

[4] *But if you have not* perish'd *all your reason,*] i. e. *destroyed:* thus in a former passage;

"to such perfection as no flattery
Of art can *perish* now."

The verb is no longer in use in an active sense.

[5] Peevish *girl,*] i. e. *foolish, captious,* or, it may be (as it evidently is in a former passage, p. 274), *perverse,* as Castamela seems at cross-purposes with her brother. That it bore all these senses in Ford's time cannot be doubted, any more than that the more ancient meaning of *peevishness* was weakness, imbecility of body or of mind.—It is not a little curious that this unfortunate word (*peevish*) was mainly operative in effecting the condemnation of Archbishop Laud. He was accused, on the evidence of his memorandum-book (of which his enemies had tyrannically possessed themselves), of a *treasonable* minute to this effect at a council-board, Strafford and Hamilton being present; "A resolution voted at the board to assist the king in extraordinary ways, if the Parliament should prove *peevish,* and refuse," &c. There was no proof that Laud had advised that vote; and he demanded "whether, though the epithet *peevish* were a very *peevish* word, he might not write it in his private notes without *treason?*" Now, in what sense was the word used? Laud's accusers seem to have given it the meaning of *wayward, perverse;* he himself apparently gives it that of *foolish;* and such was then its usual import.

A gray beard, wrinkled face, a dried-up marrow,
A toothless head, a— ?—this is but a merriment,
Merely but trial. Romanello loves thee;
Has not abundance, true, yet cannot want:
Return with me, and I will leave these fortunes,
Good maid, of gentle nature.

Cast. By my hopes,
I never plac'd affection on that gentleman,
Though he deserv'd well; I have told him often
My resolution.

Liv. Will you hence, and trust to
My care of settling you a peace?

Cast. No, surely;
Such treaty may break off.

Liv. Off be it broken!
I'll do what thou shalt rue.

Cast. You cannot, Livio.

Liv. So confident! young mistress mine, I'll do't.
[*Exit.*

Enter TROYLO.

Troy. Incomparable maid!

Cast. You have been counsellor
To a strange dialogue.

Troy. If there be constancy
In protestation of a virtuous nature,
You are secure, as the effects shall witness.

Cast. Be noble; I am credulous: my language
Hath prejudic'd my heart; I and my brother
Ne'er parted at such distance: yet I glory
In the fair race he runs; but fear the violence
Of his disorder.

Troy. Little time shall quit him.
[*They retire.*

Enter SECCO, *leading* NITIDO *in a garter with one hand, a rod in the other; followed by* MOROSA, SILVIA, FLORIA, CLARELLA; SPADONE *behind laughing.*

Sec. The young whelp is mad;[6] I must slice the worm out of his breech. I have noosed his neck in the collar; and I will once turn dog-leech. Stand from about me, or you'll find me terrible and furious.

Nit. Ladies, good ladies, dear Madam Morosa!—

Flo. Honest Secco!

Sil. What was the cause? what wrong has he done to thee?

Clar. Why dost thou fright us so, and art so peremptory
Where we are present, fellow?

Mor. Honey-bird, spouse, cat-a-mountain! ah, the child, the pretty poor child, the sweet-faced child!

Spa. That very word halters the earwig.

Sec. Off! I say, or I shall lay bare all the naked truth to your faces; his fore-parts have been too[7] lusty, and his posteriors[8] must do penance for't.—Untruss, whiskin, untruss!—Away, burs! out, mare-hag moil! avaunt! thy turn comes next;[9] avaunt! the horns of my rage are advanced; hence, or I shall gore ye!

Spa. Lash him soundly; let the little ape show tricks.

Nit. Help, or I shall be throttled!

Mor. Yes, I will help thee, pretty heart; if my tongue cannot prevail, my nails shall.—Barbarous-minded man, let go, or I shall use my talons. [*They fight.*

6 *The young whelp is* mad, &c.] See vol. i. p. 118. [*dog-leech* is dog-doctor. D.]

7 *too*] The 4to has "so." D.

8 *posteriors*] The 4to has "posterions." D.

9 *avaunt, thy turn comes next;*] The printer has repeated these words by mistake; they are [the repetition is] now removed from the text.

Spa. Well played, dog! well played, bear! sa, sa, sa! to't, to't!

Sec. Fury, whore, bawd, my wife and the devil!

Mor. Toss-pot, stinkard, pander, my husband and a rascal!

Spa. Scold, coxcomb, baggage, cuckold!

Crabbèd age and youth[10]
Cannot jump together;
One is like good luck,
T' other like foul weather.

Troy. Let us fall in now. [*Comes forward with Cast.*]—What uncivil rudeness
Dares offer a disturbance to this company?
Peace and delights dwell here, not brawls and outrage.
Sirrah, be sure you show some reasons why
You so forget your duty; quickly show it,
Or I shall tame your choler: what's the ground on't?

Spa. [*aside*] Hum, how's that? how's that? is he there, with a wannion![11] then do I begin to dwindle.—*O, O, the fit, the fit;*[12] *the fit's upon me now, now, now, now!*

10 *Crabbèd age and youth,* &c.] This is patched-up from a despicable ditty in the *Passionate Pilgrim,* foolishly attributed to Shakespeare. Spadone seems to have a sort of natural taste for these tuneful parodies.

11 *with a wannion!*] A kind of petty imprecation, often used by our old dramatists, and equivalent to the modern vulgarism *with a vengeance!* with a plague! &c. Mr. Nares wishes to derive it "from the Saxon *wanung,* detriment." In the last edition of Shakespeare it is said to be a corruption of *winnowing:* had the editor ever visited the western counties, he would have found a more probable derivation in *whang,* a lash or thong, which, as well as *whanging,* is in daily use for a *beating.* In fact, however, the word comes from neither; but from *wan* (*vaande,* Dutch, a rod or wand) [?], of which *wannie* and *wannion* are familiar diminutives. In one of Andrew Borde's humorous prescriptions for the cure of what he calls "the disease of lourdane," or laziness, he recommends "the application of a *wan,* or stick, of the bigness of a man's finger, to the patient's shoulders."

12 *O, O, the fit, the fit,* &c.] The burthen of an old song, not worth quoting. It is found also in Shirley.

Sec. It shall out. First, then, know all Christian people, Jews and infidels, hes and shes, by these presents, that I am a beast; see what I say, I say a very beast.

Troy. 'Tis granted.

Sec. Go to, then; a horned beast, a goodly tall horned beast; in pure verity, a cuckold:—nay, I will tickle their trangdidos.

Mor. Ah, thou base fellow! wouldst thou confess it an it were so? but 'tis not so; and thou liest and loudly.

Troy. Patience, Morosa.—You are, you say, a
cuckold?

Sec. I'll justify my words, I scorn to eat 'em: this sucking ferret hath been wriggling in my old cony-burrow.

Mor. The boy, the babe, the infant! I spit at thee.

Cast. Fie, Secco, fie!

Sec. Appear, Spadone! my proofs are pregnant and gross; truth is the truth; I must and I will be divorced: speak, Spadone, and exalt thy voice.

Spa. Who? I speak? alas, I cannot speak, I.

Nit. As I hope to live to be a man—

Sec. Damn the prick of thy weason-pipe!—where but two lie in a bed, you must be bodkin, bitch-baby, must ye?—Spadone, am I cuckold or no cuckold?

Spa. Why, you know I [am] an ignorant, unable trifle in such business, an oaf, a simple alcatote, an innocent.[13]

Sec. Nay, nay, nay, no matter for that; this ramkin hath tupped my old rotten carrion-mutton.

[13] *a simple* alcatote, *an innocent.*] This is pretty nearly the sense which the word still bears in the north of Devon, where I have frequently heard it: to Ford it must have been quite familiar. Totle and alcatotle are both used in the *Exmoor Dialogues*, as in the text, for *silly elf* or *foolish oaf*.

Mor. Rotten in thy maw, thy guts and garbage!

Sec. Spadone, speak aloud what I am.

Spa. I do not know.

Sec. What hast thou seen 'em doing together,—doing?

Spa. Nothing.

Mor. Are thy mad brains in thy mazer[14] now, thou jealous bedlam?

Sec. Didst not thou, from time to time, tell me as much?

Spa. Never.

Sec. Hoy-day![15] ladies and signor, I am abused; they are agreed to scorn, jeer, and run me out of my wits, by consent. This gelded hobet-a-hoy is a corrupted pander, the[16] page a milk-livered dildo, my wife a whore confest, and I myself a cuckold arrant.

Spa. Truly, Secco, for the ancient good woman I dare swear point-blank; and the boy, surely, I ever said, was to any man's thinking a very chrisome[17] in the thing you wot; that's my opinion clearly.

Clar. What a wise goose-cap hast thou show'd thyself!

Sec. Here in my forehead it sticks, and stick it shall. Law I will have: I will never more tumble in sheets with thee, I will father no misbegotten of thine; the court shall trounce thee, the city cashier thee, diseases devour thee, and the Spittle confound thee.

[*Exit.*

Cast. The man has dream'd himself into a lunacy.

Sil. Alas, poor Nitido!

[14] *mazer*] i.e. head. D.

[15] *Hoy-day!* Gifford printed "Hey-*day*." D.

[16] *the*] Gifford printed "this." D.

[17] *a very* chrisome] i.e. an infant, a child within the first month. Thus Fuller, in a pretty passage; "They say when *crysomes*" (*infants*, as he explains it) "smile, it is because of some intercourse between them and their guardian angels."

Nit. Truly, I am innocent.

Mor. Marry, art thou; so thou art. The world says, how virtuously I have carried my good name in every part about me these threescore years and odd; and at last to slip with a child! there are men, men enough, tough and lusty, I hope, if one would give their mind to the iniquity of the flesh: but this is the life I ha' led with him a while, since when he lies by me as cold as a dry stone.

Troy. This only, ladies, is a fit of novelty;
All will be reconcil'd.—I doubt, Spadone,
Here is your hand in this, howe'er denied.

Spa. Faithfully, in truth, forsooth,—

Troy. Well, well, enough.—Morosa, be less troubled;
This little jar is argument of love,
It will prove lasting.—Beauties, I attend ye.
[*Exeunt all but Spa. and Nit.*

Spa. Youngling, a word, youngling; have not you scaped the lash handsomely? thank me for't.

Nit. I fear thy roguery, and I shall find it.

Spa. Is't possible? Give me thy little fist; we are friends: have a care henceforth; remember this whilst you live—

And still the urchin would, but could not do[18]—

pretty knave, and so forth; come, truce on all hands.

Nit. Beshrew your fool's head; this was jest in earnest. [*Exeunt.*

[18] Spadone alludes to his threat of avenging himself on Nitido, who had twitted him with this scrap: p. 237.

SCENE II. *A room in* ROMANELLO'S *house.*

Enter ROMANELLO.

Rom. I will converse with beasts; there is in mankind
No sound society; but in woman—bless me!—
Nor faith nor reason: I may justly wonder
What trust was in my mother.

Enter Servant.

Serv. A caroche, sir,
Stands at the gate.

Rom. Stand let it still and freeze there!
Make sure the locks.

Serv. Too late; you are prevented.

Enter FLAVIA, *followed by* CAMILLO *and* VESPUCCI, *who stand apart.*

Flav. Brother, I come—

Rom. Unlook'd for;—I but sojourn
Myself; I keep nor house nor entertainments,
French cooks compos'd,[19] Italian collations;
Rich Persian surfeits, with a train of services
Befitting exquisite ladies such as you are,
Perfume not our low roofs;—the way lies open;
That, there. [*Points to the door.*] Good-day, great madam!

Flav. Why d'ye slight me?
For what one act of mine, even from my childhood,

[19] *entertainments,*
French cooks compos'd,] i.e., perhaps, "*which* French cooks composed:" but the pointing of the 4to is so indistinct, that it is not easy to discern what the author meant to say. Mr. Heber's copy has a full-point after "entertainments;" if that be correct, "*composed*" must be a misprint.

Which may deliver my deserts inferior
Or to our births or family, is nature
Become, in your contempt of me, a monster?

Ves. [*aside to Cam.*] What's this, Camillo?

Cam. [*aside to Ves.*] Not the strain[20] in ordinary.

Rom. I'm out of tune to chop discourse;[21] however,
You are a woman.

Flav. Pensive and unfortunate,
Wanting a brother's bosom to disburthen
More griefs than female weakness can keep league with.
Let worst of malice, voic'd in loud report,
Spit what it dares invent against my actions,
And it shall never find a power to blemish
My mention other than beseems a patient:
I not repine at lowness; and the fortunes
Which I attend on now are, as I value them,
No new creation to a looser liberty;
Your strangeness only may beget a change
In wild opinion.

Cam. [*aside to Ves.*] Here's another tang
Of sense, Vespucci.

Ves. [*aside to Cam.*] Listen, and observe.

Rom. Are not you, pray ye,—nay, we'll be contented,
In presence of your ushers, once to prattle
Some idle minutes,—are you not enthron'd
The lady-regent by whose special influence
Julio, the Count of Camerine, is order'd?

Flav. His wife 'tis known I am, and in that title
Obedient to a service; else, of greatness
The quiet of my wish was ne'er ambitious.

[20] *strain*] Means *style of conversation.*
[21] *discourse*] The 4to has "discourses." D.

Rom. He loves you?

Flav. As worthily as dearly.

Rom. And 'tis believ'd how practice quickly fashion'd
A port of humorous anticness in carriage,
Discourse, demeanour, gestures.

Cam. [*aside*] Put home roundly.

Ves. [*aside*] A ward for that blow?

Flav. Safety of mine honour
Instructed such deceit.

Rom. Your honour?

Flav. Witness
This brace of sprightly gallants, whose confederacy
Presum'd to plot a siege.

Cam. Ves. We, madam!

Rom. On, on;
Some leisure serves us now.

Flav. Still as Lord Julio
Pursu'd his contract with the man—O, pardon,
If I forget to name him!—by whose poverty
Of honest truth I was renounc'd in marriage;
These two, intrusted for a secret courtship,
By tokens, letters, message, in their turns
Proffer'd their own devotions, as they term'd them,
Almost unto an impudence, regardless
Of him on whose supportance they relied.

Rom. Dare not for both your lives to interrupt her.

Flav. Baited thus to vexation, I assum'd
A dulness of simplicity; till afterwards,
Lost to my city-freedom, and now enter'd
Into this present state of my condition,—
Concluding henceforth absolute security
From their lascivious villanies,—I continu'd
My former custom of ridiculous lightness,

As they did their pursuit; t' acquaint my lord were
T' have ruin'd their best certainty of living:
But that might yield suspicion in my nature;
And women[22] may be virtuous without mischief
To such as tempt them.

Rom. You are much to blame, sirs,
Should all be truth is utter'd.

Flav. For that justice
I did command them hither; for a privacy
In conference 'twixt Flavia and her brother
Needed no secretaries such as these are.
Now, Romanello, thou art every refuge
I fly for right to; if I be thy sister,
And not a bastard, answer their confession,
Or threaten vengeance, with perpetual silence.

Cam. My follies are acknowledg'd; you're a lady
Who have outdone example: when I trespass
In aught but duty and respects of service,
May hopes of joys forsake me!

Ves. To like penance
I join a constant votary.

Rom. Peace, then,
Is ratified.—My sister, thou hast waken'd
Intranc'd affection from its sleep to knowledge
Of once more who thou art; no jealous frenzy
Shall hazard a distrust: reign in thy sweetness,
Thou only worthy woman; these two converts
Record our hearty union. I have shook-off
My thraldom, lady, and have made discoveries
Of famous novels;[23]—but of those hereafter.
Thus we seal love: you shall know all, and wonder.

[22] *women*] The 4to has "woman." D.

[23] *Of famous* novels;] i.e. novelties. Ford uses either of the words indifferently, and as they chance to suit his metre.

Enter LIVIO.

Liv. Health and his heart's desire to Romanello!
My welcome I bring with me.—Noblest lady,
Excuse an ignorance of your fair presence;
This may be held[24] intrusion.

Flav. Not by me, sir.

Rom. You are not frequent here, as I remember;
But since you bring your welcome with you, Livio,
Be bold to use it; to the point.

Liv. This lady,
With both these gentlemen, in happy hour
May be partakers of the long-liv'd amity
Our souls must link in.

Rom. So; belike the marquis
Stores some new grace, some special close employment,
For whom your kind commends, by deputation,
Please think on to oblige; and Livio's charity
Descends on Romanello liberally,
Above my means to thank!

Liv. Sienna sometimes
Has been inform'd how gladly there did pass
A treaty of chaste loves with Castamela
From this good heart; it was in me an error,—
Wilful and causeless, 'tis confest,—that hinder'd
Such honourable prosecution,
Even and equal: better thoughts consider
How much I wrong'd the gentle course which led ye
To vows of true affection, us of friendship.

Rom. [*aside*] Sits the wind there, boy!—Leaving formal circumstance,
Proceed; you dally yet.

Liv. Then, without plea,—

[24] *held*] The 4to has "bold." D.

For countenancing what has been injurious
On my part, I am come to tender really
My sister a lov'd wife t' ye; freely take her,
Right honest man; and as ye live together,
May your increase of years prove but one spring,
One lasting flourishing youth! she is your own;
My hands shall perfect what's requir'd to ceremony.

Flav. Brother, this day was meant a holiday,
For feast on every side.

Rom. The new-turn'd courtier
Proffers most frankly, but withal leaves out
A due consideration of the narrowness
Our short estate is bounded in. Some politics,
As they rise up, like Livio, to perfection,
In their own competencies gather also
Grave supplement of providence and wisdom;
Yet he abates in his.—You use a triumph
In your advantages; it smells of state:
We know you are no fool.

Flav. Sooth, I believe him.

Cam. Else 'twere imposture.

Ves. Folly rank and senseless.

Liv. Enjoin an oath at large.

Rom. Since you mean earnest,
Receive in satisfaction; I'm resolv'd
For single life. There was a time,—was, Livio,—
When indiscretion blinded forecast in me;
But recollection, with your rules of thriftiness,
Prevail'd against all passion.

Liv. You'd be courted;
Courtship's the child of coyness, Romanello,
And for the rules, 'tis possible to name them.

Rom. "A single life's no burthen; but to draw
In yokes is chargeable, and doth require
A double maintenance:" Livio's very words;

"For he can live without a wife, and purchase:"[25]
By'r lady, so you do, sir; send you joy on't!
These rules, you see, are possible, and answer'd.

Liv. Full answer was late made[26] to this already;
My sister's only thine.

Rom. Where lives the creature
Your pity stoops to pin upon your servant?
Not in a nunnery for a year's probation.
Fie on such coldness! there are Bowers of Fancies
Ravish'd from troops of fairy nymphs, and virgins
Cull'd from the downy breasts of queens their mothers,
In the Titanian empire, far from mortals;
But these are tales:—troth, I have quite abandon'd
All loving humour.

Liv. Here is scorn in riddles.

Rom. Were there another marquis in Sienna
More potent than the same who is vicegerent
To the Great Duke of Florence, our grand master;
Were the Great Duke himself here, and would lift up
My head to fellow-pomp amongst his nobles
By falsehood to the honour of a sister,
Urging me instrument in his seraglio;
I'd tear the wardrobe of an outside from him,
Rather than live a pander to his bribery.

Liv. So would the he you talk to, Romanello,
Without a noise that's singular.[27]

Rom. She's a countess,
Flavia, she; but she has an earl her husband,
Though far from our procurement.

Liv. Castamela

[25] "*For he can live without a wife, and purchase:*"] Romanello retorts the words of Livio (p. 240); and the drift of his argument is—"Marriage is expensive; but if I do not charge myself with a wife, I shall not only be able to live, but to buy an estate."

[26] *made*] The 4to has "mate." D.

[27] *Without a noise that's singular.*] i.e. without making such an extraordinary clamour about it.

Is refus'd, then?

Rom. Never design'd my choice,
You know, and I know, Livio;—more, I tell thee,
A noble honesty ought to give allowance
When reason intercedes: by all that's manly,
I range not in derision, but compassion.

Liv. Intelligence flies swiftly.

Rom. Pretty swiftly;
We have compar'd the copy with th' original,
And find no disagreement.

Liv. So my sister
Can be no wife for Romanello?

Rom. No, no,
One no, once more and ever:—this your courtesy
Foil'd me a second.[28]—Sir, you brought a welcome;
You must not part without it; scan with pity
My plainness; I intend nor gall nor quarrel.

Liv. Far be't from me to press a blame.—Great lady,
I kiss your noble hands;—and to these gentlemen
Present a civil parting.—Romanello,
By the next foot-post thou wilt hear some news
Of alteration; if I send, come to me.

Rom. Questionless, yea.

Liv. My thanks may quit the favour.
[*Exit.*

Flav. Brother, his intercourse of conference
Appears at once perplex'd, but withal sensible.

Rom. Doubts easily resolv'd; upon your virtues
The whole foundation of my peace is grounded.
I'll guard ye to your home; lost in one comfort,
Here I have found another.

Flav. Goodness prosper it! [*Exeunt.*

[28] *this your courtesy
Foil'd me a second.*] I was deceived for an instant by your kindness.

ACT V.

SCENE I. *An apartment in the palace.*

Enter OCTAVIO, TROYLO, SECCO, *and* NITIDO.

Oct. No more of these complaints and clamours! Have we
Nor enemies abroad nor waking sycophants,
Who, peering through our actions, wait occasion
By which they watch to lay advantage open
To vulgar descant, but amongst ourselves,
Some whom we call our own must practise scandal—
Out of a liberty of ease and fulness—
Against our honour? We shall quickly order
Strange reformation, sirs, and you will find it.

Troy. When servants' servants, slaves, once relish license
Of good opinion from a noble nature,
They take upon them boldness to abuse
Such interest, and lord it o'er their fellows,
As if they were exempt from that condition.

Oct. He is unfit to manage public matters
Who knows not how to rule at home his household.
You must be jealous, puppy,—of a boy too!
Raise uproars, bandy noise, amongst young maidens;
Keep revels in your madness; use authority
Of giving punishment: a fool must fool ye;
And this is all but pastime, as you think it!

Nit. With your good lordship's favour, since, Spadone
Confess'd it was a gullery put on Secco
For some revenge meant me.

Troy. He vow'd it truth,

Before the ladies, in my hearing.

Oct. Sirrah,
I'll turn you to your shop again and trinkets,
Your suds and pan of small-coal: take your damsel,
The grand old rag of beauty, your death's-head,
Try then what custom reverence can trade in;
Fiddle, and play your pranks amongst your neighbours,
That all the town may roar ye: now ye simper,[1]
And look like a shav'd skull.

Nit. This comes of prating.

Sec. I am, my lord, a worm; pray, my lord, tread on me;
I will not turn again;—'las, I shall never venture
To hang my pole out,—on my knees I beg it,
My bare knees; I will down unto my wife,
And do what she will have me, all I can do;
Nay, more, if she will have it, ask forgiveness,
Be an obedient husband, never cross her,
Unless sometimes in kindness:—Signor Troylo,
Speak one sweet word; I'll swear 'twas in my madness,
I said I knew not what, and that no creature
Was brought by you amongst the ladies:—Nitido,
I'll forswear thee too.[2]

Oct. Wait awhile our pleasure;
You shall know more anon.

Sec. Remember me now.

[*Exeunt Sec. and Nit.*

Oct. Troylo, thou art my brother's son, and nearest
In blood to me; thou hast been next in counsels.
Those ties of nature—if thou canst consider

[1] *now ye* simper,] This, I think, should be, "now you *whimper;*" as Secco seems little disposed to indulge a smile of any kind.

[2] *Nitido,*
I'll forswear thee too.] Secco had sworn that Troylo and Nitido were privy to the introduction of Prugnuolo; the former he had already exculpated, and, in his fright, now offers to deny what he swore of the other.

How much they do engage—work by instinct
In every worthy or ignoble mention
Which can concern me.

Troy. Sir, they have, and shall,
As long as I bear life.

Oct. Henceforth the stewardship,
My carefulness for the honour of our family
Has undertook, must yield the world account
And make clear reckonings; yet we stand suspected[3]
In our even courses.

Troy. But when time shall wonder
How much it was mistaken in the issue
Of honourable and secure contrivements,
Your wisdom, crown'd with laurels of a justice
Deserving approbation, will quite foil
The ignorance of popular opinion.

Oct. Report is merry with my feats; my dotage,
Undoubtedly, the vulgar voice doth carol it.

Troy. True, sir; but Romanello's late admission
Warrants that giddy confidence of rumour
Without all contradiction; now 'tis oracle,
And so receiv'd: I am confirm'd the lady
By this time proves his scorn as well as laughter.

Oct. And we with her his table-talk:—she stands not
In any firm affection to him?

Troy. None, sir,
More than her wonted nobleness afforded
Out of a civil custom.

Oct. We are resolute
In our determination, meaning quickly
To cause these clouds fly off; the ordering of it,
Nephew, is thine.

Troy. Your care and love commands me.

[3] yet *we stand suspected*] i.e. *hitherto, up to this period.*

Enter LIVIO.

Liv. I come, my lord, a suitor.

Oct. Honest Livio,
Perfectly honest, really; no fallacies,
No flaws are in thy truth: I shall promote thee
To place more eminent.

Troy. Livio deserves it.

Oct. What suit? speak boldly.

Liv. Pray, discharge my office,
My mastership; 'twere better live a yeoman,
And live with men,[4] than over-eye your horses,[5]
Whiles I myself am ridden like a jade.

Oct. Such breath sounds but ill-manners: know, young man,
Old as we are, our soul retains a fire
Active and quick in motion, which shall equal
The daring'st boy's ambition of true manhood
That wears a pride to brave us.

Troy. He's my friend, sir.

Oct. You're weary of our service, and may leave it;
We can court no man's duty.

Liv. Without passion,
My lord, d'ye think your nephew here, your Troylo,
Parts in your spirit[6] as freely as your blood?
'Tis no rude question.

Oct. Had you known his mother,
You might have sworn her honest; let him justify
Himself not base-born: for thy sister's sake,
I do conceive the like of thee; be wiser,

[4] *'twere better* live *a yeoman,*
And live *with men,*] One of these words was apparently caught from the other: I should like to exchange the first of them for "*be.*"

[5] *horses,*] The 4to has "houses." D.

[6] *d'ye think your nephew here, your Troylo,*
Parts *in your spirit*] i.e. partakes of your nobleness of mind, your high courage, &c. In other words, "will he fight?"

But prate to me no more thus.—[*To Troy.*] If the gallant
Resolve on my attendance, ere he leave me
Acquaint him with the present service, nephew,
I meant to employ him in. [*Exit.*

Troy. Fie, Livio, wherefore
Turn'd wild upon the sudden?

Liv. Pretty gentleman,
How modestly you move your doubts! how tamely!
Ask Romanello; he hath, without leave,
Survey'd your Bowers of Fancies, hath discover'd
The mystery of those pure nuns, those chaste ones,
Untouch'd, forsooth! the holy acadèmy!
Hath found a mother's daughter there of mine too,
And one who call'd my father father; talks on't,
Ruffles in mirth on't; baffled to my face
The glory of her greatness by it.

Troy. Truly?

Liv. Death to my sufferance, canst thou hear this misery,
And answer it with a "truly"? 'Twas thy wickedness,
False as thine own heart, tempted my credulity;
That, her to ruin: she was once an innocent,
As free from spot as the blue face of heaven
Without a cloud in't; she is now as sullied
As is that canopy when mists and vapours
Divide it from our sight and threaten pestilence.

Troy. Says he so, Livio?

Liv. Yes, an't like your nobleness,
He truly does so say. Your breach of friendship
With me must borrow courage from your uncle,
Whiles your sword talks an answer; there's no remedy,
I will have satisfaction, though thy life
Come short of such demand.

Troy. Then satisfaction,

Much worthier than your sword can force, you shall have,
Yet mine shall keep the peace. I can be angry,
And brave aloud in my reply; but honour
Schools me to fitter grounds: this, as a gentleman,
I promise, ere the minutes of the night
Warn us to rest, such satisfaction—hear me,
And credit it—as more you cannot wish for,
So much not think of.

Liv. Not? the time is short;
Before our sleeping hour: you vow?

Troy. I do,
Before we ought to sleep.

Liv. So I intend too:[7]
On confidence of which, what left the marquis
In charge for me? I'll do't.

Troy. Invite Count Julio,
His lady, and her brother, with their company,
To my lord's court at supper.

Liv. Easy business;
And then—

Troy. And then, soon after, the performance
Of my past vow waits on ye; but be certain
You bring them with ye.

Liv. Yet your servant.

Troy. Nearer,—
My friend: you'll find no less.

Liv. 'Tis strange: is't possible?

[*Exeunt.*

[7] *So I* intend *too*:] i.e. such is my meaning; such is the way in which I also *understand* it.

SCENE II. *Another room in the same.*

Enter CASTAMELA, CLARELLA, FLORIA, *and* SILVIA.

Cast. You have discours'd to me a lovely story,
My heart doth dance to th' music ; 'twere a sin
Should I in any tittle stand distrustful,
Where such a people, such as you are, innocent
Even by the patent of your years and language,
Inform a truth. O, talk it o'er again!
Ye are, ye say, three daughters of one mother,
That mother only sister to the marquis,
Whose charge hath, since her death,—being left a widow,—
Here in this place preferr'd your education ;
Is't so?

Clar. It is even so ; and howsoever
Report may wander loosely in some scandal
Against our privacies, yet we have wanted
No graceful means fit for our births and qualities,
To train us up into a virtuous knowledge
Of what and who we ought to be.

Flo. Our uncle
Hath often told us, how it more concern'd him,
Before he show'd us to the world, to render
Our youths and our demeanours in each action
Approv'd by his experience, than too early
Adventure on the follies of the age,
By prone temptations fatal.

Sil. In good deed, la,
We mean no harm.

Cast. Deceit must want a shelter
Under a roof that's covering to souls
So white as breathe beneath it, such as these are :
My happiness shares largely in this blessing,

And I must thank direction of the providence
Which led me hither.

Clar. Aptly have you styl'd it
A providence; for ever in chaste loves
Such majesty hath power. Our kinsman Troylo
Was herein his own factor; he will prove—
Believe him, lady—every way as constant
As noble: we can bail him from the cruelty
Of misconstruction.

Flo. You will find his tongue
But a just secretary to his heart.

Cast. The guardianess, dear creatures, now and then,
It seems, makes bold to talk.

Clar. Sh'as waited on us
From all our cradles; will prate sometimes oddly;
However, means but sport: I am unwilling
Our household should break-up, but must obey
His wisdom under whose command we live;
Sever our companies I'm sure we shall not:
Yet 'tis a pretty life this and a quiet.

Enter MOROSA, *and* SECCO *with his apron on, carrying a basin of water, scissors, comb, towels, razor, &c.*

Sec. Chuck, duckling, honey, mouse, monkey, all and everything, I am thine ever and only; will never offend again, as I hope to shave clean, and get honour by 't: heartily I ask forgiveness; be gracious to thine own flesh and blood, and kiss me home.

Mor. Look you provoke us no more; for this time you shall find mercy.—Was 't that hedgehog set thy brains a-crowing? be quits with him; but do not hurt the great male-baby.

Sec. Enough; I am wise, and will be merry.—
Haste, beauties; the caroches will sudden receive ye:

a night of pleasure is toward; pray for good husbands a-piece, that may trim you featly, dainty ones, and let me alone to trim them.

Mor. Loving hearts, be quick as soon as ye can; time runs apace: what you must do, do nimbly, and give your minds to 't: young bloods stand fumbling! fie, away! be ready, for shame, beforehand.—Husband, stand to thy tackling, husband, like a man of mettle.—Go, go, go! [*Exit with the Ladies.*

Sec. [*aloud*] Will ye come away, loiterers? shall I wait all day? am I at livery, d'ye think?

Enter SPADONE *ready to be trimmed, and* NITIDO.

Spa. Here, and ready; what a mouthing thou keepest! I have but scoured my hands and curried my head to save time. Honest Secco! neat Secco! precious barbarian! now thou lookest like a worshipful toothdrawer: would I might see thee on horseback in the pomp once![8]

Sec. A chair, a chair! quick, quick!

Nit. Here's a chair, a chair-politic, my fine boy; sit thee down in triumph, and rise one of the Nine Worthies: thou'lt be a sweet youth anon, sirrah.

Spa. [*sits down*] So; to work with a grace now. I cannot but highly be in love with the fashion of gentry, which is never complete till the snip-snap of dexterity hath mowed-off the excrements of slovenry.

Sec. Very commodiously delivered, I protest.

Nit. Nay, the thing under your fingers is a whelp of the wits, I can assure you.

8 *Would I might see thee on horseback in the* pomp *once!*] That is, I suppose, in the procession of the city "companies of trades and callings," as a barber-surgeon. The *chair-politic* mentioned in the next line was, not improbably, the "engine" introduced in *The Broken Heart*, vol. i. p. 302; at least, it appears to have prevented Spadone from using his arms.

Spa. I a whelp of the wits! no, no, I cannot bark impudently and ignorantly enough. O, an a man of this art had now and then sovereignty over fair ladies, you would tickle their upper and their lower lips, you'd so smouch and belaver their chops!

Sec. We light on some offices for ladies too, as occasion serves.

Nit. Yes; frizzle or powder their hair, plane their eyebrows,[9] set a nap on their cheeks,[10] keep secrets, and tell news; that's all.

Sec. Wink fast with both your eyes: the ingredients to the composition of this ball are most odorous camphire, pure soap of Venice, oil of sweet-almonds, with the spirit of alum; they will search and smart shrewdly, if you keep not the shop-windows of your head close.

[*Spa. shuts his eyes while Sec. besmears the whole of his face.*

Spa. News! well remembered: that's part of your trade too;—prithee do not rub so roughly;—and how goes the tattle o' the town? what novelties stirring, ha?

Sec. Strange, and scarce to be credited. A gelding was lately seen to leap an old mare; and an old man of one hundred and twelve stood in a white sheet for getting a wench of fifteen with child here hard by:[11] most admirable and portentous!

Spa. I'll never believe it; 'tis impossible.

[9] *plane their eyebrows,*] i.e. pluck-out the straggling hairs.

[10] *set a nap on their cheeks,*] i.e. give a freshness and bloom to them by the application of the usual cosmetics. See vol. ii. p. 32.

[11] Here seems to be an allusion to Old Parr. When he was presented to Charles I., that monarch said to him, "You have lived much longer than other men, what have you done more remarkable?" "Please your majesty," replied the hoary profligate, "I did penance in a white sheet for a bastard when I was above a hundred years old." The king sternly rebuked the ill-advised old man, and dismissed him from his presence. The former part of the speech refers to Spadone and Morosa.

Nit. Most certain. Some doctor-farriers are of opinion that the mare may cast a foal, which the master of their hall conclude[s], in spite of all jockeys and their familiars, will carry every race before him without spur or switch.

Spa. O rare! a man might venture ten or twenty to one safely then, and ne'er be in danger o' the cheat. —This water, methinks, is none of the sweetest; camphire and soap of Venice, say ye?

Sec. With a little *Græcum album* for mundification.

Nit. *Græcum album* is a kind of white perfumed powder, which plain country-people, I believe, call dog-musk.

Spa. Dog-musk! pox o' the dog-musk!—what! dost mean to bleach [?] my nose, thou givest such twitches to't? Set me at liberty as soon as thou canst, gentle Secco.

Sec. Only pare-off a little superfluous down from your chin, and all's done.

Spa. Pish, no matter for that; dispatch, I entreat thee.

Nit. Have patience, man; 'tis for his credit to be neat.

Spa. What's that so cold at my throat, and scrubs so hard?

Sec. A kind of steel instrument ycleped a razor, a sharp tool and a keen: it has a certain virtue of cutting a throat, if a man please to give his mind to't. —Hold up your muzzle, signor.—When did you talk bawdily to my wife last? tell me, for your own good, signor, I advise you.

Spa. I talk bawdily to thy wife! hang bawdry! Good, now, mind thy business, lest thy hand slip.

Nit. Give him kind words, you were best, for a toy that I know.

Sec. Confess, or I shall mar your grace in whiffing tobacco, or squirting of sweet wines down your gullet; —you have been offering to play the gelding we told ye of, I suppose;—speak truth;—move the semicircle of your countenance to my left-hand file;—out with the truth; would you have had a leap?

Nit. Spadone, thou art in a lamentable pickle; have a good heart, and pray if thou canst; I pity thee.

Spa. I protest and vow, friend Secco, I know no leaps, I.

Sec. Lecherously goatish, and an eunuch! This cut, and then—

Spa. Confound thee, thy leaps and thy cuts! I am no eunuch, you finical ass, I am no eunuch, but at all points as well provided as any he in Italy, and that thy wife could have told thee. This your conspiracy! to thrust my head into a brazen tub of kitchen-lee, hoodwink mine eyes in mud-soap, and then offer to cut my throat in the dark, like a coward? I may live to be revenged on both of ye.

Nit. O scurvy! thou art angry: feel, man, whether thy weason be not cracked first.

Sec. You must fiddle my brains into a jealousy, rub my temples with saffron, and burnish my forehead with the juice of yellows! Have I fitted ye now, sir?

Enter MOROSA.

Spa. All's whole yet, I hope.

Mor. Yes, sirrah, all is whole yet; but if ever thou dost speak treason against my sweeting and me once more, thou'lt find a roguy bargain on't.—Dear, this was handled like one of spirit and discretion; Nitido has paged it trimly too: no wording, but make ready and attend at court.

Sec. Now we know thou art a man, we forget what hath passed, and are fellows and friends again.

Nit. Wipe your face clean, and take heed of a razor. [*Exeunt Mor. Sec. and Nit.*

Spa. The fear put me into a sweat; I cannot help it. I am glad I have my throat mine own, and must laugh for company, or be laughed at. [*Exit.*

SCENE III. *A state room in the same.*

Enter LIVIO *and* TROYLO.

Liv. You find, sir, I have prov'd a ready servant,
And brought th' expected guests: amidst these feastings,
These costly entertainments, you must pardon
My incivility, that here sequesters
Your ears from choice of music or discourse
To a less pleasant parley. Night draws on,
And quickly will grow old; it were unmanly
For any gentleman who loves his honour
To put it on the rack;[12] here is small comfort
Of such a satisfaction as was promis'd,
Though certainly it must be had: pray tell me,
What can appear about me to be us'd thus?
My soul is free from injuries.

Troy. My tongue
From serious untruths; I never wrong'd you,
Love you too well to mean it now.

Liv. Not wrong'd me?
Bless'd heaven! this is the bandy of a patience
Beyond all sufferance.

[12] *To put it on the rack;*] i.e. to stretch the period of redeeming it to the utmost. Livio is impatient for the moment of satisfaction; and his reproof is delicate and forcible.

Troy. If your own acknowledgment
Quit me not fairly, ere the hours of rest
Shall shut our eyes up, say I made a forfeit
Of what no length of years can once redeem.

Liv. Fine whirls in tame imagination! On, sir:
It is scarce mannerly at such a season,
Such a solemnity,—the place and presence
Consider'd,—with delights to mix combustions.

Troy. Prepare for free contents, and give 'em welcome.

A flourish. Enter OCTAVIO, JULIO, FLAVIA, ROMANELLO, CAMILLO, *and* VESPUCCI.

Oct. I dare not study words, or hold a compliment,
For this particular, this special favour.

Jul. Your bounty and your love, my lord, must justly
Engage a thankfulness.

Flav. Indeed,
Varieties of entertainment here
Have so exceeded all account of plenty,
That you have left, great sir, no rarities
Except an equal welcome, which may purchase
Opinion of a common hospitality.

Oct. But for this grace, madam, I will lay open
Before your judgment,[13] which I know can rate 'em,
A cabinet of jewels rich and lively,
The world can show none goodlier; those I prize
Dear as my life.—Nephew!

Troy. Sir, I obey you. [*Exit.*

Flav. Jewels, my lord?

Oct. No stranger's eye e'er view'd them,
Unless your brother Romanello haply
Was woo'd unto a sight for his approvement;
No more.

[13] *judgment*] The 4to has "judgments;" and so Gifford. D.

Rom. Not I, I do protest: I hope, sir,
You cannot think I am a lapidary:
I skill in jewels!
Oct. 'Tis a proper quality
For any gentleman; your other friends,
May be, are not so coy.
Jul. Who, they? they know not
A topaz from an opal.
Cam. We are ignorant
In gems which are not common.
Ves. But his lordship
Is pleas'd, it seems, to try our ignorance.—
For passage of the time, till they are brought,
Pray look upon a letter lately sent me.
Lord Julio, madam, Romanello, read
A novelty; 'tis written from Bonony.
Fabricio, once a merchant in this city,
Is enter'd into orders, and receiv'd
Amongst the Capuchins a fellow; news
Which ought not any way to be unpleasant:[14]
Certain, I can assure it.
Jul. He at last has
Bestow'd himself upon a glorious service.
Rom. Most happy man!—I now forgive the injuries
Thy former life expos'd thee to.
Liv. [*aside*] Turn Capuchin!
He! whiles I stand a cipher, and fill-up
Only an useless sum to be laid out
In an unthrifty lewdness, that must buy
Both name and riot; O, my fickle destiny!

[14] *news Which ought not any way to be unpleasant:*] The news is satisfactory enough; but surely it is awkwardly introduced both as respects the time and the company. [Here Gifford printed "ways;" and, a few lines before, "Bononia." D.]

Rom. Sister, you cannot taste this course but bravely,
But thankfully.

Flav. He's now dead to the world,
And lives to heaven; a saint's reward reward him!—
[*Aside*] My only lov'd lord, all your fears are henceforth
Confin'd unto a sweet and happy penance.

Re-enter TROYLO, *with* CASTAMELA, CLARELLA, FLORIA, SILVIA, *and* MOROSA.

Oct. Behold, I keep my word; these are the jewels
Deserve a treasury; I can be prodigal
Amongst my friends: examine well their lustre;
Does it not sparkle? wherefore dwells your silence
In such amazement?

Liv. [*aside*] Patience, keep within me,
Leap not yet rudely into scorn of anger.

Flav. Beauties incomparable!

Oct. Romanello,
I have been only steward to your pleasures:
You lov'd this lady once; what say you now to her?

Cast. I must not court you, sir.

Rom. By no means, fair one;
Enjoy your life of greatness. Sure, the spring
Is past, the BOWER[15] OF FANCIES is quite wither'd,
And offer'd like a lottery to be drawn;
I dare not venture for a blank, excuse me.—
Exquisite jewels!

Liv. Hark ye, Troylo.

Troy. Spare me.

Oct. You, then, renounce all right in Castamela?
Say, Romanello.

Rom. Gladly.

[15] *Bower*] The 4to has "Bowers." D.

Troy. Then I must not:
Thus I embrace mine own, my wife; confirm it
Thus—When I fail, my dearest, to deserve thee,
Comforts and life shall fail me![16]

Cast. Like vow I,
For my part.

Troy. Livio, now my brother, justly
I have given satisfaction.

Cast. O, excuse
Our secrecy; I have been—

Liv. Much more worthy
A better brother, he a better friend
Than my dull brains could fashion.

Rom. Am I cozen'd?

Oct. You are not, Romanello: we examin'd
On what conditions your affections fix'd,
And found them merely courtship; but my nephew
Lov'd with a faith resolv'd, and us'd his policy
To draw the lady into this society,
More freely to discover his sincerity;
Even without Livio's knowledge; thus succeeded[17]
And prosper'd:—he's my heir, and she deserv'd him.

Jul. [*to Rom.*] Storm not at what is past.

Flav. A fate as happy
May crown you with a full content.

Oct. Whatever
Report hath talk'd of me abroad and these,
Know they are all my nieces, are the daughters

[16] *confirm it Thus—When I fail*, &c.] The old copy places the point after "*it*." I have not disturbed the arrangement without some hesitation; but it seems as if Troylo meant to confirm the act of taking possession of his mistress by imprecating a curse on himself, if he proved unworthy of her love.

[17] thus *succeeded*, &c.] Meaning, perhaps, thus *he* (Troylo) succeeded: if this be not admitted, it will be expedient to read "*this* succeeded" for "*thus*."

To my dead only sister; this their guardianess
Since they first saw the world: indeed, my mistresses
They are, I have none other; how brought up
Their qualities may speak. Now, Romanello
And gentlemen, for such I know ye all,
Portions they shall not want both fit and worthy;
Nor will I look on fortune; if you like,
Court them and win them; here is free access
In mine own court henceforth: only for thee,
Livio, I wish Clarella were allotted.

Liv. Most noble lord, I am struck silent.

Flav. Brother,
Here's noble choice.

Rom. Frenzy, how didst thou seize me!

Clar. We knew you, sir, in Prugnuolo's[18] posture.

Flo. Were merry at the sight.

Sil. And gave you welcome.

Mor. Indeed, forsooth, and so we did, an't like ye.

Oct. Enough, enough.—Now, to shut-up the night,
Some menial servants of mine own are ready
For to present a merriment; they intend,
According to th' occasion of the meeting,
In several shapes, to show how love o'ersways
All men of several conditions,—Soldier,
Gentry, Fool, Scholar, Merchantman, and Clown;
A harmless recreation.—Take your places. [*Music.*

Enter SPADONE, SECCO, NITIDO, *and other* Maskers, *dressed respectively as the six characters mentioned above.*

A DANCE.

Your duties are perform'd.—Henceforth, Spadone,
Cast-off thy borrow'd title:—nephew Troylo,

[18] *Prugnuolo's*] The 4to has "Prugniolo's." Gifford printed "Pragnioli's." See note, p. 267. D.

His mother gave thee suck; esteem him honestly.—
Lights for the lodgings! 'tis high time for rest.—
Great men may be mistook when they mean best.

[*Exeunt.*[10]

[10] Much cannot be said in favour of the plot of this drama, as Ford has conducted it. He has imperfectly executed his own design; for the story is capable of furnishing, in judicious hands, a series of events neither uninstructive nor unamusing; but, with his usual ill-fortune, he entangled himself at the outset with a worthless rabble of comic characters, and after debasing his plot to the utmost, is compelled, by their outrages on decorum, to terminate it prematurely. The Fancies are wholly insignificant; and the "great marquess" must have imbibed strange notions of female elegance and delicacy, when he confided the education of his nieces to the vulgar and profligate set who conduct his boasted academy.

All, however, is not in this reprobate strain. The leading characters are well conceived and judiciously sustained; Castamela, in particular, is beautifully depicted. Though indigent, and affectionately attached to her brother, she indignantly resents the compromise which she supposes him to have made with fortune at her expense; and when he appears willing to abandon his hopes, and, apprehensive of her danger, to return with her to their pristine poverty, she rejects the thought with scorn, and, secure in her high sense of female decorum and of virtue, resolves to brave the severe trial to which his impatience of want had exposed her. Livio is only inferior to his sister; and his struggles to extricate himself with honour from the toils which appear to lie in his way are described in that strong, free, and vivid language which marks the more serious parts of this singular play.

The second or under-plot of Julio and Flavia, like most of our author's *intermedes*, contributes nothing to the advancement of the main story: it is not, however, without merit. Flavia is skilfully drawn, and has many touches of sensibility, for which we are not prepared by her first appearance; and her brother Romanello, *perplexed*, like Livio, *in the extreme*, but less fortunate, is entitled, both for language and sentiment, to considerable praise.

EPILOGUE.

Spoken by MOROSA, CLARELLA, CASTAMELA, *and* FLAVIA.

Mor. Awhile suspected, gentlemen, I look
For no new law, being quitted by the book.
Clar. Our harmless pleasures free in every sort
Actions of scandal ; may they free report !
Cast. Distrust is base, presumption urgeth wrongs;
But noble thoughts must prompt as noble tongues.
Flav. Fancy and judgment are a play's full matter:
If we have err'd in one, right you the latter.

END OF VOL. II.

ROBSON AND SONS, PRINTERS, PANCRAS ROAD, N.W.

www.ingramcontent.com/pod-product-compliance
Lightning Source LLC
Chambersburg PA
CBHW021214270326
41929CB00010B/1128
9783744710633